SILBURY

SILBURY

RESOLVING THE ENIGMA

MICHAEL DAMES

To my beloved wife

First published 2010

The History Press
The Mill, Brimscombe Port
Stroud, Gloucestershire, GL5 2QG
www.thehistorypress.co.uk

British Library Cataloguing in Publication Data.
A catalogue record for this book is available from the British Library.

ISBN 978 0 7524 5450 4

Typesetting and origination by The History Press
Printed in Great Britain
Manufacturing managed by Jellyfish Print Solutions Ltd

CONTENTS

one

EXCAVATORS' TALES

First Impressions

Silbury, in Avebury parish, Wiltshire, is an artificial hill and the tallest prehistoric monument in Europe. Carved from the tip of a chalk spur and overlooking the River Kennet's headwater meadows, the edifice rises in a steep-sided, truncated cone to a height of 130ft. In the eyes of most British archaeologists the monument's original purpose is an unsolved and probably insoluble enigma.

However, in my 1976 book *The Silbury Treasure*, I argued that the hill and its surrounding moat, if viewed together, could be seen as a vast architectural image of an earth and water goddess, worshipped by the Neolithic or New Stone Age farming community who designed, built and used this temple.[1]

The goddess is displayed heavily pregnant to match every forthcoming annual harvest, with the hill denoting her full womb. The moat (still visible, though now somewhat clogged with silt) described the rest of her reclining body. This gigantic effigy, depicted squatting on her right side in the act of giving birth, was their divine 'Lady of the Lake'. She *was* that lake, deliberately dug and shaped into a superhuman female form.[2] The rock excavated in order to make this watery icon was then piled up 130ft high to symbolise her earth-womb and its crops. Both were seen as extensions of her living cosmic self and as her sacred progeny. Such was the interpretation put forward in *The Silbury Treasure*.

Substantial discoveries that have recently been made, both inside and immediately around the monument, lend extra weight to this hypothesis, especially if this new archaeological data is viewed within the wider scholarly context now available. Comparative religion, the literature and art of classical antiquity, place-name evidence and the rich folklore heritage of the British Isles can, in their different ways, contribute to a better all-round view of Silbury.[3] By re-integrating these studies we may improve our chance of reconnecting with the hill builders' outlook and intentions, while also revealing Silbury's possible significance to later peoples.

What underlies the sense of continuity proposed here is the fact that we share with our ancestors essentially the same terrestrial, subterranean and celestial realms; the same bodies and brains; the same need for food; and a strong desire to make overall sense of things. Thus Silbury's story may be far from over. Rather, the old Hill can both illuminate several layers of the past *and* rise to address our current predicaments.

Before the threat of erosion to Silbury Hill's grassy flanks from a growing number of sightseers put the flat, circular summit out of public bounds, those who laboured, panting, to the top in former times could enjoy a splendid 360-degree view over the undulating spurs and ridges of Wiltshire's Marlborough Downs.

1(a) Silbury Hill, drawn by William Stukeley, 1724, with the Swallowhead spring (*left*), the River Kennet (*foreground*) and Avebury's church tower. (b) Silbury Hill from the south, AD 2000. Wheat has been grown here since *c*.4000 BC.

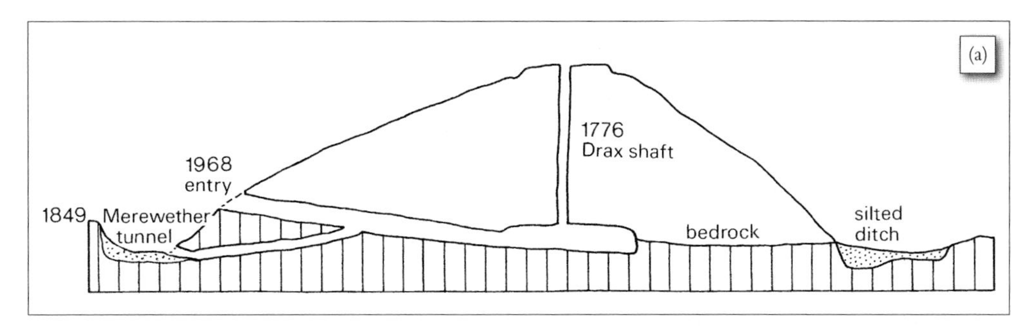

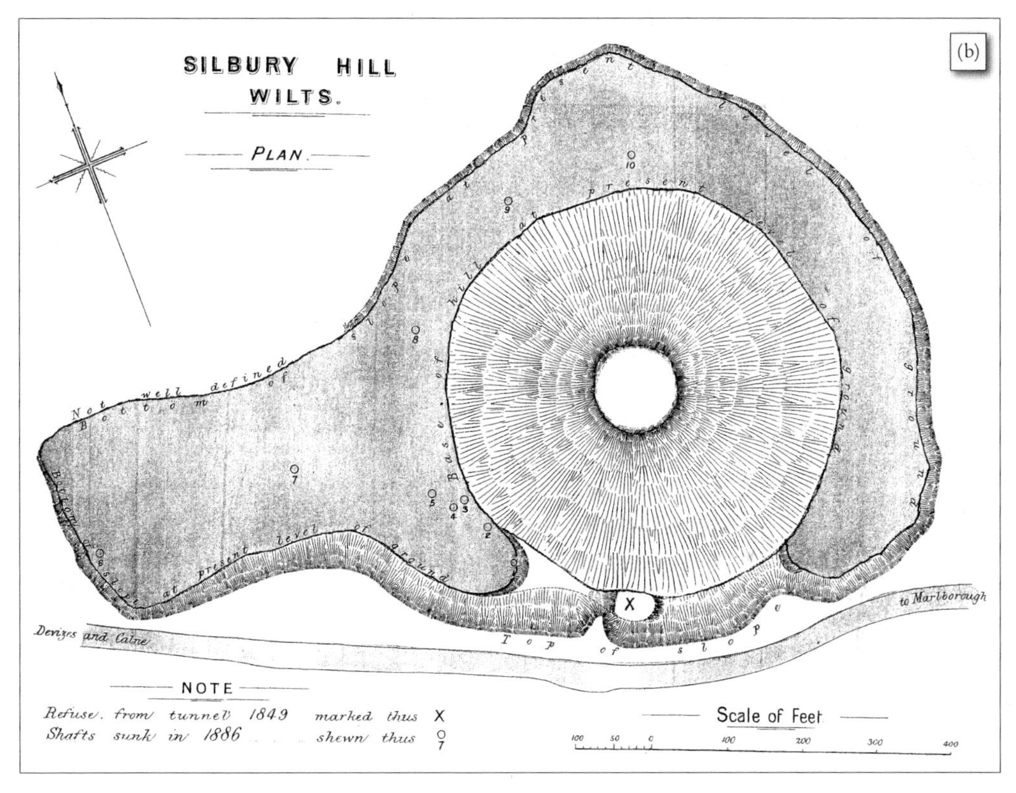

2(a) Shafts and tunnels dug into Silbury Hill. (b) Plan of Silbury by A.C. Pass, 1887, based on survey by G.C. Ashmead & Co. of Bristol. Pass concluded: 'I have ascertained that Silbury Hill was originally surrounded by a deep trench or moat, at all times containing water.' His discovery and its possible significance were ignored until *The Silbury Treasure* appeared in 1976.

In all directions, the rolling landscape is adorned with an extraordinary range of prehistoric monuments. Amongst these, the embanked megalith-studded disc known as the Avebury Henge lies a mile north of Silbury, while southwards the finest long barrow in England is plainly visible. Nearby, an avenue of standing stones winds from an ancient temple site, which in turn overlooks traces of vast wooden stockades, which were built in the Stone Age. A few miles further off are three 'causewayed camps', the earliest type of ceremonial enclosure known in Britain. In addition, clusters of Bronze Age round barrows join the array.[4]

These structures are gathered like the variously shaped instruments of a gigantic orchestra around Silbury's stupendous 'rostrum', as if to perform a sacred composition, superhuman in scale and timeless in scope. The whole area is now designated a World Heritage site of global value.

To visitors, stout Silbury makes a challenging eruption that impinges upon the eyes, emotions and mind, encouraging an unlikely intimacy with its silent 'foreignness'. Though an outdated residue, battered by treasure hunters, Silbury seems to defy chronological time, standing instead for an endless 'now'.

But we are trained to reject that possibility as irrational. The modern concept of linear history, even when illogically projected onto *pre*history, insists that we keep our distance from 'the past', while science tells us that any scrutiny of the hill must be of a strictly objective kind, devoid of empathy.[5]

Yet Silbury's study calls for extra more appropriate methods of enquiry to supplement science and chronology, before the monument's *pre*-scientific nature and purpose can be read. Accordingly, this book tries to address Silbury primarily on its own terms; that is to say those that operate within the sacred and *cyclical* world of myth, from which the hill arose.[6]

When so viewed, Silbury's rich legacy, both deep and wide, becomes apparent. These neglected connections help change the monument from an ossified relic into the centre of a living network. The edifice defines a continuity that we can no longer afford to neglect.

Desecrations

Something of Silbury's original meaning and function survives despite the passage of time and attacks by the Christian Church, who were determined to prohibit pre-Christian forms of worship at long-revered pagan sanctuaries. Though Silbury was far too big to dismantle, the fourteenth-century toppling and burial of Avebury's great circle stones, authorised by the Church, provides evidence of the hostile ecclesiastical attitude towards a religion inherited from the Neolithic founders of these temples.[7]

In more recent centuries Silbury has also suffered vandalism by treasure hunters. They came in three waves, coincidentally matching the rise, apogee and fall of the British Empire, and the Industrial Revolution's mining of coal, iron, tin and other irreplaceable minerals.

First, in 1776, the Duke of Northumberland commissioned a party of Cornish tin miners, supervised by Colonel Drax, to dig a vertical shaft from top to bottom of the hill. The duke had heard a rumour that a king named Sel or Zel was interred beneath the mighty edifice accompanied by a life-sized golden effigy, mounted on an equally golden horse. But neither bones nor equestrian statue were found.[8] However, because the shaft was inadequately refilled by the eighteenth-century miners, it was inclined to collapse. On 29 May AD 2000 a large hole appeared in the summit of the hill. By February 2008 this crater was 8 yards wide and 16 yards deep.

In 1849 Dean Merewether of Hereford Cathedral organised a second hunt for Silbury's hidden grave goods. He arranged for a railway engineer, Mr Holford, to excavate a 300-yard-long horizontal tunnel from the south base of the hill to its central core. When this gallery failed to locate the hoped-for burial chamber, the dean ordered an extra semicircular tunnel and two side branches to be dug around the base of the Drax shaft, which yielded the same negative result.[9]

Since Holford's timber-propped works were never backfilled, the tunnels' subsequent distortion and partial collapse, due to the enormous weight pressing down from above, further destabilised the hill. In 1922, following the exposure through erosion of the tunnel mouth, an iron door was inserted to keep trespassers from crawling to the hill's dark centre. (At the conclusion of the 1849 dig Merewether had preached to a mixed congregation of antiquaries and Avebury villagers, assembled on neighbouring Waden Hill, on the need to treat Silbury and all ancient monuments with respect.)[10]

Despite the negative outcome of these intrusions, the twentieth century saw renewed attempts to prove that Silbury was a mid-second millennium Bronze Age burial mound, of unprecedented size, designed for an unusually powerful chieftain and presumably furnished with artefacts of appropriate splendour.

In 1922 Egyptologist Sir Flinders-Petrie dug into the south-east perimeter of the hill, with the knowledge that the entrance to a pharaoh's tomb is usually orientated in that quadrant. Yet beneath the turf, instead of the expected passageway, constructed of locally available sandstone slabs, leading to a corbelled vault of the same rock, he found only 'cells' of quarried chalk blocks filled with finer chalk rubble, of which the massive cone is, in fact, almost entirely built.[11] Silbury was not a pyramid.

The Atkinson Dig

Instead, according to R.J.C. Atkinson, Professor of Archaeology at Cardiff University, the monument was more likely to have been made as a mausoleum for the ruler who conceived and supervised the construction of Stonehenge. He wrote:

> I believe that Stonehenge itself is evidence for the concentration of political power in the hands of a single man who alone could create and maintain the conditions necessary for this great [Silbury] undertaking. Who he was, whether native or foreign, we shall never know, but who but he should sleep like Arthur or Barbarossa in the quiet darkness of a sarsen vault beneath the mountainous pile of Silbury Hill?[12]

By the time Atkinson's Silbury project was announced in September 1967 he was inclined to believe that the interred leader, creator of Stonehenge, came from Mycenae in Greece, *c.*1600 BC. He therefore asked BBC2 television, sponsors of the excavation, to make some Mycenaean-type armour and other artefacts to complement those he hoped to find under Silbury. These props were duly prepared.

What was new about Atkinson's 1968–70 approach to Silbury compared to earlier assaults (in addition to the promise of continuous television coverage) was the emphasis that he placed on his commitment to a scientific methodology. He stated: 'We shall be deploying every latest scientific skill and modern resource to solve the mystery. We shall concentrate deliberately upon instrumental methods of exploration, so as to define as narrowly as possible the questions to be asked.'[13] His narrow gaze brought extra meaning to the phrase 'tunnel vision'.

Some mining techniques had, of course, been involved in the earlier digs, though systematic science was almost absent. Indeed, Emmeline Fisher's 'Silbury' poem, a copy of which was buried under the hill in 1849, laments: 'O that … the eagle glance of Science could call back thy history lost'.

The professor's analytical zeal (Wordsworth's 'murdering to dissect'?) could readily merge with the treasure-hunting enthusiasm of his predecessors. But whereas the Duke of Northumberland wanted to conceal Silbury's booty in the privacy of his Sion House mansion, the 1967 project, by contrast, offered the common viewer a share in the spoils. The public was promised nightly five-minute television news flashes from the excavation. Millions of us could instantaneously savour the hoard without having to understand the science.

Yet the Silbury Project leader went to some trouble to offer intelligent guesswork in advance of his instrumentally measured quantities. For instance, we learnt that the hill's volume was

3(a) 2 April 1968; Professor Richard Atkinson (*far right*) starts his Silbury excavation.

approximately 12.5 million cubic feet, or 350,000 cubic metres.[14] Estimates of how many men (700) spent how many man hours (3 million) doing the original work were also publicised. In this way, statistics led towards, or at least hinted at, a realm of pure number, which might temper and perhaps dignify our vulgar lust for gold.

In practical terms, a new downward-sloping tunnel would be driven into the hill, aligned directly above Merewether's point of entry. It would follow the prehistoric soil line, to join the nineteenth-century tunnel about 100ft inside the mound. The 1849 gallery would then be widened and its headroom increased to a height of 6ft 6in. In charge of the engineering work was Dr Jon Taylor of Cardiff University's Department of Mining. He eventually erected more than 80 steel arches or 'rings' to support the roof. A light railway, mains lighting, forced air supply and telephones were then installed, along with the television cameras. In this manner, modern and ancient worlds were set to collide.

However, two years into the intended three-year campaign, the BBC abruptly withdrew its funding and interest. The entire project was prematurely closed down. Silbury had proved a disappointment for the television executives and the archaeologists. The Bronze Age ruler had declined to present himself. No burial chamber, no human bones and no treasure could be found.

In fact, for sponsors and excavators, the news from Silbury was worse than none at all. Atkinson had found the body of a winged ant in the prehistoric grass of the hill's central primary mound of stacked turf that had probably been born in the year of the hill's foundation. To discover the age

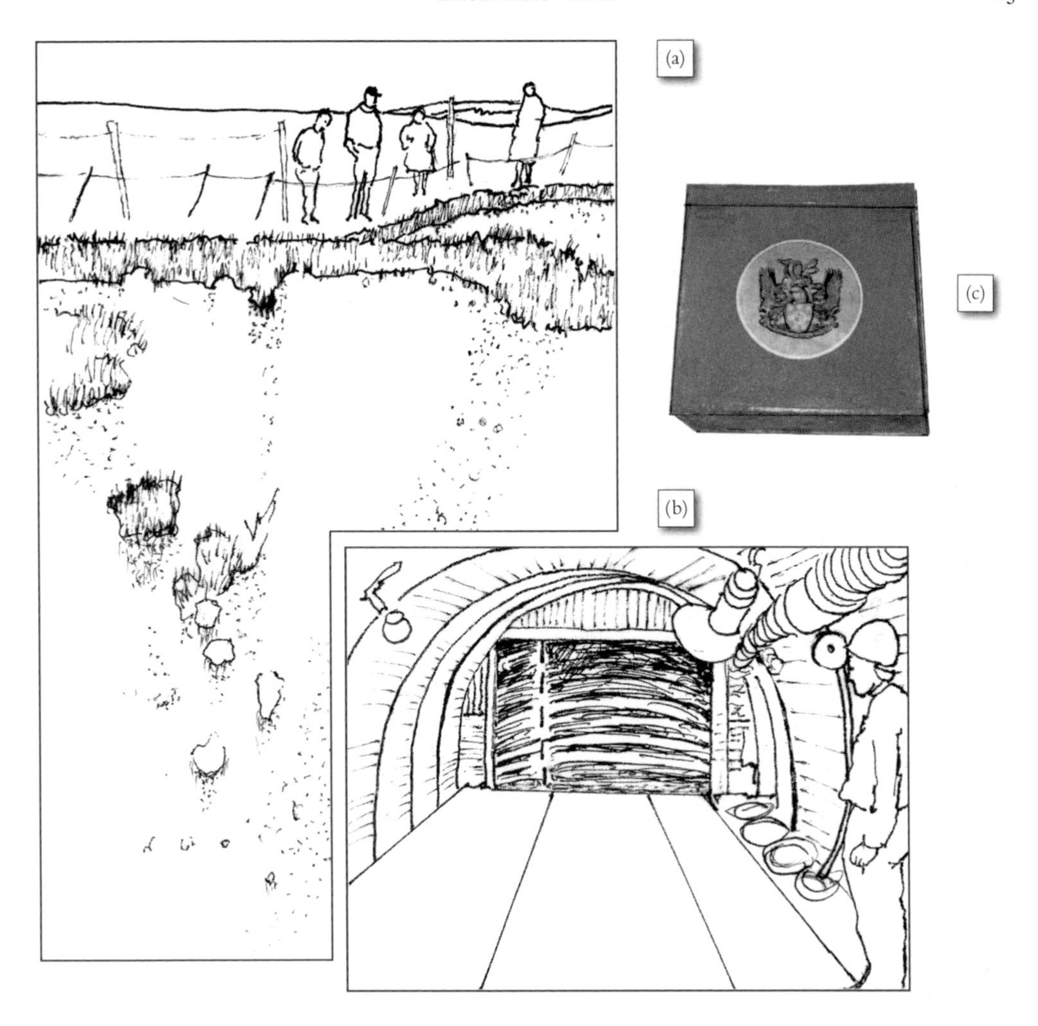

4(a) Following heavy rain, a crater, 4m deep and 7m wide, appeared in Silbury's summit on 29 May 2000. This collapse was caused by the inadequate infilling of the Drax shaft of 1776, combined with the void left over the monument's core in 1969 by Atkinson. For seven years the crater was filled with polystyrene blocks. (b) Inner end of the 1969 tunnel when new, showing the dark organic matter of the primary mound. By 2000 this tunnel had collapsed. (c) The 'Time Capsule' metal box, left by Atkinson at Silbury's core in 1969, containing film of his dig.

of this insect and of the organic material in which it was embedded was therefore essential. So the insect was flown to New Jersey, USA, for radiocarbon dating.

The tests proved beyond doubt that Silbury was not a Bronze Age monument at all. The Hill was a thousand years too old to fit into a Bronze Age *milieu*, where gold ornaments, bronze weapons, heroic rulers and individual burial beneath a round barrow were characteristic. Instead, Silbury was built in the mid-third century BC, in an era when the features listed above were unknown in Britain.[15]

Thus science, conducted in a US laboratory, carried Silbury Hill's vast bulk a distance of one millennium backwards in time, and set it down in different age entirely. Overnight the edifice had betrayed our hopes. From now on, the hill was bound to speak a New Stone Age or Neolithic language, involving radically different priorities from those that Drax, Merewether, Flinders-Petrie, Atkinson and the general public had, for three centuries, imagined.

After digesting this unwelcome development, BBC2 predicted that their 1969 television audience would dwindle to a handful of enthusiasts for Neolithic ants and grass, which would only benefit the viewing figures of rival channels. Therefore the camera crews were ordered to leave the site. They went, as did Atkinson and his team. Neither media nor academics seemed interested in what a Stone Age Silbury might have to say.

When the entertainment ratings of a television show drop, the plug is understandably pulled. But for an archaeologist professing an attachment to science, the equally sudden collapse of Atkinson's interest in Silbury was surprising. In scientific terms, far from being a 'disappointment' (his words), the unexpected Silbury date was a significant discovery, pointing to the need to study the monument in a different context, calling for revised conclusions. Indeed, Atkinson himself had stated: '*When* Silbury was built is crucial; for if we can answer this, we already know enough to define, at least in outline, the culture concerned and by inference the society which it represents.'[16]

To this he attached another perceptive remark: 'In a text-free prehistory, a society manifests itself to us most directly … through the exceptional achievements [like Silbury] that required the concerted effort of the society as a whole.'[17] In other words, a Neolithic Silbury was the key to understanding the essence of Neolithic values.

As regards the need for full publication of any excavation's results, Atkinson's students at Cardiff recalled his oft-repeated lecture room maxim: 'an excavation is only as good as its published report.' Thus the Silbury Project required him to follow his own precept. Instead he confined himself to a few factual paragraphs in the journal *Antiquity* (1970) and wrote no full report during the remaining 20 years of his life.

Time Capsule and Void

After 1970 a profound silence fell over Silbury. For several reasons the hill was in disgrace. The expense, the embarrassment to BBC2, an aroused public let down; these misfortunes somehow became the hill's fault. Above all, because the monument had been transported to the Stone Age and now stood on the wrong side of a major cultural watershed, where even the possibility of a heroic son buried beneath seemed lost, the hill had become 'illegitimate'. For years thereafter archaeologists steered clear of the troublesome monument.

The Atkinson dig left an intellectual and physical void. His decision not to backfill his excavation under Silbury's central core undoubtedly contributed to the major summit collapse on 29 May 2000 around the Drax shaft. In 2007, to their surprise, Skanska engineers discovered several other dangerous voids inside the hill, created by the failure of the 1968 steel supporting 'rings'. In less than 40 years many of these inverted U-shaped girders had either been severely distorted under huge pressure from above or pushed downwards by as much as 1m.[18]

In January and February 2008, deep scars appeared and then deepened on the hill's south side, over the line of the 1967 main tunnel, which in 1970 had been inadequately refilled with road chippings.[19] What did remain intact was a concrete lintel, inscribed '1968' and installed over the tunnel's mouth at the start of the project. This date stone effectively reduced Silbury's timeless presence to a fleeting historical event, an 'I Woz Here' of 12 months' duration.

So diminished, the monument became 'Atkinson's Hill'. Accordingly, he devised a time capsule: a metal tin, resembling a shallow biscuit box, in which were sealed (for posterity) three spools of television colour film of himself and his assistants shot during the previous years' work. The container was laid in a place of honour at the furthest end of his tunnel. Thanks to this film, the professor was installed as an action man replacement for the missing Bronze Age hero. So, from the lintel on the peripheral door, to the canned footage at the hill's centre, Silbury had a new master.[20]

Unfortunately the time capsule was badly sealed and leaked. The 2007 team found the contents waterlogged and removed them and the box from the tunnel,[21] while above their heads the mauled Hill threatened further collapse. The heavy rains of July 2007 exacerbated the peril to such a degree that work was stopped on the 26th of that month. The project director Rob Harding

5 Silbury Hill, south side, January 2008. In July 2007 Skanska engineers found 'instability and voiding within Silbury ... much more significant than predicted', resulting from the 1776, 1849 and 1968 digs. Ten months into the restoration project, fresh collapses occurred over the line of Atkinson's tunnel. Here chalk paste is piped and pumped to fill the summit crater.

reported: 'At best the work has been delayed... At worst, the stability of the whole structure has been weakened by the huge amount of rain.'[22] Emptied of substantial meaning, Silbury now seemed to be about to implode.

And yet this wreck, abandoned on modernity's nihilistic shore and surrounded for a year by the ugly paraphernalia essential to the rescue effort, remained at heart a green and white cone, full of hidden possibilities, perhaps prehistory's finest gift to us.

Despite her recent travails, the great Hill continues to prey on the feelings and thoughts of passing motorists and truck drivers as they consider what kind of wealth or virtue might lie wrapped within its awesome simplicity. Was the hill, despite ill treatment, willing to release her archaic meaning into modern recognition and relevance?

Pluggings and Purposes

In May 2007, seven years after the huge crater appeared in the top of Silbury Hill, English Heritage, its official guardian, commissioned Skanska Engineering to patch up the entire monument. During several months of this restoration a team of archaeologists, led by Jim Cleary, took the opportunity to re-examine the interior.

Dr R. Bewley, regional head of English Heritage, remarked: 'It is a privilege for us to be able to get so close to people that originally built the hill, through the work we are doing over the coming months, deep inside it.'[23]

For Cleary, the examination involved asking many questions. As he told the journal *Current Archaeology*, 'foremost among them is: why? What is the purpose of Silbury Hill? What did it represent, what function did it perform, what was its meaning to the people who went to such great efforts to build it?'[24]

However, as Dr Bewley had warned at the start of the new investigation: 'It is very unlikely that we shall ever know why it was built.'[25] This pessimism reflected that of another archaeologist: Professor Alastair Whittle. He had spent years gathering together and trying to make sense of Atkinson's scattered notes, before concluding that 'Silbury demands yet thwarts explanation'.[26] Whittle was sure what Silbury *was not* (a royal tomb), but not what it is.

The same may be said of David Field. His *Analytical Survey of Silbury Hill*, commissioned by English Heritage and published in 2002, claimed on page one to have 'provided detail about construction *and use* [author's italics] of the monument'. But in fact the report offers almost no suggestions as to the hill's original role.

On 24 October 2007, close to the end of his subterranean period of study, Jim Cleary shared both these men's puzzlement. To a news conference packed with the nation's media he remarked: 'We know that something about this site was incredibly special and sacred to generations of people, but we have no idea what.' He added: 'It is not a big clock, it wasn't built for a big laugh, or to give people something to do.'

The *Daily Telegraph* duly reported that 'the original purpose of the hill is still a mystery', while *The Times* sighed: 'If mankind endures ten million years we may never discover the who and why of the most tantalising enigma in the British landscape.' For his part, Michael Hanlon, in the *Daily Mail*, voiced dissatisfaction with the vagueness of Cleary's reference to the builders' supposedly 'sacred' motivation, and complained: 'this is pretty much what archaeologists *always* say when faced with an object they don't understand: "It must have something to do with Religion".'

From November 2007 to April 2008, Silbury's shaft, tunnels and subsequent voids were gradually filled to the brim with chalk rubble and paste. The mixture soon solidified. By this necessary act, the hill's prehistoric purposes were seemingly locked in, concealed from human understanding forever.

One positive consequence of the operation was the announcement of a firm date for Silbury's core. Improved radiocarbon technology enabled A. Bayliss to state that the earliest organic material was laid down in 2400 BC, and that a small but substantial chalk hill was then erected over the primary mound – all being completed 'within one human lifetime'. Grass, found growing on top of this initial chalk heap, indicated that there was then a pause of several years, possibly as long as four centuries, before the massive hill took its final shape.[26A]

As for the monument's purpose, the public was left with some nebulous words, such as 'ritual, reverence, ceremonial, and place of pilgrimage', volunteered (when pressed) by the 2007 experts. Like former Prime Minister Blair, Silbury's archaeologists do not seriously *do* religion, yet these terms now jostled with the 'demonstration of power and wealth' explanation for Silbury, favoured in the 1980s. But for the *Daily Mail*, the new terminology was as insubstantial as the body of the absent Bronze Age monarch.

Science and Antiquity

Underlying these tentative theological utterances was the dawning recognition among a few British archaeologists that, by definition, science *alone* is incapable of conducting a fruitful discourse with *pre*-scientific antiquity. As the Silbury Hill impasse indicates, the language of modern science, including Field's emphasis on analysis, is radically different from that employed and understood throughout antiquity. So different in their fundamental assumptions are these two worlds, as to be mutually incomprehensible to each other.

Today's archaeologists often restate the importance of chronological dating to their work. ('Nothing matters more than the dates', wrote A. Bayliss prior to the 2007 re-sampling of Silbury's primary mound.)[27] But they tend to forget an equally important dateline, namely that which separates their world of analytical reductionism and a techno-scientific frame of reference, introduced during the eighteenth century 'Enlightenment', from all previous eras of human life on earth.

This orthodoxy of unadulterated reason has retained its dominance into the twenty-first century. It tends to regard all previous rationales as based on deluded, irrational superstition. Where these discredited attitudes linger on, either in folklore or in religion, science typically ignores them or turns their 'outdated beliefs' into dry, value-cleansed, quantified data.

Ironically, the same estrangement from the past is prevalent among British prehistorians. Yet of all specialists, it surely behoves *them* to make a particular effort to escape from an exclusive faith in scientific procedures and assumptions. Otherwise they risk the self-entrapment of colonial officials, who, by displaying total loyalty to their own prestigious cultural baggage, inevitably return from their travels into the 'primitive' with little to show for their efforts.

Nevertheless, around Stone Age Silbury, faith in science as the foremost interpreter of ancient wisdom remains strong. For example, BBC News 24 announced in May 2007 that 'archaeologists will be going into Silbury, hoping that modern science can solve the mystery of why the hill was built'. This is not so much a case of Silbury's purpose now being 'lost in translation', but rather of little or no translation being attempted at all. Consequently, prehistoric meaning is largely absent from our reports.

Some experts are now well aware of this situation. For instance, at the end of his two-year analytical study of Silbury, David Field reflects on the need for a different future approach, considering that: 'the ultimate goal might be to obtain some insight into the perception of those who constructed the site'. Tellingly, he adds: '*To do so will necessarily involve dispensing with 20th century western preconceptions about both the prehistoric past and perceptions of landscape*' (author's italics).[28]

But even assuming a willingness to set aside his modern outlook, he does not say how a perspective typical of the third millennium BC can possibly be acquired.

The World of Myth

For help he could turn to the works compiled by students of comparative religion, myth and anthropology. From many of these studies one finds that, despite substantial variations, certain attitudes recur among pre-scientific communities. These include the following characteristics:

Active ritual engagement, as distinct from scientific objective scrutiny.
A belief in metamorphosis between humans, animals and plants.
A poetic zeitgeist, with an emphasis on synthesis rather than analysis.
Employment of multivalent symbols rather than single-function signs.
Supernatural narrative as the template of human morality and social life.
The total absence of abstract concepts or theory.
An awareness of the numinous quality of topographic features.
Experience of creation as a sacred, divinely given, living organism.
A cyclical, repeatable, festival-orientated attitude to time.
The integration of physical, emotional and intellectual aspects of being.

An appreciation of the union between macrocosm and microcosm.
A multi-layering of 'reality', involving 'this world' and a divine 'otherworld'.

To explore and understand these attitudes depends in part on the range of methods that the enquirer is prepared to use. Yet David Field, who is Silbury's English Heritage appointee, recommends the opposite. Perhaps because he is fluent in only one language, the scientific, he declares: 'As ever, it is imperative that a scientific approach to this [widening of scope] is adopted.'[29]

Thus, 'as ever', we are told that further investigations must be bound within a single methodological straight jacket. Scientific logic is to remain the *only* valid means of approach to the questions posed by Silbury's *pre*-scientific outlook.

Yet in seeking ways to mitigate this self-defeating mismatch one is faced with the complete dumbness of prehistory. How can the illiterate Neolithic, with no written texts, pass on its key religious beliefs after its oral voices have died away? In Atkinson's opinion the task of recovering these convictions was almost impossible:

> When finally the prehistorian comes to matters of faith and religion, he is usually inclined to take refuge altogether in silence [because] … the plain fact is that on such points there can be no certainty, or even any very high degree of probability, as long as written evidence is lacking.[30]

Professor G. Daniel shared his defeatism. He stated: 'the history of ideas begins with writing; there is not and never can be a history of prehistoric thought.'[31] Neither man appreciated that in preliterate eras a single work of art or architecture could display a 'book-full' of ideas.

6 The Neolithic Goddess. (*Left*) Wooden figurine found waterlogged under the Bell Track, Westhay, Somerset, 15in high, *c.* 2890 BC. (*Right*) Stone image of a goddess from Capdenac, Lot, France, *c.*3000 BC.

Neolithic Religion

By contrast, the Lithuanian archaeologist Professor Marija Gimbutas *did* understand this possibility, as she demonstrated in her book on the European Neolithic, *The Goddesses and Gods of Old Europe*.[32] She followed this with another book, entitled *The Language of the Goddess*.[33] Both were copiously illustrated. Numerous clay, stone and bone figurines of a female Neolithic deity were interrelated with sculpted and incised animal and plant motifs. She found the same vocabulary of shapes among the pots and utensils of the same period. When re-combined, these images presented an eloquent iconography of Neolithic belief in visual form; hence the second book's title.

These pictorial accounts, sympathetically interpreted, effectively gave voice to the prehistoric silence and vividly showed pan-European evidence of goddess-centred beliefs as the intellectual context for Silbury's construction. And this 'influx of European cultures' was particularly strong at that time, as Jim Cleary concedes.

As Gimbutas has revealed, the Neolithic ethos was centred upon the figure of a Great Goddess, the creator and mistress of the universe, who imbued all earthly life forms with her fecund persona and received the dead into her 'Mother Earth' mode, in a rotating continuum.

One effect of *The Language of the Goddess* was to lend more weight to a substantial body of evidence previously published by a few British researchers. They had brought together Stone Age visual imagery with similar material found in ethnography and folklore. In doing so, they, like Gimbutas, had shown that the Neolithic's spiritual heart did not necessarily lie beyond the bounds of modern enquiry.

Among these pioneering texts are O.G.S. Crawford's *The Eye Goddess* (1957), E.O. James' *The Cult of the Mother Goddess* (1959), and two books by M. Dames, both specifically concerned with the Avebury group of monuments.

The Protestant Blockade

But in Protestant England these works inevitably encountered a 500-year-old obstruction. Erected during the sixteenth-century Reformation, this cut us off from, and demanded a negative attitude towards religious imagery. A State Injunction, issued in 1548, ordered the removal of all images from every place of worship. It was followed by a nation-wide smashing of stained glass windows, the obliteration of sacred murals beneath lime wash, the decapitation of sculpted images of the godhead and his saints, and the despoliation of most rural shrines.

English historians have often deplored this iconoclasm, yet beneath an outward show of dismay, they have also inherited a discomfort with the very notion of sacred imagery, of whatever period. The sixteenth-century Reformation has to some degree remoulded the national psyche. Our minds have been whitewashed against the re-emergence of idols, including those bequeathed by prehistory.

This is confirmed in *The Oxford English Dictionary*. There 'idol' is defined as 'image of a deity worshipped by pagans, hence in scriptural language a false god, or fictitious divinity' and 'applied polemically to images of divine beings or saints'.

Therefore, when it is suggested that Silbury Hill may be part of the body of a Neolithic deity, drawn on an architectural scale, the proposition is likely to be dismissed as both repugnant and absurd. Likewise, how many contemporary Anglican bishops would share the commonly held view of their pre-Reformation counterparts, that the cruciform shape of Christian churches displays the spirit of the crucified Christ, contained within his mother's physical frame, as defined by walls and roof?

Where 'idols' have undeniably survived until recently, as in rural images of the female corn deity, annually plaited from straw, their potency has been diminished and disparaged by the term 'corn *dollies*', fit only for childish, superstitious peasants.

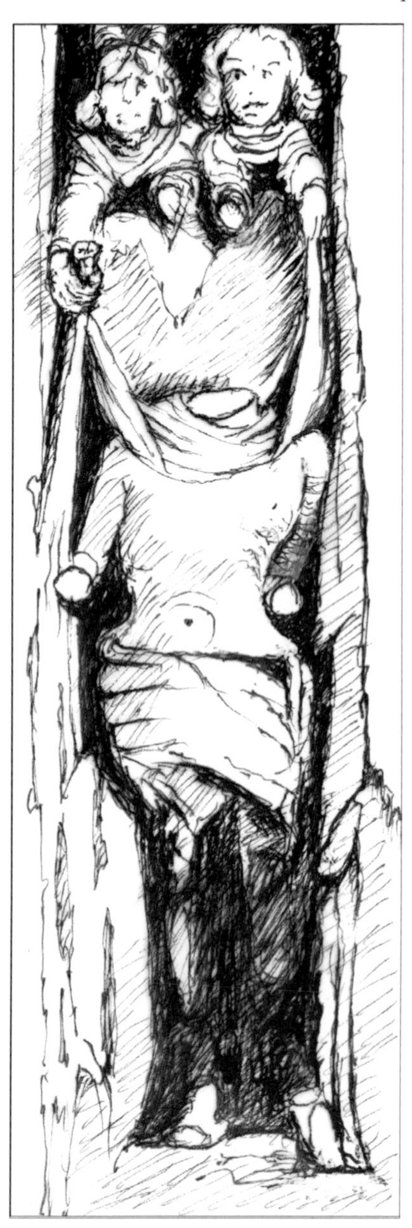

7 Iconoclasm in England. A beheaded, limbless remnant of Christ's deposition; Prince Arthur's chapel, Worcester Cathedral, carved *c.* 1504.

Opposite 8 No art, please. (*Above*) Horse head engraved on bone, *c.* 10,000 BC, Cresswell Crags, Derbyshire, denounced as a fake by Dr Wilson of the British Museum, but since authenticated following the discovery of Stone Age cave drawings (*below*) at Cresswell.

Below 9 Silbury summit repair. Eighty-three tonnes of crushed chalk and 497 tonnes of chalk paste were poured into the crater. The work was completed in April 2008. One year later consolidation had produced a 2ft-deep saucer-shaped depression here.

The iconoclasm, that began in mid-Tudor times and continued under Cromwell's seventeenth-century Protectorate, has left its mark on the reflexes of this country's modern prehistorians. For example, in 1990 I asked Dr Wilson, head of the British Museum's Palaeolithic (Old Stone Age) department, for permission to study a horse-engraved bone from Creswell Crags, Derbyshire. She stated that the item was not in her collection. Then, after an assistant produced the bone, Dr Wilson declared that it was a nineteenth-century forgery and that there was *no* figurative Palaeolithic art anywhere in Britain. Subsequently, a cave at Creswell has been found which displays several authenticated Stone Age drawings of herbivores, bison and birds, similar in style to those of south-west France.[34] (The horse-head bone has now been re-instated.)

Similarly, many British Neolithic scholars suffer from a blind spot regarding the art and architectural imagery of that period. This has been a major impediment to Silbury's elucidation. A failure to *see* brings an inability to interpret. To cast a sidelight onto our insular problem, one only has to consider the willingness of most continental archaeologists and museum curators to identify and label *their* Stone Age effigies, whether realistically rendered or highly stylised, as divinities.

The response to the self-same images by visiting British academics, adopting a fashionably secular stance, is often to trivialise them. For instance, the London-based P.J. Ucko toured Europe and the Near East in the 1960s and measured numerous Neolithic goddess figurines to the nearest millimetre. He concluded that these effigies were mainly 'toys or dolls, made for and by children', partly on the grounds that their fabric was typically fired clay rather than 'a more costly material'.[35]

In 1969, a comparable Stone Age 'demolition' was directed at the fully authenticated Mother Goddess engravings of Neolithic Brittany, by a Sheffield archaeologist, Andrew Fleming. He appealed to his male colleagues: 'The Mother Goddess has detained us for too long; let us disengage ourselves from her embrace.'[36]

The message from England was clear: 'No prehistoric religious art, *especially* not if female'! The Bristol historian, Professor R. Hutton, has greeted Ucko and Fleming's work as definitive, declaring that 'there was no possible answer' to their analysis. The very existence of a Stone Age goddess, in Hutton's opinion, has been 'shattered, blown to pieces for ever' by them.[37]

Silbury to the Devil

Another tactic used by British academics to deflect attention away from the internationally acknowledged Neolithic goddess (the divinity most likely to have inspired Stone Age Silbury) is to invoke the Devil. Although Satan first entered Wiltshire millennia after Silbury Hill was built (and thereby plays havoc with archaeology's rigorous pursuit of linear chronology and with its secular scientific outlook), his help is eagerly sought by these scientists.

For example, at a Silbury news conference on 10 March 2007, Dr Amanda Chadburn of English Heritage told the science editor of *The Telegraph* that the Devil was Silbury's rumoured founder. She chose to pluck this particular tale from a tangle of much more credibly archaic folk belief that surrounds the monument. Dr Chadburn's 'devil talk' flew round the world at internet speed, and effectively threw the global public off the Stone Age scent. Satan has a PhD in false trails. His Wiltshire story tells how he was intending to bury the nearby town of Marlborough under a shovelful of earth, but when a cobbler informed him that he had a vast distance still to go, the weary miscreant dropped his load, thereby accidentally creating Silbury Hill.[38]

Dr Chadburn did not mention that in one version of story the Devil carries the earth not in a shovel, but in his *apron*, a remarkably feminine garment.[39] This accords with the frequently encountered Welsh folk explanation for the origin of Neolithic megalithic tombs and monuments, namely that their constituent rocks were spilled from a giantess's apron.[40] Thus the apron-attired, Silbury 'Devil' might well hint at a pre-Christian giantess, still intent on claiming Silbury as her own apron's 'offspring', though here obliged to parade under an imposed Christian title. Since the apron, as a symbol of the womb, is known throughout Eurasia, Silbury's 'Devil-Giantess' may, in turn, represent the long after-shadow thrown by a lost Neolithic goddess, in whose name the hill was originally raised.

two

EARTHING THE MONUMENT

Silbury and the Goddess

However improbable it may seem, it was Professor Atkinson who was indirectly responsible for revealing Silbury as a Neolithic goddess, for it was he who recognised the monument as Neolithic. Moreover, as a prelude to his dig he had asked Bristol University's Geography Department to make him an accurate plan of the entire site, including the carefully shaped ditch. This plan (which closely resembles an earlier one published in 1887 by A.C. Pass) was printed on the back of a BBC pamphlet, issued to accompany the 1968 excavation.[1]

Hey presto! Thanks to that cartographic outline, a squatting goddess re-emerged, closely resembling hundreds of Neolithic figurines, albeit on a greatly enlarged scale. Here, in a flash, at – *and as* – Silbury, the archaic maternal deity reappeared. Student geographers (whose subject starts with 'Ge', the ancient Greek earth goddess) were the agents who unwittingly helped resolve the Silbury enigma.

Their map shows with extraordinary clarity that ditch and hill are two parts of a single design, in which hole and hill, negative and positive, underworld and sky, combine. The chalk that formed the great Hill was dug out from the surrounding quarry with antler picks. It was carefully shaped around the edge by the Neolithic architects in order to describe the harmonious outline of their squatting goddess's plump 'pond-body'. (As is well known, people are also mostly water.) The Neolithic builders were engaged in far more than extraction of material. Rather, they were creating a gigantic image of their presiding deity. From the pit, successfully made to contain the waters that still form most of her shape, her hill-womb literally grew. It was a matter of give and take.[2]

Through more than four millennia Silbury Hill, together with sun, moon and stars, has been reflected in this 'Lady of the Lake's' watery head and maternal form. The Hill is her full womb, set in, belonging to and rising from her body, described by water. Her Hill's promise of fecundity amounts to the highest and arguably the most important monument in European prehistory.

One expert in modern times who recognised Silbury as a rock *and* water monument was Sir Flinders-Petrie. In 1923 he concluded that Silbury's valley bottom position was chosen in order to create a water feature around the hill,[3] though later workers seemed unaware of this insight. Thus David Field, after a lengthy survey of the hill in 2001, could write of a 'lack of emphasis on the ditch', adding 'it is perhaps surprising that there has been so little investigation of the ditch'.[4]

In fact, a quarter of a century earlier I had proposed that Silbury was planned as a ditch-contained water temple, in the image of the Neolithic squatting goddess. Today, as originally intended, she measures 1109ft from the top of her westward pointing head to the underside of her eastward facing thigh. Her breast points southwards, her straight back lies towards the Avebury Henge. So disposed, she incorporates the cardinal points and the four quarters into her metabolism.

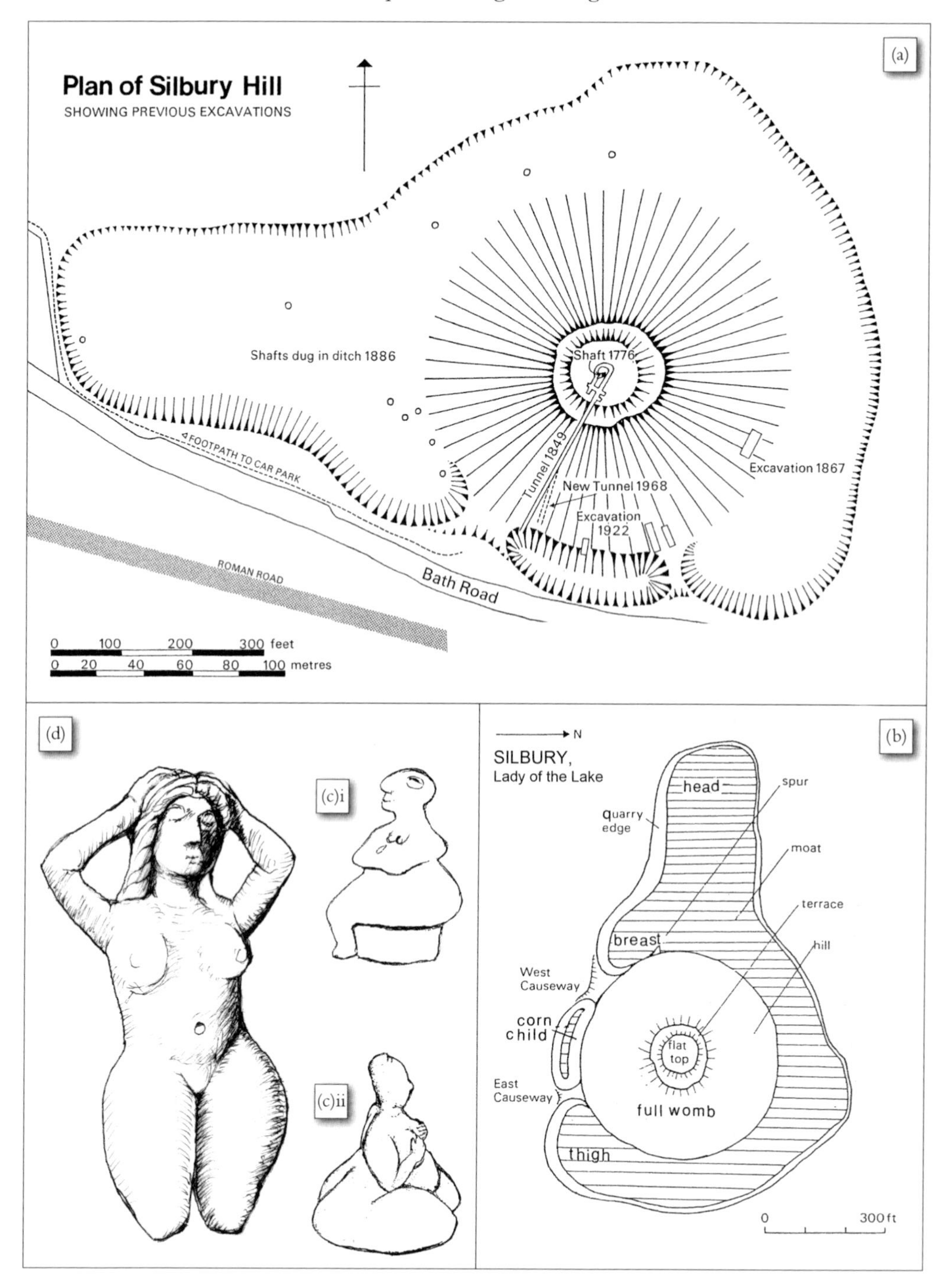

10(a) Plan of Silbury, drawn in 1968. (b) Silbury's moat and hill, seen together as an architectural image of the Neolithic squatting goddess. (ci and cii) Neolithic goddess figurine from Pazardzik, Bulgaria (*top*) and Catal Huyuk, Anatolia. (d) Archaic Greek terracotta statuette of the goddess Ge, alias Gaia, 'Earth'.

Her central axis is precisely aligned with equinoctial sunrise and sunset, when night and day are always of equal length. She is perfectly balanced.[5]

Between her watery knee and breast, two 'causeways' of natural chalk were left undisturbed by the Stone Age architects. In addition to providing access to the hill, they define a dry section of ditch as a possible 'child', pressed against its mother's belly wall.

As many Neolithic figurines demonstrate, the squatting pose was favoured because it represented the moment of divine parturition or childbirth. To emphasise this, in sculpts the unborn infant is depicted about to emerge from between its mother's thighs.[6] At Silbury, the architects employed the same squatting pose, but laid in a horizontal plane, essential for water containment, thereby giving extra emphasis to the vertically rising womb-hill.

Today's summertime visitors to Silbury may find the surrounding ditch completely dry. This is partly because the fast growing nearby town of Swindon is drawing increasing amounts of water from the underlying chalk strata. In addition, a 3m-deep layer of silt has accumulated in the ditch since it was first dug. Without the silt, the ditch would be full of water all year round, as A.C. Pass realised in 1887. His 10 trial shafts sunk into the ditch encountered water over 2m deep.[7] Even in the twenty-first century, despite handicaps, the Silbury water goddess often reappears above the silt in winter and spring. Swans are then to be seen, floating on her body. At other times she can wear an all-encompassing garment of translucent ice.

In August 1969 Atkinson sunk a trench to the original ditch floor and was astonished by the power and persistence of the invading floodwaters. He brought in several pumps to suck it out, not realising that the ditch was deliberately based on a thin layer of natural clay (known to geologists as Plenus marl), in order to create the necessary body-lake.[8] This supply is supplemented by water entering the moat at the west or 'head' end, delivered by a brook flowing from Beckhampton.

That the water table was as high, if not higher, during the period of Silbury's construction was proved in 2007 by researchers exploring beneath the hill. From there, F. McAvoy reported: 'The Neolithic workmen were struggling with wet ground conditions.'[9] A recent survey by J.G. Evans of the water-born alluvium on the valley floor confirms this view.[10]

Objections

Since 1976, when *The Silbury Treasure: The Great Goddess Rediscovered* first appeared in print, most (but not all) archaeologists have either ignored or dismissed its interpretation of the monument. In the official English Heritage account of the Avebury monuments, written in 1989 by C. Malone, curator of Avebury's Keiller Museum, she gave two reasons for rejecting the Silbury lake goddess hypothesis: 'This theory rests much of its argument on an aerial view of the site, and on comparison with goddess figurines from distant parts of the world, neither of which would have been available to Neolithic people.'[11]

Her first point suggests that the moat can only be seen from an aircraft or balloon. But this is not the case. An 'aerial' view of the entire water figure can be obtained by walking around the terrace just below the hill's summit. In Atkinson's unchallenged opinion, this broad ledge is an original Neolithic feature of the monument. Neolithic people would surely have taken advantage of this 'sky-high' opportunity to gaze at the surrounding water goddess who they had laboured so hard to create.

Malone also asserts categorically that Silbury 'cannot be seen from within the Avebury circles'.[12] Yet its flat top is clearly visible from the middle of the henge's south circle to anyone who cares to glance upwards. This inter-visibility of two major contemporary monuments, apparently a Neolithic intention, is lost on Malone, though the inter-monument sightline is only 200 paces from her museum door. However, she *does* concede that the Avebury Henge describes a circle, even if its sprawling size (much more extensive than Silbury's moat), makes it impossible to see the whole ring from any one point. Yet she nowhere insists that *it* can only be read from the air.

Narrative, Icon, Ritual

Another way to comprehend Silbury is to perambulate the moat at ground level. To those who are inclined to 'do the rounds' of the moat's circumference, the divine image is gradually revealed, feature after feature, as is the case with all deities conceived on an architectural scale, such as Christ – referencing cruciform churches.

A similar journey is traced on foot during Easter 'Stations of the Cross' processions. Likewise, people who undertake mountain pilgrimages in Ireland and elsewhere find that topography's suggestive shapes amalgamate with their prayers and the mythic storyline as the walk proceeds.[13] Such fusions, brought to life both in recent practices and earlier cultures, are probably at one with Stone Age tradition.

In most eras, worship typically involves the integration of three elements: (1) divine narrative; (2) visual icons – both natural and of human making, and on every scale; (3) ritual acts. Because these basic ingredients are employed worldwide, it is safe to assume that the Silbury goddess was seasonally 'reactivated' by a communal re-tracing of her outline, ritual submergence in her waters, facilitated by the chalk steps that lead under her water-breast, and ascent of her womb-hill. In almost any pre-scientific society this type of behaviour would have been expected.

However, to appreciate the lake lady's effigy, lying at the heart of Silbury's original meaning, requires more than a febrile 'snap shot' mentality. As with the first encounter between two people, time is required for a relationship to develop. The same applies to the study of an ancient edifice such as Silbury. Architecture, like sculpture, can only be fully known 'in the round'. Therefore, if time is spent wandering the profile of the supposed water lady's reclining form, leaving aside the opportunity (now out of bounds) to absorb the entire image from the hilltop or from its surrounding Neolithic viewing terrace, the chances of seeing her will be proportionally increased. Helicopters are not required.

The Silbury Lake remains more than an inconvenient swamp in a utilitarian quarry, complained of by Skanska engineers in 2008, as they drove their heavy equipment across the unrecognised goddess's waterlogged thigh. Indeed, both Field and Cleary are now prepared to acknowledge the importance of water to Silbury's siting, though 'the connection to water was completely under-estimated and under-valued by archaeologists until very recently', according to their Regional Director, Dr R.H. Bewley, writing to me in 2007.[14]

One puzzle facing a purely functionalist attitude towards the Silbury moat is what Field terms its 'western extension' (i.e., the goddess's neck and head). This lobe is hard to account for on strictly practical grounds. Indeed, 30 years after *The Silbury Treasure* was published, some English Heritage thoughts are now beginning to turn to a religious justification for the entire moat. For instance, Field has floated the idea that water may have been considered necessary to repel evil spirits![15] Is Satan coming again?

Figurines

Malone's second objection to interpreting Silbury as a large-scale pregnant female image concerns my use of 'comparison with Goddess figurines from distant parts of the world, which would not have been available to Neolithic people' in Britain. Here, apparently, despite being physically attached to it until relatively recently, we had no contact with mainland Europe – a claim so bizarre as to require no refutation.

Equally untrue is the assertion that there were no small-scale models in Britain for Silbury to draw on. In the first instance female figurines were everywhere inspired by and modelled after real women. The pregnant women of Neolithic Britain were the dependable life models for that society's goddess. (Who could reasonably argue for a Neolithic Britain, flourishing for thousands of years, *without* pregnant women and human mothers?)

Throughout the world, including Britain, veneration of the woman as a living image representing the source of new life in general has also inspired the creation of female figurines as objects of worship. This attitude, inherited from the Old Stone Age, is known to have risen to particular prominence wherever farming was introduced. There and then, the poetic interconnection with seed sowing and germination within 'Mother Earth' gave an additional metaphoric scope to womankind, with female connotations of universal renewal further enhanced.

Why should Britain have been excluded from this sacred perception of the feminine? In truth it was not. For our Old Stone Age of hunter-gatherers, the Palaeolithic expert, S. Aldhouse-Green, has identified three carved bone 'goddess' figurines from Paviland cave, South Wales, made *c.*23,000 BC. As he remarks, the cavern (as uterus?) is set into a white limestone cliff of a truncated cone shape. He believes that this natural feature (a proto-Silbury Hill) was probably venerated by those who deposited the figurines in the cave at its base.[16]

The same writer convincingly compares the Paviland figurines with others of the same age and similar design from Moravia and from sites on the Russian plain.[17] These 'distant parts of the world' (to use Malone's phrase) show how unified Palaeolithic Europe was in its goddess iconography. From Britain eastwards, Aldhouse-Green discerns 'a far-flung social and exchange network, extending to the very gates of Asia'. In truth, attempts to deprive Britain of this heritage have been based more on 'Little Englander' parochialism and a puritanical distaste for 'idols', than on the archaeological record. Life in the British Mesolithic or Middle Stone Age, *c.*12,000–7000 BC, may also have revolved around a goddess image, such as that found at Nab Head, Pembrokeshire. This 41mm-long shale figurine, with large buttocks and an elongated neck, is presumed to have served as a fertility amulet. It (she) was found with 33 shale beads.[18]

While many British Neolithic squatting goddess figurines have disintegrated in the testing British climate, a wooden image found beneath the Bell Track in the Somerset marshes has survived, thanks to its waterlogged placement. This big-breasted squatting female, shown in the act of giving birth, was carved from ash wood, radiocarbon-dated to *c.*2890 BC.[19] She is 15.5cm tall and was discovered set upside down in the marsh within a group of pegs, beneath the overlaid wooden

11 The pre-Neolithic goddess in Britain. (a) A carved bone female figurine from Goat's Hole, Paviland, South Wales, *c.*21,000 BC. (b) This 200ft-high limestone cliff is naturally endowed with a brow, mouth, shoulders and vulva, and was probably seen overall as a gigantic 'humanoid' female deity. Palaeolithic interments in Goat Hole (*centre*) include a red ochre-coated human body, a mammoth skull and three goddess figurines. The cave received more offerings in Roman times.

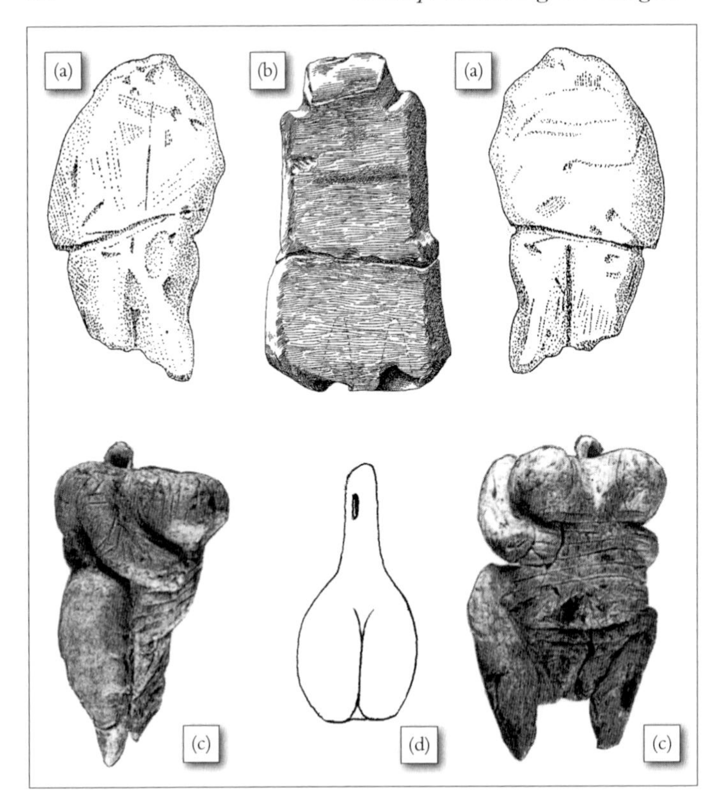

12 Goddess figurines (a–a) from Windmill Hill, Avebury, fourth millennium BC; carved chalk with emphasised groin and 'belt'. (b) Neolithic chalk figurine from Maiden Castle, Dorset. (c–c) Mammoth ivory figurine from Hohle Fels, Germany, 6cm tall, carved *c.*28,000 BC. (d) Figurine from Nab Head, Pembrokeshire, *c.*10,000 BC.

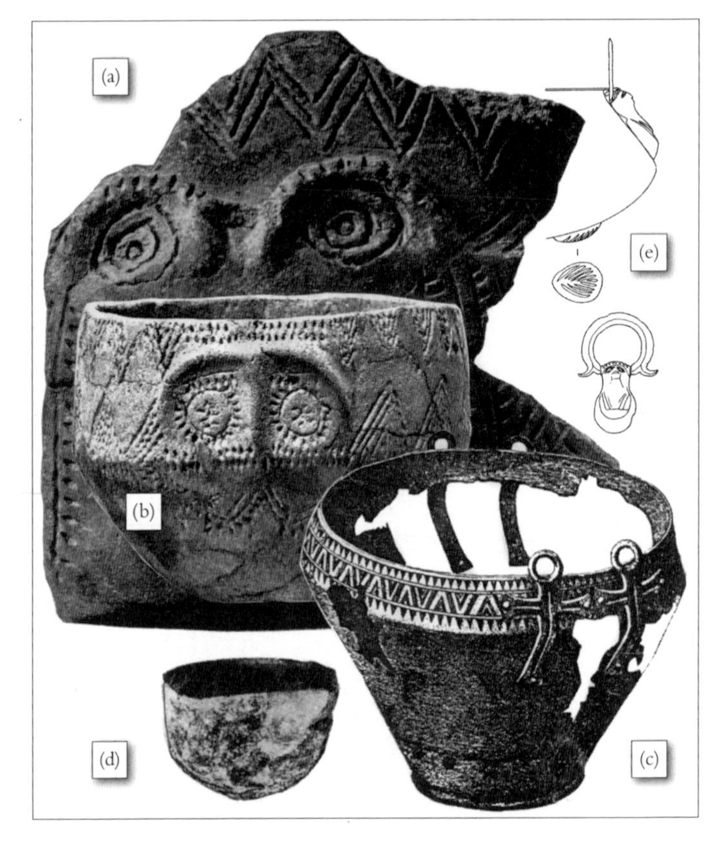

13 Goddess as pot. (a) In Denmark 'The goddess still gazes at us from the clay vessels of the [Neolithic] passage graves', writes P.V. Glob. (b) Neolithic 'eye goddess' pot from Svino, Kong parish; 15cm diameter. (c) Bronze Age bucket from Birkendegaardd, Zealand, with handle mounts as four deities spinning the solar wheel. (d) Skull-shaped pot, fourth millennium BC, Avebury. (e) A Romano-British bronze hanging bowl with female deity-shaped escutcheons and 'vulva' emblems on base; found Westbury, Wiltshire.

track. In the excavator's view she was probably a votive offering, carved to guide and ensure the success of the work. He classified her as a 'dolly', in line with the1960s reductive terminology, but with a 'god' rather than a 'goddess' prefix, hence 'god-dolly', because he saw her emerging 'child of renewal' as phallic.

To find Silbury's equivalent in female figurine size, we can therefore either look overseas or travel no further than the neighbouring counties of Somerset or Dorset. At Maiden Castle in Dorset Sir Mortimer Wheeler found an early Neolithic female figurine, sculpted out of chalk and with peg holes intended for her detachable limbs.[20]

Despite Malone's belief that no Neolithic figurines have been found in Britain, it is well known that two female figurines, dated *c.*3350 BC, were discovered in the early Neolithic camp on Windmill Hill, less than 2 miles from Silbury. Unearthed by A. Keiller, and now displayed at the Avebury Museum bearing his name, they have been accepted as authentic by the very conservative Neolithic authority I.F. Smith. In 1965 she drew and described them. Carved from chalk, they are 10cm and 6cm high. Both have 'a deep groove between the thighs', while the taller has 'an irregular groove about the buttocks that might represent a belt'.[21]

These stylised human females closely resemble the chief deity of a much earlier time and a distant place, such as the similarly 'abstract' figurine, carved from ivory, found at Dolne Vestonice, in Moravia (fig. 12 c, d). It is at least 10,000 years older than the pair from Windmill Hill. This effigy also displays the deep groove between the thighs and the characteristic Old Stone Age woman's belt. The Moravian figure 'symbolizes the potential fertility of the mature female', according to A. Marshack.[22]

As at Windmill Hill, the symbol in question embodies the epitome of fruitfulness in a supernatural womanly form. Through such depictions, both Old and New Stone Ages maintained a common adherence to their pivotal goddess. Her images silently spoke for many thousands of years. Appropriately, the Windmill Hill figurines were set in a pit overlooking the valley where Silbury was later to arise.

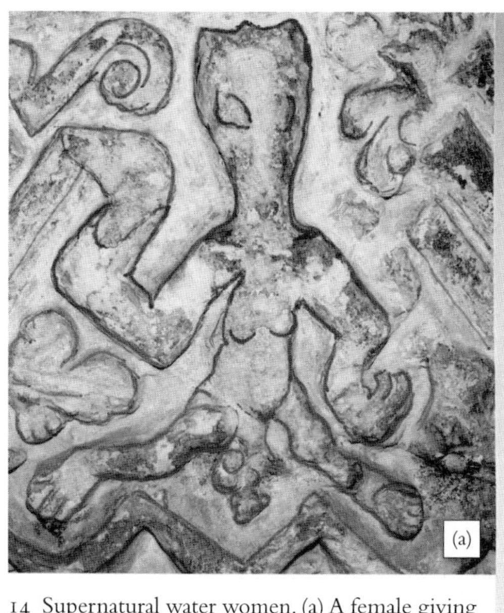

14 Supernatural water women. (a) A female giving birth to vegetation on the twelfth-century font at Winterbourne Monkton, near Avebury. (b i) The Neolithic Westhay idol, deposited in a swamp, compared with (ii) Silbury as water-deity. In many early myths the entire earth is born from water and human embryos are believed to originate in water.

Moreover, the goddess outlived the entire prehistoric era and even managed to survive the arrival of Christianity in Britain. So vital was her presence to the rural community's hopes of good fortune, that her image was incorporated into many parish churches. For example, the twelfth-century font at Winterbourne Monkton, a village only 2 miles north of Silbury, shows her depicted in low relief, with legs apart and a sprig of vegetation issuing from her vulva. In her right hand she holds a sickle.

The Goddess at Sea

As Jim Cleary has pointed out, the mid-third millennium, the period of Silbury's construction, 'was a time when Britain was being influenced by an influx of European cultures'.[23] And since, throughout prehistory, all societies were fundamentally deity based, such an influx implies a further strengthening of divine ties between Britain and the Continent, where goddess imagery abounds. In effect, Cleary's statement implies the coming of yet another wave of New Stone Age goddess culture, diffused, east to west, across Europe, from the eighth millennium onwards, with each surge further broadening and deepening the earlier Palaeolithic devotion to her image.

To have taken and adopted the Continent's Neolithic benefits of ploughing, weaving, pottery manufacture and architecture, but *not* the divinity worshipped as the sacred mother of these innovations, as Malone implies, is hardly credible. Admittedly, in today's largely secular England, museum curators tend to set religious artefacts only at the end of their displays, after more 'serious' practical matters have been dealt with. Yet even now, Sunday, nominated as God-the-Creator's day, remains the first, not the last day of the week. This was also the pattern in Neolithic Britain, where all practical innovations were believed to come from divinely granted prototypes.

It is safe to assume that however far she had travelled from the east, the Eurasian goddess was given a place of honour in the cross-channel boats, and not left behind on the Continental shore. At Silbury we see evidence of her 're-arrival' and renewed influence during the mid-third millennium BC. Silbury fulfilled the human urge, already deeply rooted in our soil, to furnish goddess worship with a working image; and here it was imagined and delivered on an unprecedented scale.

Silbury Stirring

Shortly after the 1969 Silbury dig had ended, a 2ft-high concrete plinth was set into the ground, overlooking the west end of the hill's moat. Riveted into this reinforced block was a bronze-coloured metal plate, embossed with lettering which informed the visitor that Silbury Hill was a prehistoric monument of unknown purpose. There the empty message stood for decades. If not a tomb, better that it should mean nothing, and *be* nothing to us. In this way Silbury's official guardians sought to protect the public from the possibility of infection by heretical books such as *The Silbury Treasure: The Great Goddess Rediscovered* (1976).

Twenty-two years later, a review appeared in the journal *British Archaeology*, under the headline: 'Silbury Hill and the New Age Angle'. It was of Professor A. Whittle's book, *Sacred Mound, Holy Rings.* The sacred mound in question was Silbury Hill, and the text was Whittle's new gloss on Atkinson's old excavation notes. Frances Lynch, Professor of Archaeology at Bangor University, wrote the review and was taken aback by the words 'Sacred' and 'Holy' in Whittle's title. Had Atkinson survived until 1998 he would doubtless have shared Lynch's unease, given his views on the near impossibility of interpreting prehistoric religions.

Yet Whittle discerned in Silbury evidence for a 'spiritual ethos of voluntarily accepted authority' and saw religious enthusiasm as the motivating passion behind the hill's construction. Both it and the nearby Avebury monuments were, he wrote, designed to celebrate 'the mythic, ritual, or sacred dimensions of Neolithic life'.[24]

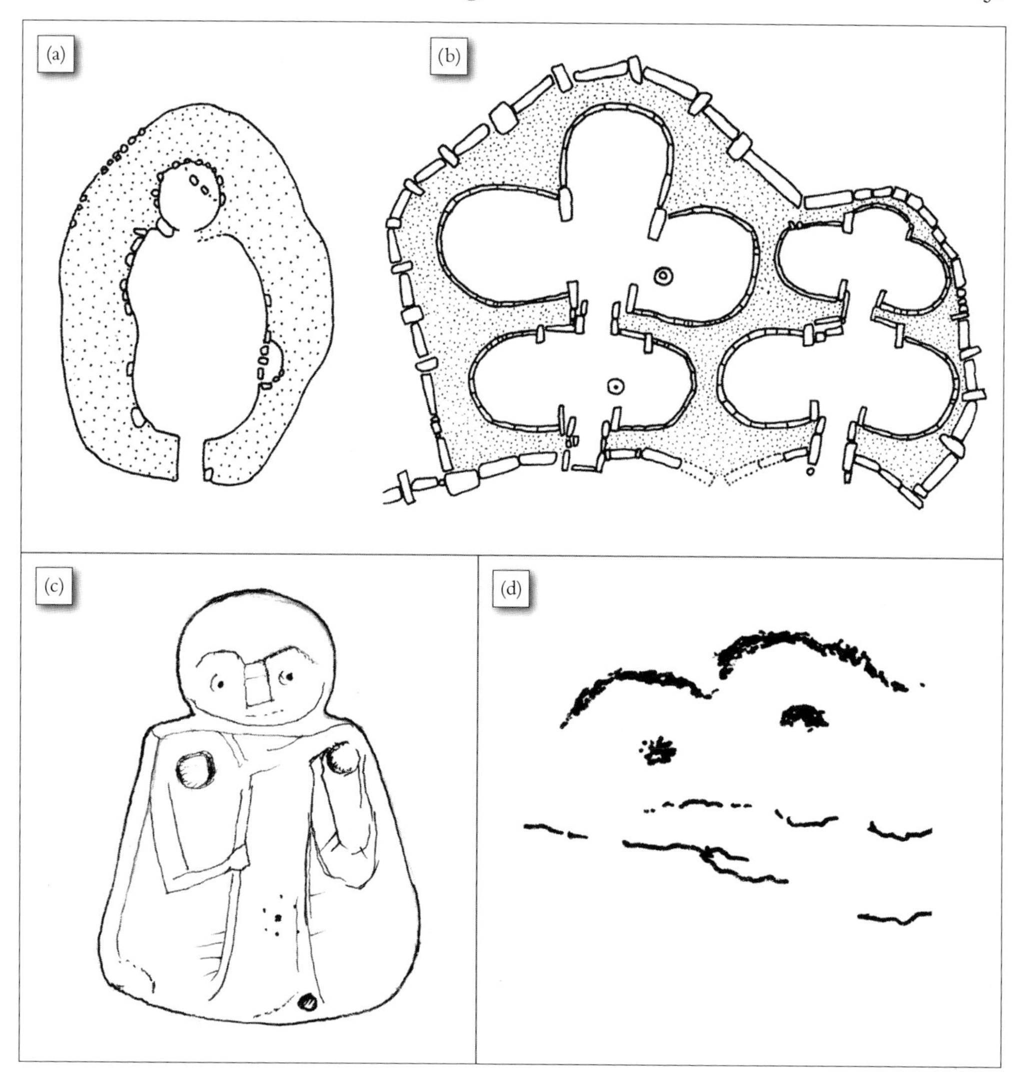

15 Figurine and architecture. (a) Neolithic house at Gruting School, Shetland. (b) Neolithic temple of Ggantija, Malta, planned as gigantic divine mother and offspring. (c) Engraved sandstone figurine, *c.*2500 BC, 3.4cm high, buried under a Neolithic house on Westray, Orkney; found by J. Kainz in 2009. The goddess draws back her cloak while her left hand points to a breast. (d) Eye-dot and eyebrow motif carved on a Neolithic chambered tomb at Holm of Papa, Orkney. From figurine to monument, the Neolithic deity was represented on every scale.

Perhaps the English 'Ice Age' was about to thaw. Whittle's work presaged a welcome, if belated, attempt to contact a non-prosaic prehistoric reality, from which British archaeology had for so long largely debarred itself. But, for her part, Lynch preferred to savour whatever 'factual elements in this book' she could find. She assumed that any religious speculation was bound to be insubstantial and of short-lived value. What she described as Whittle's 'New Age' drift, redolent of pot-smoking hippies, offered 'at best a hazy way' to approach the Stone Ages, old or new. Absurdly, any attempt to approach prehistoric religion, which undoubtedly formed the nucleus that transmitted overall cohesion and meaning to prehistoric communities, was to be disparaged from the outset as a 'New Age' jaunt. Lynch spoke for many experts who claim to be offering a valid account of our remote past.

At the start of his work, Whittle rightly attributes sacredness to the hill's entire fabric. No longer an oversized tomb mound, it was to stand instead as a heap of ultimate worth. From the organic material in the primary core, through the skilfully stacked chalk blocks and their chalk rubble infill, to the soil and grass that form the hill's protective clothing against the ravages of frost and rain – all these ordinary ingredients were to be transformed under the 'Sacred' banner of his book's title. In a word, Silbury was made over, consecrated to a supernatural power and purpose.

What is more, his text showed that this change was entirely compatible with a meticulous *scientific* analysis of Silbury's organic components, based on documentation from the 1968 dig. Science was at last encouraged to feel at home within a sacred context. For instance, his Table 5 lists pollen counts from grains found in the hill's core. They came from oak trees, alder, lime and hazel.[25] All were present in the late Neolithic woods. These fringed the farmlands, where (as most of Silbury's buried pollen showed) a wide range of grasses flourished, indicating a predominantly open grassland habitat for the locality. In addition, plough marks, found under the South Street long barrow close to Silbury, showed that arable agriculture was also in full swing long before Silbury's construction. Other Silbury pollens listed by Whittle are from flowers familiar to us, including buttercups, madder, cow parsley and wild roses, all mixed with those of blackberry and nettle.[26]

For these gifts Atkinson and Whittle deserve sincere thanks. From the dry record we can almost inhale the Neolithic air and recognise its scent as that of today's countryside! It wafts across the millennia to the 'here and now', as naturally as breathing. So too does the hope that by sharing (as we do) these ancestrally populated meadows, our own inherited spiritual capacities may be enhanced.

Sacred Abstract

The English word 'sacred' comes from Latin *sacer*, 'consecrated to a deity' and 'placed under its divine patronage or protection'. Similarly, in plain English, 'sacred' is: (i) 'Consecrated to, or esteemed especially dear to a deity'; (ii) 'Associated with religious symbolism'; (iii) 'Safeguarded by religion, inviolable, sacrosanct'.

Silbury has not remained sacrosanct. Instead, the temple has been violated at least three times in the last three centuries, including once by a high-ranking Church of England cleric. By now, one might think its holiness has been destroyed beyond recall. Indeed, as Lynch's reaction shows, most scholars are unwilling to study the monument in religious terms or to concede that such an approach is feasible.

Given this consensus, Whittle's account of Silbury is understandably tentative in tone, as if he has just landed on an unknown island and has stumbled upon a random scatter of abstract nouns and adjectives, derived from lost religious languages, the nature of which he is reluctant to guess at. Yet with these fragments he gamely juggles.

When summarising his findings, he writes of 'special ritual knowledge' (unspecified) and (equally vaguely) of 'ancestors, spirits or gods'. His key sentence, beginning 'My emphasis on the mythic, ritual or sacred dimensions of Neolithic life', is left dangling without enlargement or justification.[27] Though myth always involves one or more deities engaged in a divine drama, he names no divinities, nor their likely Silbury deeds. And because the well-established Neolithic goddess remains an apparently taboo subject for him, and no other gods come to his aid, he is left with a vacuum.

To fill the void, references to Mesopotamian ziggurats, Egyptian pyramids, Madagascar and Mississippian earth mounds are listed, but not assimilated. Instead, after a few unfocussed references to landscape and 'some association with water flow', he contemplates Silbury's summit, musing: 'Perhaps we could envisage prophets shouting at the sky from the top'.[28] (Of what, he does not say. Are they advocating his immediate return to a strict diet of pure science?)

Yet, with the benefit of hindsight, one can see that in 1998 Whittle set a trend which has since been followed by other Silbury professionals. He pioneered a genre of well-intentioned evasion, which serves as a convenient refuge for those who seem determined to exclude the Silbury deity from her own monumental effigy.

Now, guided by Whittle, Britain's prehistorians can relax in a bath of ill-defined, 'sacred' generalisations. For example, on 11 May 2007 an English Heritage spokeswoman stated that Silbury 'may have been a sacred place of pilgrimage. We don't know exactly what it was for, but it was probably part of a sacred ceremonial landscape which centred on the Avebury Henge.'[29]

In the same vein, Jim Cleary summed up the meaning of Silbury, speaking on 21 November 2007: 'We know that something about this site was incredibly sacred and special to generations of people, but we have no idea what.'[30] In short, Silbury's voids have been plugged but the public is left feeling hollow inside, for as one solitary, courageous archaeologist, T. Insoll, has recently admitted: 'religion has been almost completely neglected by the archaeological community'. He adds: 'The absence of religion seems like a basic omission [because] a spiritual dimension has been important to humankind since at least the Upper Palaeolithic.'

A curious symmetry has developed around Silbury studies. In place of the vanquished imaginary monarch under the hill-as-mausoleum, there is now an officially unmentionable, unnamed, perhaps non-existent deity *somehow* linked to the whole site, but debarred by a feat of collective self-censorship from reuniting with her physical form. Yet from the crown of her moat-head, to the watery thigh beneath her pregnant womb-hill, she continues to recline full length and on the surface, for all, including her appointed guardians, to see.

Synthesis and Departmentalism

The sequence of recent events at Silbury demonstrates how far our own culture has drifted away from the synthesis portrayed by Silbury's design. For if 'bringing together' was a Neolithic priority, by contrast a harmful subdivision of skills is the price paid for modernity's many achievements.

Silbury studies have suffered from the departmentalised, fragmented state of British academia. Therein, the unity of spirit with material life, normal in antiquity, has been systematically dismantled. In today's universities, where over-specialisation in self-isolated departments is the norm, theology is barely on speaking terms with archaeology, while folklore (which *does* contain vestiges of the archaic synthesis) is rarely considered at all.

Archaeologists seem largely unaware that beyond the confines of their discipline, other groups of equally isolated scholars have for centuries been studying comparative religion and mythology, thereby creating an invaluable resource that has been at best under used. Conversely, comparative religion's explorations into our fascinating mythic heritage have sometimes been hampered by an insufficient familiarity with the physical structures left behind by ancient societies – a shortcoming that archaeology is qualified to rectify. The Silbury enigma might be resolved if these and other perspectives could be induced to cross-pollinate. By merging the approaches, Silbury's purpose *and* the values of the 'lost' civilisation for which it stands might then be recovered, then to assume unexpected contemporary relevance.

To set Silbury's apparently inert mass within a context of basic religious ideas, common to all humanity, was a task first attempted with youthful enthusiasm and insufficient knowledge in *The Silbury Treasure* (1976). The following chapters enlarge on that hazardous interdisciplinary enterprise, here undertaken for a second time, and (it is hoped) with more skill than was initially shown.

three

SILBURY AND SWALLOWHEAD

Chalk Valleys

The primary 'document' in this study of Silbury is the landscape in which it is set. The same topographic features that we see now were here from the start of the human adventure. The discovery of Mesolithic flint tools in the vicinity prove that by 10,000 BC hunter-gatherers were familiar with the forest-clad dry valleys of the Marlborough Downs, long before farmers and herders of domesticated livestock appeared on the scene.[1]

What the earliest wanderers had in common with the later arrivals was a need for water. This they found in the River Kennet valley. In particular, they were likely to have been drawn to that river's dramatic springhead, called Swallowhead, still the acknowledged birthplace of the Kennet, even though a substantial headwater of the same river, now named Winterbourne, rises 5 miles further north, at NG 099763, near the village of Broad Hinton.

Holy Spring

The Winterbourne's ill-defined source lacks the dramatic allure of Swallowhead, where, as throughout the Stone Ages, from a natural tunnel at the base of a chalk cliff, pure water comes gurgling, as it gleams and trickles into view, bringing underworld and surface reality together. It was at Swallowhead that the *genius loci* of the area 'spoke' to people.

The porosity of chalk, combined with a drop in the level of the water table, a million years ago, has caused the Swallowhead rivulet to run underground for the first 2 miles of its valley's length from Beckhampton Plantation. (To find this subterranean waterway, a 20ft-deep modern well shaft was sunk a mile above Swallowhead.) In geological terms, the emergence of the stream at Swallowhead occurs because there it strikes a thin layer of clay, the Plenus marl. To prehistoric eyes this spring was seen as a land-lady giving birth to a river.[2]

An inclination to regard topography in superhuman terms prevailed throughout pre-scientific times. Therefore, Neolithic people were disposed to regard Swallowhead with awe, as an epiphany of their living goddess. At her spring they witnessed the Earth Mother in labour, repeatedly delivering her holy river-child.

Today this same 'water-baby' wanders 22 yards to join the Winterbourne, thereby changing that stream's name to Kennet, or Cunnit. Both these names are related to the ancient word 'cunt'. (Thanks to the Judeo-Christian doctrine of Original Sin, blamed primarily on Eve, 'cunt', which previously indicated the sacred vulva, gateway to new life, became a shocking blasphemy.)

16 Swallowhead flowing, 29 July 1971. This spring is regarded as the source of the River Kennet, which flows eastwards to join the Thames at Reading. Silbury is 520 yards from and within sight of Swallowhead. Throughout antiquity supernatural powers were believed to have created nature and then hovered around their creations as 'spirits of place'.

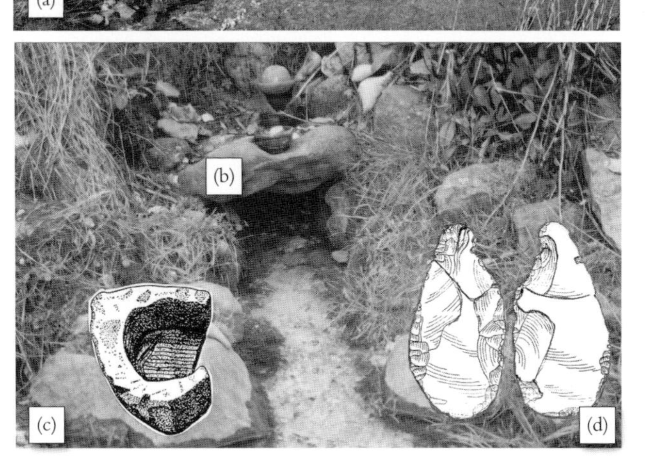

17(a) Swallowhead (*bottom left*) with its water running against the base of the natural bank and with Silbury (*top right*). (b) Swallowhead outflow, 2007, with the chalk face protected by natural sarsen stone. (c) A fourth millennium BC carved chalk 'springhead' image from the Windmill Hill early Neolithic enclosure, 2 miles from Swallowhead. (d) A Swallowhead mother? Two views of a worked Neolithic flint found at the G55 site, overlooking the spring.

18 (*Top*) A mother and child at the Swallowhead spring, 2007. (*Bottom*) Its water flows into and renames the Winterbourne stream as River Kennet (or Cunnit). A symbol of birth, this spring helped inspire 'Mother Silbury's' temple, built nearby. Through such visual metaphors organic cohesion was achieved.

Evidence abounds from the Old Stone Age onwards for the veneration of underground watercourses, emerging from white limestone caverns, where the walls often display human vulva symbols, as at La Ferrassie.[3] Also in France, the Peche Merle[4] and Lascaux caves,[5] like those of Altamira in Spain,[6] illustrate the same impulse which inspired the ritual art found in Britain's late Palaeolithic grottoes of Creswell Crags,[7] Paviland,[8] Kendrick's Cave on Great Orme's Head,[9] and Kent's cavern, Devon.[10] Likewise at Swallowhead, the rocky enclave and its emerging stream were probably worshipped as the source of all life.

Though the 18in-high Swallowhead tunnel was always too small for human entry, to Stone Age people the exposed rock around the springhead drew attention to her inaccessible generative organs, identified with the 'cave' within the coomb.

To judge by the surviving convictions of many 'primitive' societies, the earth does not necessarily need a male partner to produce her children. It was believed that women could receive an ancestral spirit, stored in a cavern, directly into their wombs, before returning it to life as a new-born child.[11] In one way or another, the Neolithic population of the Avebury district may have regarded the Swallowhead cave as *their* underground place of origin.

Folk Customs

When William Stukeley visited Avebury in 1719 he encountered whisps of this archaic devotion. He noted:

> Swallowhead or true fountain of the Kennet, which the county people call by the true name of Cunnit ... is not a little famous among them... To this day the country people have a particular regard for herbs growing about the springhead, and a high opinion of their virtue.[12]

In the Neolithic, these herbs, which included the white flowering water plant *apium nodiflorum*, may have been revered as the immortal goddess's pubic hair *and* as her vegetable progeny.

Silbury rises a mere 520 paces north of and is inter-visible with Swallowhead. However, in his review of *The Silbury Treasure*, written shortly after the book was published, Professor Atkinson rejected the idea that the spring had any bearing on Silbury's placement. He implied that the Kennet's underground watercourse (many million years old) was not *there* in the Neolithic.[13] He also discounted the geological faults, which, long before humanity's arrival, had locked the river's course against steep cliffs for 200 yards on either side of Swallowhead, giving a remarkably stable configuration and a striking topographic image of the Earth Mother's widespread thighs, a pose frequently depicted in Neolithic figurines and medieval Sheila-na-gig figures.

Recently, some archaeologists *have* begun inching towards an acceptance of Swallowhead's likely prehistoric significance. For example, with regard to Silbury's location, D. Field writes tentatively of 'the importance of the landscape ... with the focus perhaps being a natural feature that we can at present only guess at[14] ... [though] springs may be considered sacred'.[15] With equal circumspection, in 2005 Dr Chadburn favoured 'a natural feature, – tree, swallow hole or spring as Silbury's original focus'.[16] Then, on 25 October 2007, J. Cleary of English Heritage told a *Daily Mail* reporter: 'I personally feel that this monument [Silbury] is bound up with Swallowhead Springs, head of the River Kennet.'[17] So they dare to sip.

As I pointed out in 1976, the inhabitants of the district had been actively *demonstrating* this connection for centuries. Stukeley wrote in 1743: 'the country people have an anniversary meeting on the top of Silbury-hill, on every Palm Sunday, when they make merry with cakes, figs, sugar, and water fetched from the Swallow head, or spring of the Kennet.'[18] This custom was kept up well into the second half of the nineteenth century.[19]

Figs? In 1923 C. Harvey published the recollections of Avebury's oldest surviving inhabitants. They remembered the road at Silbury's foot lined with stalls, selling toys, sweets, nuts, ginger beer, round gingerbread cakes (which they afterwards took home to eat) and figs. The fair was known as Fig Sunday. The figs were imported dried and sold loose or in packets. They were considered very important. (The fig is a long-established Mediterranean symbol of fecundity. Its tree is called 'the many breasted' from the pendulous shape of the fruit, first brought to Britain by the Romans.)

Harvey's informants recalled how every year on Fig (alias Palm) Sunday 'hundreds of people, dressed in their best clothes, gathered from the surrounding villages' for the festival's 'merry-making and drinking', with young people of both sexes dragging planks to the hilltop and tobogganing down the precipitous slope to the bottom.[20]

Even in 1932 F.S. Thacker could report that 'a few children still climb Silbury Hill on Fig Sunday, the only relic of the generally observed event of 100 years ago'.[21] Children, it seems, were the last to abandon the old mother hill, even if they carried no more Swallowhead water to the summit for her to drink.

Springhead Consensus

Every inhabited continent has natural founts regarded in terms of human parturition, with the two 'metabolisms' integrated into the working body of a local goddess. In India, for example, worship of these water deities is performed at the point of outflow, and typically involved dancing, drinking and immersion in the 'sacred waters of rebirth'.[22] From the Neolithic onwards, these rituals were often further formalised within a goddess temple, as at the source of the River Ganges. Silbury is a massive, yet orthodox, example of just such a tendency, and the worldwide coupling of springhead and temple supports the Silbury-Swallowhead connection.

Swallowhead and Silbury are both maternal life-giving images that rely on the use of metaphor to enable their meaning. Metaphor involves a deliberate conflation of categories, in which 'this' can become 'that'; for example, a springhead 'is' a giantess' vulva; a range of hills 'is' an outstretched human body. And this is not so much a matter of *replacing* one thing by another, but rather a *doubling* of possible meanings that are asked to exist simultaneously.

Such poetic mergers have typified the mythic outlook and utterance through the ages, and, as far as creation myths are concerned, the stories often involve water. In Egyptian, Hindu, Greek, Babylonian and Hebrew creation myths life emerges from the waters, the primal substance, containing the seeds of all things. Water was seen as the source of life, rebirth and immortality. As the supreme magical and medicinal substance, it was the divine solvent that ran through and sustained all life. Swallowhead's Kennet, springing from beneath a winding dry valley, was so regarded.

Mircia Eliade, a world-renowned authority on primitive mythology, writes:

> the waters are *fons et origo*, 'spring and origin', the reservoir of all the possibilities of existence; they precede every form and *support* every creation... In whatever religious complex we find them, the waters invariably retain their function... They are at once purifying and regenerating. Their destiny is to precede Creation and to reabsorb it.[23]

That pre-eminence is encapsulated and shared between Silbury's moat, Swallowhead and the River Kennet or Cunnit. As the river's name indicates, it is both ever new and of a very old language stock. Thus the proto-Indo-European root *ken*, meaning 'fresh, new', is found in Vedic *kanistha*, 'youngest', Greek *kainos*, 'new', Avestan *kaine*, 'maiden', and Gaulish *cintu-gnatus*, 'first-born'.[24] Add to these, in plain English, the true language word 'cunt', neither slang nor originally a blasphemy, which accurately describes both the Swallowhead birthplace and her Cunnit river offspring, which flows past the former Roman town of *Cun*etio, sited on her bank 7 miles downstream.

What more propitious location could be imagined as a site for Silbury, a major earth and water temple, designed to replicate Mother Nature's own achievement? To the Neolithic builders the intervisibility of monument and sacred spring announced more than the *inter-dependence* of nature and culture, for here they all but merged, in sacred union; two expressions of one universal truth.

The G55 Site

If Swallowhead was so important to the late Neolithic community as to inspire Silbury's creation, what archaeological evidence is there of that spring's appeal in earlier Neolithic times? Today, the nearest *visible* fourth millennium monument to the spring is the West Kennet long barrow, which lies 500 yards to the south-east. But aligned halfway between that mighty barrow's east end and Swallowhead is an important Neolithic settlement site.

Now known somewhat bleakly as G55 (after the denuded early Bronze Age bell barrow subsequently erected at its centre), this of a patch of land, 100 yards in diameter, was densely strewn with evidence of Neolithic occupation.

This consists of more than 1000 worked flint implements of that period, including chiselled arrowheads, knives, scrapers, a sickle blade and a saddle quern. This equipment were mostly made before Silbury was built. In addition, over 600 sherds of Neolithic pottery were found, ranging in date from Windmill Hill type of *c*.4000 BC, through Peterborough, Mortlake, Ebbsfleet and Fengate wares, and their successors – Rinyo-Clacton sherds, followed by those from late Neolithic

19 Dog daisies and grass cover the Neolithic campsite, now known as G55, used for more than a millennium from *c.*3600 BC. G55 lies midway between the West Kennet long barrow and Swallowhead spring, which rises between the foreground trees and hedge.

beakers, introduced just prior to Silbury's construction. These finds, along with innumerable animal bones, suggest that the site was a regular assembly place for more than a thousand years, with people coming from afar, some carrying Mendip pebbles.[25]

In addition, nine storage pits were discovered, the biggest over 4ft across, containing worn down red deer antlers, interpreted as hoes. These and several postholes sunk amidst the spread of debris are further signs of the Neolithic gatherings on this shoulder of down land, sited above the Kennet's flood plain, yet within 200 yards of Swallowhead. That spring's grip on the Neolithic imagination and behaviour has left a substantial trace behind around G55's site. The camp was in use from *c.*4000 BC, up to and *including* the time when Silbury was built, as the late Neolithic 'long-necked' beaker sherds indicate. Further, a worked microlithic flint rod, made *c.*10,000 BC, unearthed from Pit 2, implies that Swallowhead's allure ignored our artificially imposed archaeological divisions.[25A]

Swallowhead and Silbury's Moat Image

In 1976 I proposed that the Swallowhead-Silbury duo exemplified a basic nature-culture partnership. In the twenty-first century the reaffirmation of such an accord is recognised as indispensable to our civilisation's survival.

One unexpected consequence of *The Silbury Treasure*'s publication was that for the first time in more than a century, people began to pay visits to Swallowhead. Some came out of curiosity; others to venerate the spring. Ribbons and small offerings, including 'goddess' figurines, were set around the outflow or hung, along with dedicatory messages in English and many other languages, from the overarching willow trees.

20(a) Offerings left at Swallowhead in 2007 include a dancing figurine (*left*), flints, a 'grape' cup and candle, money, flowers and a pregnant seated clay image. (b) Swallowhead, with the mile-long dry valley above. (c) Well shaft near Beckhampton Penning, 15ft deep, tapping the underground stream that emerges at Swallowhead further down this dry coomb. (d) Sheila-na-gig, Kilpeck church, Herefordshire; twelfth century. A flint axe, made *c.*10,000 BC, found close to Swallowhead at Grid 105682, is evidence of pre-Neolithic interest in the spring.

The historian Jon Cannon described what he found there since 1994 as:

> a rich assemblage of objects, including carvings and vessels, all deposited in and around the [Swallowhead] water ... Ritual activity on the site began in the last 20–25 years, and is almost certainly the result of the publication in 1976 of Michael Dames' *The Silbury Treasure* ... Dames' ideas fill the landscape with significance, imagery and meaning.[26]

These 'ideas' arose in the first instance from an instinctive sense of connection with that spring, subsequently confirmed by a study of humanity's spring-fed reservoir of mythic narratives, which describe how cosmos-creating divinities, locally witnessed, were responsible for life on Earth. Such timeless, cyclical tales, along with their associated human rites and effigies have been explored and described by numerous writers, including J. Campell, E. Cassirer, K.W. Bolle, G. Dumezil, J. Puhvel and M. Eliade, D. Eck, H. Frankfort, S. Giedion, A. Marshack and M. Gimbutas.[27] Available to all who can read, their findings help to illuminate, from an encompassing religious perspective, the landscape and prehistoric remains of the Avebury district, including Silbury and its supernatural setting.

Avebury's grand monuments and lesser earthworks have accumulated over several millennia, yet they all share in Swallowhead's deceptive simplicity. A little flow of water from white rock provided a unifying symbol, charged with ambiguous import.

Complementary Opposites

The Swallowhead spring is a birthplace, set into a 'graveyard' cliff, composed of marine shells, raised *en bloc* from the bottom of the 60-million-year-old Cretaceous Sea.[28] Salt water and fresh, death and renewal, rising and sinking – Swallowhead is the common denominator for every organism and human culture, which issues from the dark tunnel of pre-existence and as surely will return to underworld oblivion. As the name suggests, Swallowhead gives *and* consumes in equal measure. No wonder this mistress of extremes attracted and continues to draw attention.

In several respects Swallowhead and Silbury appear as opposites. Swallowhead is a small cave, Silbury a big hill. While the cave and Kennet valley are concave, the hill is convex. One leads to subterranean realms, the other addresses the sky. Spring and river emphasise a horizontal plane; the hill boasts a vertical axis. Swallowhead dispenses running water; Silbury displays a still lake. The springhead is dressed in wild weeds; the hill is clothed in cattle farmers' turf and corn growers' soil. The cave mouth is natural; the monument artificial.

Yet the two features (like most opposites) are also complementary. This interdependence grows even closer if one takes into account the belief, common to many myth-based societies, that the world and the entire cosmos was generated from water.

Primary Waters

The combination of water's fluidity, transparency, elusiveness, life-giving and -promoting qualities may partly account for it being so often identified as the substance from which all creation arose. For example, in the Babylonian epic *Enuma elish*, only water existed in the beginning and was identified with the goddess Tiamat.[29] Indian myth links the origin of the cosmos to the churning of the Waters of Chaos,[30] while in Egypt creation was believed to have begun when a tiny mud bank arose in the primordial waters, identified with the Nile.[31]

In these terms, Silbury's biggest idea may have been to present the same turbulent 'pre-universe waters' but arranged into a coherent 'Mother of Everything' shape. This First Mother could then be seen to produce both the universe *and* the world from her own watery womb.

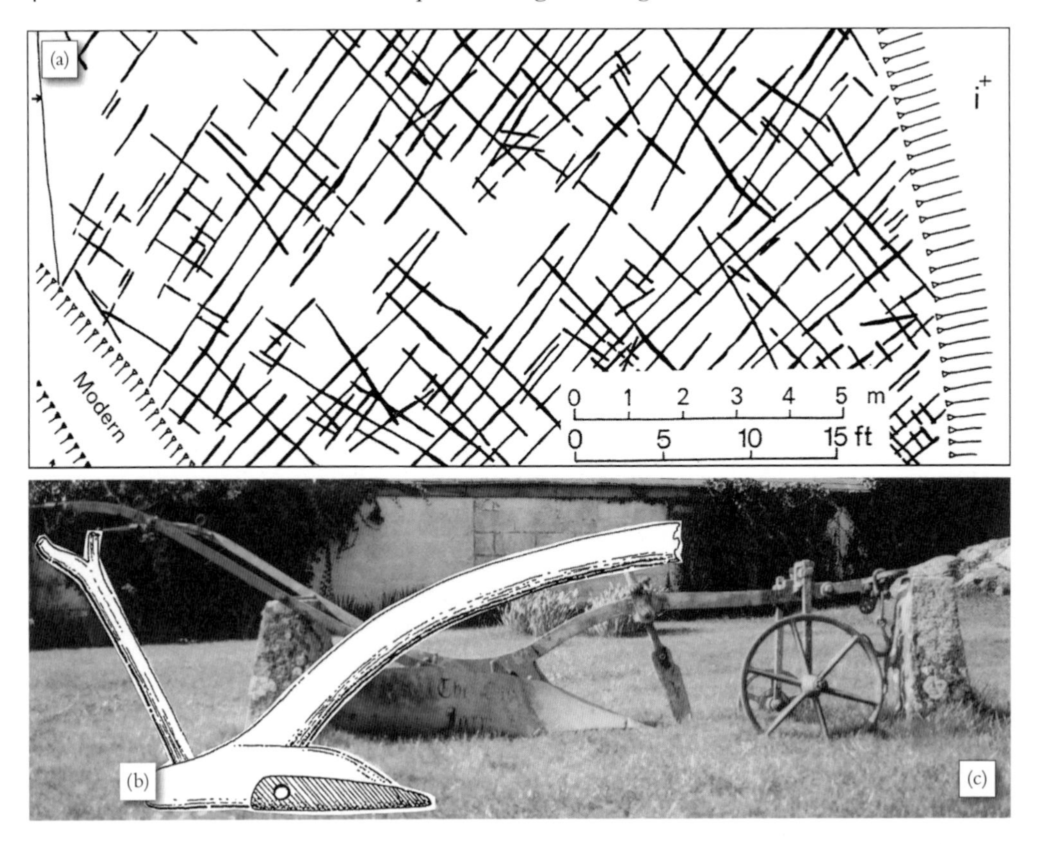

21 The fruitful underworld. (a) Early Neolithic plough furrows (fourth millennium) found beneath the South Street long barrow, half a mile from Silbury. (b) Reconstructed Neolithic wooden plough with stone coulter. (c) Nineteenth-century horse plough and granary staddle stones, Berwick Basset, near Avebury. Interest in and dependence on the underworld increased with the adoption of agriculture.

Jim Cleary, who led Silbury's 2007–08 investigation, told a *Daily Mail* reporter: 'We believe the top of the hill was literally lopped off around the time of the Battle of Hastings … or when the Danes attacked in 1006, to create flat land to use as a military base.'[32] If so, prior to AD 1006 Silbury Hill displayed half the entire 'round earth-in-miniature'. Seen together with its inverted reflection, the hill could then be read as a 'cosmic egg'. Just such an egg-shaped universal nucleus was imagined in ancient Greece and Egypt.[33]

Whether or not Cleary's 'lopped' belief is well founded, Silbury Hill's present flat-topped inverted reflection can also suggest the half-born, original divine child, stirring with every breeze within the goddess's amniotic waters, stored within its mother's lake body where sacred fish occasionally broke the surface.

Silbury Hill's pregnant gift to the world was the cosmos, including its pantheon of gods and humanity's annual harvests. Pilgrims and worshippers coming to the monument, like those in every religion, probably intended to participate, through their rites, in her universe-creating (or re-creating) act. By miming the founder-deity's labour pains, they could share in her work of re-staging the primal birth from her waters and thereby assist in the fulfilment of their own good fortune, as an aspect of her infinite fecundity.

Silbury was designed to bring elemental forces together within the persona of the Great Goddess, to the benefit of the community. So rock and earth were joined by wind-rippled water, glazed by the sun's fire and by moon and starlight, all merged within her recumbent body. This union accords with Gimbutas' view of the pan-Eurasian Neolithic deity as 'the Goddess-Creatrix in her many aspects'.

Archaeologists have shown that before the moat quarry was dug, the builders' first act was to take *water-born* silt and gravel from the nearby Kennet's riverbed. Cleary confirmed previous findings, when, in 2008, he stated: 'A lot of the gravel core of the hill looks like river gravel and a lot of the mud looks like it came from the river.'[34] (It was possibly this evidence that convinced him of Silbury's association with Swallowhead's Kennet outpourings.)

The founders carried the Kennet's water-lain deposits to the precise spot over which the hill was eventually to rise. There they dug a small pit, as if to mimic the holy underworld source of this Kennet-born material that they had collected. The pit continues the Old Stone Age reverence for caves as the source of life, as shown at Paviland, at Cresswell Crags and across Eurasia.[35] This Silbury pit also corresponds to the 'womb cell' (*gharba-grihya*), situated beneath the central 'mountain tower' of each Hindu temple. In that cell, the seed of the cosmos-creating divinity is housed.[36]

Over and around the Silbury pit river-born sludge was then carefully heaped, layer after layer, to make a primary mound, the core of the future chalk Hill. Perhaps they doused that core in 'amniotic' water from Swallowhead. By these means the Neolithic community ensured that their eventual 'World Foetus Hill' was descended from a silt-child, born of the divine underworld 'bloodstream', revealed at Swallowhead.

After Silbury was completed, the same libation ceremony was probably transferred to the hill's summit and repeated annually, for in many myths 're-creation' is a recurring yearly event. Those local inhabitants who, as Stukeley observed in the eighteenth century, carried Swallowhead water to Silbury's top once a year and drank it there may well have been unconsciously re-enacting a vestige of the original Neolithic rite.

The appeal of fresh water, flowing from rock, is never out of date. In common with their Stone Age ancestors, people of the twenty-first century are drawn to the springhead to share a timelessly pure and enlarged version of the individual's bloodstream and chalk-white bones. Swallowhead, like Silbury, lies permanently under our skin.

four

CENTRAL IDEAS

Yew Berry

On 26 October 2007 English Heritage announced the discovery of a single yew tree berry.[1] It was found in the small pit, sunk by the original builders into the top of the gravel core of Silbury's primary mound. Also in that cavity were a fragment of animal bone and four humanly struck flint flakes. Viewed together, this miniscule animal, vegetable and mineral deposit may have represented the 'seeds' of the entire material world, cradled in Kennet gravel at the hill's absolute centre. The berry also fits Silbury's forward-looking outlook, as a pregnant mother concerned with growth.

The choice of a yew berry is significant. The yew is one of the few native British evergreen trees. Its wood is immensely strong, yet flexible.[2] The tree can live to a great age. The Fortingall Yew in Glen Lyon, Perthshire, is believed to be older than Silbury and may have sprouted from its pea-sized red fruit more than 9000 years ago.[3] Moreover, the deadest looking old yew has the power to rejuvenate itself with new growth, while its trunk is inclined to subdivide into four vertical parts, leaving gaps around a hollow centre open to the 'four winds' and cardinal directions.

Given these characteristics, it is hardly surprising that the yew was venerated as the immortal, eternal, divine 'Tree of Life' throughout pre-Christian Europe. Like Silbury, its seed stands for eternity. This conviction has passed into the languages and folk beliefs of the British Isles. The two Welsh words for 'yew', *wyf* and *bod*, also mean 'existence' and 'being'. So the tree's dark canopy shelters and incorporates life and death. Welsh *wyf* stands for existence *per se* and *in toto.*

In Irish, 'yew', *ur*, has resurrection connotations, since *ur* also means 'fresh, new, beginning'. Ireland's Munster dynasty was referred to as 'People of the Yew', while the fabled Yew of Rossa is described in an early manuscript as 'Best of creature's, a mother's good, Banba's renown, judgment of origin, vigour of life, spell of knowledge, [and] shout of the world'. (Banba *is* Ireland, in supernatural female form.)[4]

Another Irish word for 'yew' is *eo*, found in the personal name Eogan, 'yew-born'. (*Eo* is also 'salmon' and in both Irish and Welsh medieval tales the salmon is regarded as the oldest, wisest and most sacred of beings. Fish and yew seem to share a word of primal wisdom.)[5]

The yew's sacredness has not been lost on the English. As Grigson reminds us, that tree was planted by many a cottage and was believed to be the dwelling place of the home's protective deity.[6]

Similarly, one often comes across an ancient yew growing on a mound alongside an English parish church. Four miles south from Silbury, a flourishing female yew in the churchyard at Alton Priors is 56ft tall, has a girth of 28ft and an estimated age of 1700 years, and was planted a century before the Romans left Britannia. Such trees can embody the living *genius loci* of pagan sacred

22(a) An oak tree growing between Silbury and the West Kennet long barrow festooned with ribbons in 2009. Silbury was originally seen as the Mother of the Cosmos. From zenith to abyss, she gave supernatural life to her universe-child. (b) A yew tree at Alton Priors church, Vale of Pewsey, Wiltshire. This hollow female has a girth of 28ft and is 1700 years old. Such yews sited on churchyard mounds often denote a pre-Christian site.

23 (*Left*) 'Big Belly Oak', Savernake Forest, 5 miles east of Silbury. With deep roots and towering height, the long-lasting oak acquired sacred associations. Oak trunks were used to create the Neolithic Palisades enclosures close to Silbury. (*Right*) Angels' Ladder, west front of Bath Abbey, sixteenth century. Uniting earth and heaven, here the ladder serves as an *axis mundi*, the world's sacred axis.

enclosures, later adopted by Christian church builders who used the same sites. This leads us back to the Silbury temple and its 'belly button' yew pip, set within that great Hill. Together they offer the 'tree-temple-mound' alliance employed by several faiths.

Axis Mundi (World Axis) and World Tree

In many religions a supernatural tree is imagined as the vertical axis uniting the human world with underworld, sky and hidden realms of the gods. For pre-Christian Scandinavians this was the mighty ash named Yggdrasil. Its branches formed a canopy over heavens and earth. Of its three roots, one found succour among the Aesir gods, a second reached down to the frost giants' kingdom, while the third fed on death's realm.[7] The same need to reach to the underworld is matched at Silbury by the vertical alignment of the pit dug beneath the primary mound and the yew berry's hole, inserted into the primary mound's top.

Silbury Hill's symmetrical shape also fits the *Axis Mundi*, or World Axis, idea, developed throughout Eurasia from at least the third millennium BC. For example, just as the Babylonian cosmic tree was the home of Bau, goddess of plenty[8], so the Silbury yew seed, placed centrally within the womb-hill, bears comparison with it *and* the tree rising from the navel of the Indian deity Varuna, son of infinity, as he floats in the universal waters.[9]

Numerous myths trace the emergence of the 'first people' into the world via a divine tree.[10] Here again, if Silbury's role as maternal creator of all life is accepted, the world tree (represented by its seed and embryonic essence) found at her core was an essential ingredient.

In some countries, the 'tree' can become a staff, a pillar or a ladder,[11] while retaining its principal mythic use, which is to join the natural world to the divine zones, and to improve the degree of interplay between them. So connected, the central tree becomes the symbolic Tree of Life, ensuring continued fertility, in a world benefiting from the rise of sap from the abyss and the play of light on its blossom, fruit and foliage.

When, in 1776, Drax sank his vertical shaft from Silbury's summit to the prehistoric ground in an attempt to find treasure, he discovered only 'a slip of oak' at the base. The oak is Britain's longest living deciduous tree and has long been imbued with supernatural characteristics, emphasised by Iron Age druids.[12] Perhaps Silbury's centrally set oak sliver was intended to complement the yew berry by offering a deciduous aspect of the universe tree. If so, nothing could have been more valuable. But the antiquarian J. Douglas set fire to the relic (which for 20 years had lain, cloth-wrapped, in a drawer) to show that it was not, as some had supposed, a whale's bone.[13]

The protective quality attributed to the cosmic tree may be implied in one other way at Silbury. As Atkinson reported, the hill's central organic mound, 65ft in diameter, is contained within a ring fence, supported by widely placed stakes.[14] Just as the tree of trees was sometimes believed to grow in the middle of a sacred grove, so this modest circle of hazel stakes seems to attend and support that notion. Therefore, beneath Silbury's notably symmetrical cone, at the very centre of the buried fence ring, a mere yew pip was planted. So microcosm implies macrocosm, to make a classic pairing.

Centre of the World

Silbury can be seen as a 'centre of the world' image. As such, it is only one of many. Some of these sites are physically real, while others are entirely imaginary. Both kinds have been recognised and documented by scholars.

The term 'centre of the world' refers to that place where all essential modes of being and all imagined realities intersect and come together. There, communication and even passage *between* these realms is thought possible. Such places are 'the heart of reality, where the real is fully manifest'[15] and therefore dangerous. For example, on Ireland's central mountain, Ard Eireann, it was believed that there was 'a grassy spot on the mountaintop and if anyone stepped on it the ground would give way beneath his feet, and he or she would be swallowed into the mountain for ever.'[16] To merge with the deity's essence is the feared yet longed for aim of devotees in most religions.

During prehistoric times, ultimate reality was located in the supernatural. Therefore, 'the centre' was often synonymous with 'the direct appearance of a divinity'. Thus Silbury Hill is both a deity's world-creating womb *and* the middle of the world so created. Consequently the hill is a sacred place, qualitatively different from the mundane space around. Moreover, in Ireland, as at Silbury, the deity identified with a sacred hill tended to be particularly active on 1 August. Thus children living around Ardagh Hill, Co. Longford, home to the god Midir and the goddess Etain, were warned that he might 'pull them down his "swalley-hole"' if they climbed her hill on that day.[17]

Because the 'centre of the world' idea was anchored by mythic narrative rather than latitude and longitude, a large number of spots can legitimately make the same claim. For example, in Christian Europe, Jerusalem, the scene of Christ's death and resurrection, was so nominated. Therefore medieval Christian maps arrange the entire world around that city.

Moriah, the Temple Mount in Jerusalem, was originally sanctified as the site of a pre-Judaic Canaanite threshing floor and its associated harvest rites, so making an unexpected link to Silbury as Harvest Goddess.[18] Whether the faith was Christian, Judaic, Moslem or Canaanite, from Jerusalem the entire cosmos was (and still is) arrayed as a spiritual, physical, intellectual and emotionally experienced truth, absorbing every aspect of the practical life of the believer into a divine unity. For faiths that permit imagery, the discernible presence of the deity at such a World Centre guarantees, in the devotees' eyes, its authenticity and practical effectiveness; hence the importance of the goddess's 'moat image' wrapped around Silbury Hill.

The geologically varied stone axes found in Silbury's immediate vicinity, probably offered by Neolithic pilgrims from Cornwall, North Wales and Cumbria, indicate how widespread the hill's appeal was. Similarly, big botanical differences found among the grass turfs placed in Silbury's core proved that they also had been carried, 'year after year', from a wide area to that spot. It seems that from its inception Silbury was a 'central place'.[19]

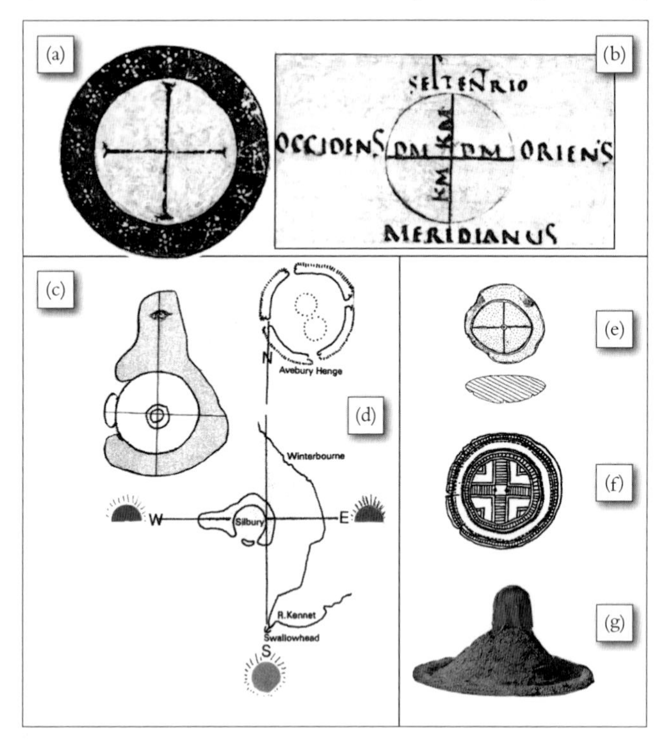

24 Divine centres. (a) Templum of the sky; from the sixth-century *Codex Arcerianus*. (b) Templum of the earth, from the same surveying manual, used by augerer-priests. (c) Silbury's long axis is orientated due east–west, to every equinoctial sunrise and sunset, when day and night are of equal length. (d) Silbury's north–south axis joins her life-giving vulva to the Avebury Henge and Swallowhead spring. This 'life line' is confirmed by each noonday sun's due south position. (e) Engraved chalk disc from Windmill Hill, Avebury; fourth millennium BC. (f) Bronze Age gold button from Ballyshannon, Co. Kildare. (g) Vermilion cloth over a pot on a mound, signifying the centring of the goddess' life force in India. (Photograph P. Mookerjee, 1987).

World Mountain

In myths a World Centre often takes the form of a mountain, such as Australia's Ayres Rock, regarded as the sacred 'dreamtime' Uluru by the indigenous population. Often seen as the kernel of the world, the Fujiyama volcanic peak in Japan is home to the goddess Sengen-Sama, while in Mexico the goddess Tonantzin's influence radiates in a comparable manner from her mountain top, named Tepeyac.[20]

As a high spiritual centre of the Neolithic world in Britain and the tallest artificial prehistoric mound in Europe, Silbury's modest altitude paradoxically amounts to a major example of the World Mountain mode, pitched midway between mental and physical realities. Since there are no mountains in the fertile chalk lands of southern England, to which early farmers were drawn, it was necessary to build one there. Thanks to the power of architectural metaphor, the Silbury temple and the sacred mountain could merge.

Nor would their stupendous efforts to achieve a valley floor pile, 130ft high, have been regarded as inadequate, given the flexibility of scale implied by symbolic representation. For instance, even though the recent dominance of quantification has now somewhat eroded the *lingua franca* of visual symbolism, the Queen of Britain's head, when depicted on a postage stamp, continues to register as the *whole* queen and as the *entire* island of Britain. On this basis, Silbury was, and still is, a World Mountain, able to match in terms of sacred meaning its physically bigger counterparts throughout the world.

The World Mountain is frequently the place where a god is born or nurtured by the Earth Mother. Thus, Ard Eireann, at 526m, is named after the goddess Eriu She who is synonymous with Eire or Ireland. There on Ard Eireann the rebirth of Lugh, young god of harvest, is celebrated annually at Lughnasa, the 1 August 'start of harvest' rites which are named after him. They were maintained, in a gradually reduced form, into the twentieth century AD.[21]

Beneath Mount Ida, Crete's highest mountain at 2456m, Cretan Zeus died and was reborn in a cave which was held in repute throughout the classical world.[22] Neolithic pottery was found there in

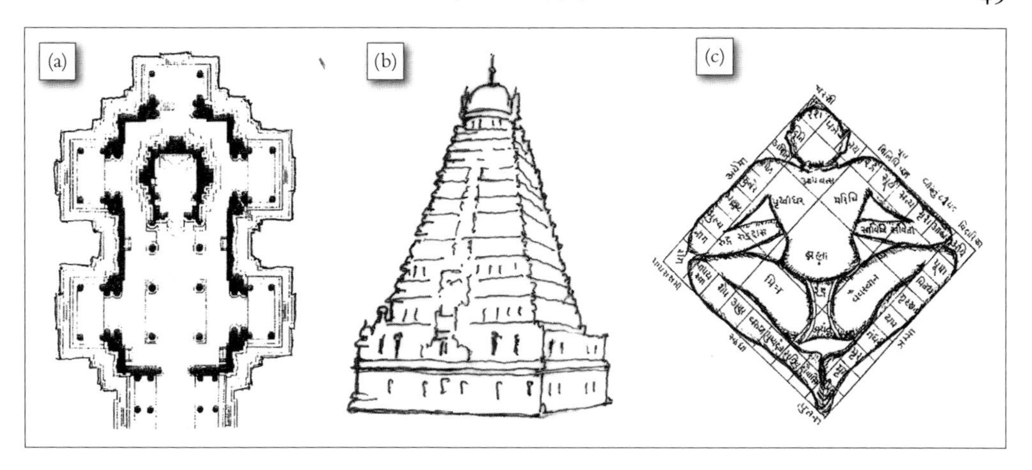

25 World Mountain. (a) Plan of Lakshmana temple, Khajuraho, India; tenth century. Its 'head', 'arms' and 'legs' refer to a deity in superhuman form. Similarly, Nordic myth sees the universe as giant-born. (b) 'Meru', the sacred mountain, is the tallest feature of a Hindu temple and contains the 'womb cell', where the image of the goddess is kept. Like Silbury, the Hindu temple tower is a mountain that nurtures divinity. (c) To show the cosmos in human form (*mahapurusha*) is the basic intention of Indian temple design. Silbury demonstrates the same ambition.

1982. As for Zeus' Mount Olympus residence on the Greek mainland, the seventh-century BC poet Homer sang: 'Never is it swept by the winds, nor touched by snow; a purer air surrounds it, a white clarity envelops it, and the gods there taste of a happiness which lasts as long as their eternal lives.'

Thus *super*natural reality can transform the 'facts'. By the same token, we may hope that the 500 tonnes of ordinary chalk paste squirted into Silbury's summit cavity during 2008 have not entirely dissipated the divine aura that was once associated with *its* summit. Silbury's fate is in our hands. The physical fabric has been saved from collapse. Its spiritual significance may or may not be restored.

In Asia, as in Europe, myth-based societies mixed the imaginary with the topographic. For instance, the *actual* Kunlun Mountains of northern Tibet are believed in Chinese myth to contain the *legendary* Mount Jade, alias Mount Flaming Fire, where deities from heaven settle in the palace of the Queen Mother of the West. There, at her banquets, she gives out peaches of immortality which ripen once every 3000 years.[23]

Woven together, Kunlun and Mount Jade show what western reductionists may regard as confusion between 'real' and 'fictitious' landscapes. But even logical positivists have real dreams, and from the mythic viewpoint all physical manifestations of reality are aspects of the divine metabolism and mind, sometimes accessible to shamans. Therefore the interplay between material world and the mythic tales it can engender contribute on equal terms to humanity's accounts of the divine.

For this reason Silbury, though only 130ft tall, was probably as much if not more a World Mountain as Snowdon (3560ft) or Ben Nevis (4406ft); not least because, thanks to Silbury being set in a lake, there one may see the archetypal mountain arising from the underworld and breaking the surface of the waters at the very moment of its orogenesis. Silbury confirms that the World Mountain idea is not so much a 'thing of the past', but a re-lived *event*.

Such is the case with Mount Kailasa, a vast pyramid of black rock that rises to 22,028ft, close to the Indian border with Tibet. Kailasa serves as *the* World Mountain where the universe is born for billions of people belonging to four different religions.[24] For Hindus it is also the abode of Lord Shiva. Like Silbury the mountain is surrounded by holy waters. Into these icy lakes, one of which is named Manosavara, 'Enlightenment', the pilgrims plunge. Yet so remote and inaccessible is Kailasa's location in south-west Tibet, and so high, that only a few thousand worshippers manage to visit it each year. In other words, for most believers the mountain is a figment of their collective imagination. Therefore it tends to merge with the entirely fictitious Mount Meru, the alternative (yet synonymous) central peak of Jain, Hindu, Buddhist and Bon cosmologies.[25]

Deity-Temple-Mountain

After considering Silbury's structure in terms of three inter-related themes, (i) *Axis Mundi*, (ii) World Centre and (iii) World Mountain, it appears that the Wiltshire monument, far from being an inexplicable freak, belongs within each of these overlapping categories. Silbury is securely embedded within Eurasian culture.

That heritage also includes strong linguistic connections, uniting the two continents. Philologists have unanimously accepted the existence of a Proto-Indo-European root language – the ancient common source of a closely related family of tongues still spoken from India to Ireland.[26] And because speech is the chief vehicle on which religious ideas ride, it is hardly surprising that Silbury Hill bears some resemblance to the mythic Mount Meru, as described on the Indian sub-continent. Thus, in plan Silbury's cone consists of concentric circles made from chalk blocks in-filled with chalk rubble. Likewise, Mount Meru is imagined to be constructed of cones, surrounded by seven rings of cosmic fields, atmospheric zones and oceans, where continents float.

Seen in elevation, Silbury (according to Atkinson) is built of seven massive steps or tiers. Similarly, Jain diagrams of Mount Meru, pictured in elevation, show a stacked sequence of terraces and pavilions, likewise diminishing in size from bottom to top. For Hindus, the sky god Indra lives on the summit. Comparable with Silbury, Meru is frequently called 'navel of the earth' and this sacred mount is so full of vegetal energy as to be regarded as another guise of the Tree of Life. Here again, Silbury's concealed yew berry comes into view.[27]

Moreover, in Hindu Tantric belief, Meru and its universe-wide array of connotations could merge, through contemplation, with an individual human being. Ultimately, the worshipper's spine would then become synonymous with Meru's vertical axis.[28] Perhaps a comparable fusion

26 Silbury as 'cosmic egg', seen in January 2002, with nine swans (*centre*) floating upon the moat. In world mythology the egg often symbolises divine perfection, containing and giving birth to all creation. Within the 'egg-womb-world-mountain' amalgam 'the unlike is joined together, and from the difference results the most beautiful harmony', as the Greek philosopher Heraclitus remarked.

was sought between the Silbury moat's long axis and the worshipper's body, so that the temple 'out there' could also be 'in here'.

Globalisation is not new and has always involved much more than banking. The anthropologist Victor Turner perceptively remarked that we, who are able to analyse the differences between peoples, are inclined to forget what they have in common.[29] This includes birth, procreation and death, the quest for food, shelter, social harmony and good relations with flora and fauna. The same sun, moon and stars help stimulate the endless worldwide search for ultimate meaning. Therefore it is hardly surprising if similar human responses occur in 'separate' parts of the world.

Temple as Cosmic Being

The earliest of India's architectural manuals stipulate that, in overall plan, a temple should depict a superhuman being known as the *Purusa*, or 'Cosmic Person', from whose gigantic body everything is said to emerge.[30] Like Silbury, the Indian temple is the condensed image of the cosmos in anthropomorphic form. Hindu temple builders continue to demonstrate this idea. In Meister's words, the temple so shaped is 'supreme reality in human form'.[31] As a divine image: 'The temple is not only a place of worship, but also an *object* of worship', involving *darshan*, which is the exchange of eye contact between images of the gods, including the 'temple-as-deity' and the worshipper.[32]

Great care is taken over a Hindu temple's site. Echoing the Silbury-Kennet link, a streamside location is usually sought. The ground on which the temple will stand is then 'seeded' for auspicious signs of germination. Finally, when the building is complete, it is 'brought to life' by the architect and priest. Together they ascend to the top of the highest tower at midnight to prick open the 'eyes' of the temple with a golden needle, possibly replicating a divine sunbeam.

Neolithic Inheritance

This ceremony may find its (super)natural architectural match at Silbury. From the west, the radial and concentric walls of its Hill make a huge 'divine eye' set in a 'water-head'. On a miniature scale, the eye motif is well attested in Neolithic Britain's smaller carvings, like the Folkton drums.[33]

The typical Indian temple is crowned by a stone 'sun disc', or *amalalaka*, which joins the celestial to the terrestrial sphere. Likewise, when seen from Silbury Hill, the noonday sun, at the apogee of its daily arc, shines directly over Swallowhead's entrance to the underworld, thereby threading the three zones onto a single sunbeam.

The Hindu temple's most arresting feature is a multi-tiered tapering tower, recognised as a stone image of Mount Meru or Kailasa. Again, the parallel with Silbury Hill is clear. Another striking resemblance may be found between Silbury's dark mud and stacked turf core, concealed under the chalk Hill, and the Indian temple's *garbha grihya* (literally 'embryo chamber'), situated under the Meru 'tower-mountain'. This cave is regarded as the goddess's womb, containing an image of her divine child, which is often the male god Siva. In the British Isles our 'Siva' is now Irish Lugh or English John Barleycorn, annually sacrificed in brewing and beer drinking, only to be re-born next harvest time.

Contemporary Hindu temple designs can be traced in an unbroken line of descent to the cult of the Great Mother that flourished in Neolithic India. This included the Mohenjo-Daro and Harappa towns of the Indus valley, which were contemporaries of Silbury's era.[34] Although invading Aryans superimposed a male pantheon, the goddess survived as consort-wife to the new gods. Moreover, as a deity in her own right she continued to encapsulate the origin and energy or *shakti* of all phenomena. Therefore she is still acknowledged as 'Mother India'.

As in Neolithic Britain, Indian goddesses continue to embody the seasonal cycle of ploughing, planting and harvesting, coupled with phases of the female life cycle, from maidenhood to old age. These essentially New Stone Age beliefs are accompanied by the annual modelling of clay images that represent the divine 'village mother'. In addition, her stone head is normally set at the centre of each village, where she is called either Amman, meaning 'mother, mistress, lady', or simply Ai or Ma.[35]

By contrast, driven from British villages by Christianity, 'Ma's' equivalent here was the fugitive 'shadow' known as the 'White Lady', who haunted the country until AD *c.*1900. She was 'a bright vision, clothed in white, but with a pale, care-worn face, bearing an expression of intense pain'. Near Llantrisant she begged a farm labourer to bring her his wife's baby 'that I might be saved by the kiss of a new-born, un-baptised child'. Near Brecon, a farmer saw her scattering seeds and she gave him some. He threw most of them away, but on returning home found several grains of gold in his pocket. The White Lady was the lost spirit of a discredited Silbury, a grief-stricken wraith lingering in the collective subconscious.[36]

Yet, as in India, the deity of our Neolithic farmers *did* remain visible in the female corn dollies (idols), plaited from straw at the end of every harvest until the early twentieth century. These were called 'Maiden', 'Mother' and 'Hag', with all three terms applied to the same subject (who sometimes took a 'harvest mare' equine form). The 'dollies' were accorded a place of honour in the farmhouse before being ploughed back into a field at the start of the following year. (Britain, after all, *is* part of Eurasia!)

Two further Indian similarities with Silbury should be noted. First, Silbury is orientated to the four cardinal directions, as are Indian temples, where the four intermediate directions (corresponding to Britain's 'quarter days' – 1 February, 1 May, 1 August and 1 November – each key moments in the farming year) are likewise honoured. In Hindu temples the presiding deity controls these spatial divisions, since they emanate from the divine architectural body, correctly aligned.[37] Moreover, a concern for fertility, both human and agrarian, is a feature of Hindu temples and of Silbury.

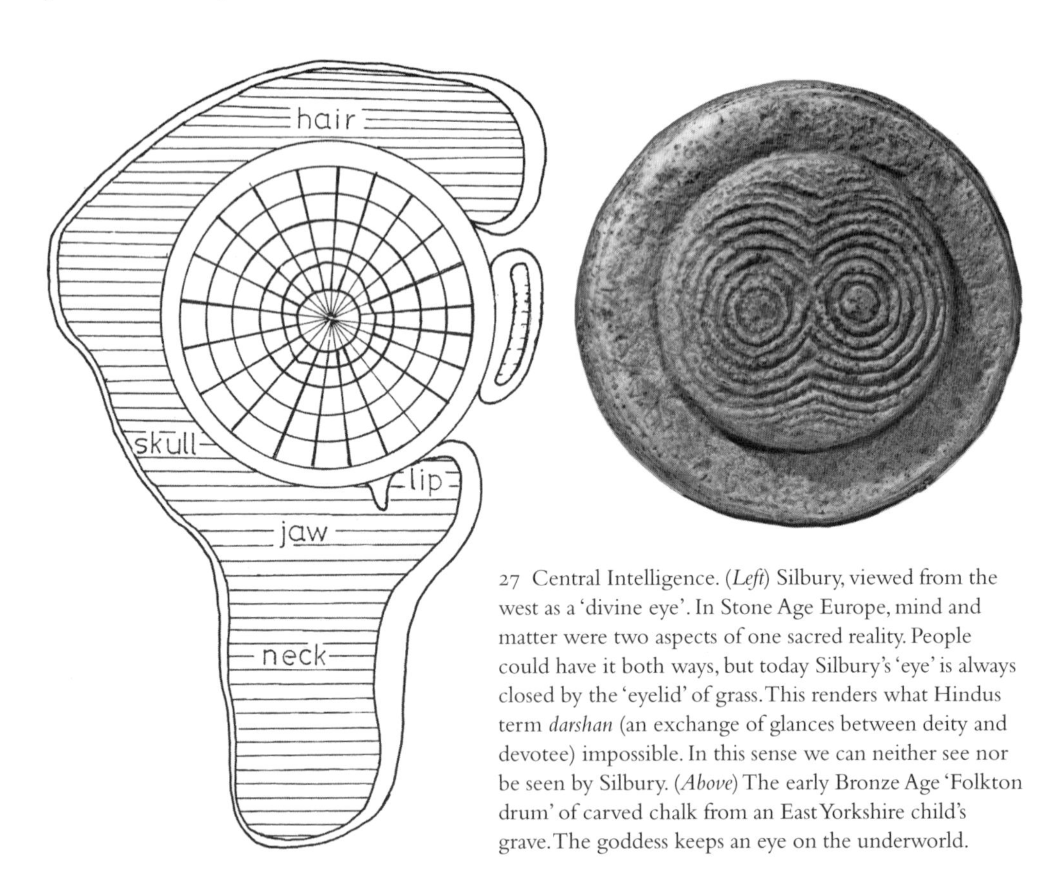

27 Central Intelligence. (*Left*) Silbury, viewed from the west as a 'divine eye'. In Stone Age Europe, mind and matter were two aspects of one sacred reality. People could have it both ways, but today Silbury's 'eye' is always closed by the 'eyelid' of grass. This renders what Hindus term *darshan* (an exchange of glances between deity and devotee) impossible. In this sense we can neither see nor be seen by Silbury. (*Above*) The early Bronze Age 'Folkton drum' of carved chalk from an East Yorkshire child's grave. The goddess keeps an eye on the underworld.

28 A Somerset corn dolly maker, *c.*1900. Made from barley, oats, wheat and the straw of each crop, these narrow-waisted, broad-hipped images are probably descended from the Neolithic goddess 'idols'. They displayed harvest fruits and seeds of renewal within a superhuman female form, believed to engender everything. Dates obtained from charred grain prove that cereal farming was well established in Britain by 3800 BC.

'Mother', that essential reality, believed to operate on human *and* superhuman levels around the globe, is audibly present in the Eurasian accord. A score of languages make a chain of similar 'mother' words, from the Bay of Bengal to the Atlantic:

> mehter (Proto-Indo-European), mata (Sanskrit), ma (Bengali), mote (Lithuanian), meter (Greek), mater (Latin), mathir (Old Irish), muoter (Old High German), mam (Welsh) and mother (English).

From word of mouth and written document, through carved, baked and woven idol, by adoration of mountain, cave and river, or by means of temple design, human multitudes have honoured a Great Goddess. She has featured as a mythic pivot of Eurasian life from the remotest beginning of human culture. Therefore we celebrate our battered but now patched up Wiltshire monument as a distinguished example among a host of notable maternal expressions. Common as dirt and pure as water, Silbury was and is an image of the elemental life-giver, reclining in our midst.

The edifice, seen as a whole, is equivalent to the Greek goddess Gaia or Ge. Although now reduced to an abstract sound, a single syllable, smaller than a yew berry, she still dwells in modern *Ge*-ology and *Ge*-ophysics, which in their turn explore the same inescapable unity of the globe from its molten core to wrinkled skin and oxygen-rich atmosphere. In this sense, at least, we perpetuate the Neolithic outlook.

five

SILBURY'S ROMAN TOWN

The Urban Surprise

In March 2007 English Heritage announced the discovery of a Roman 'township'. It was centred upon Silbury, a monument already *c.*2500 years old before the Romans arrived in Britain. Dr Neil Linford's geophysical survey of the area employed caesium magnetometers, which can detect hidden structures up to 1.5m below the ground. He revealed that this previously unknown settlement around the hill was at least the size of 24 football pitches: 'We are really excited by this discovery because we had no idea that a Roman village of this size lay so close to Silbury.'[1]

To the very edge of Silbury's moat his survey showed the rectilinear traces of Roman streets and buildings, intermingled with more irregular marks left by small enclosures of a pre- or post-Roman type. These features completely surround the north, east and south sides of the monument. The land beyond the moat's west end has yet (in 2008) to be surveyed.

A related area of Roman building runs north from Silbury and along the flank of Waden Hill towards Avebury. This was first traced in 1996 during modern pipe-laying operations, and subsequently confirmed by aerial photography parch marks. These clearly showed a rectangular layout of buildings and enclosures terraced into the hillside and branching from a central street, heading towards the prehistoric Avebury Henge monument. Excavation has since proved that the buildings in this part of the settlement used a range of materials, including roof tiles, brick, mortar, chalk blocks, flint and sarsen stone, set on deep foundations, dating from the second to early fifth century AD.[2]

What purpose did the impressive Roman township serve? On a mundane level, lying as it does on both sides of the east to west Roman road (arbitrarily named *Via Badonica* by Stukeley), the settlement appears, in one commentator's view, as a convenient overnight stopping place on the way to the sacred spring and baths of *Aquae Sulis*, modern Bath.[3] Seen from Silbury's summit, this lost road appeared to the antiquarian Wilkinson in 1867 as a 'Milky Way' of disturbed chalk subsoil, lying a few yards south of the modern A4. His section proved that the road was 18ft wide and flanked by ditches.[4]

Because Silbury stands midway (12km) between two small towns on the same road, namely Cunetio and Verlucio, the need for a hostelry in its vicinity is clear. Yet even the biggest inn would cover only a tiny fraction of 24 football pitches. So, as Dr Bewley of English Heritage states: 'To have found such a substantial and organised settlement is amazing … It may also have been a place of pilgrimage in its own right, focussed on the hill.' Perhaps with religious intent, the new east-to-west Roman highway was deliberately aligned on Silbury.[5] In social terms, Silbury may have evoked to Romans of all classes their own *Mons Sacra*. That holy hill, sited a few miles north of Rome, was where, in 494 BC, a legally binding and just accord was struck between the plebeians and their overbearing patrician masters.[5A] Silbury, like *Mons Sacra*, stood for fairness.

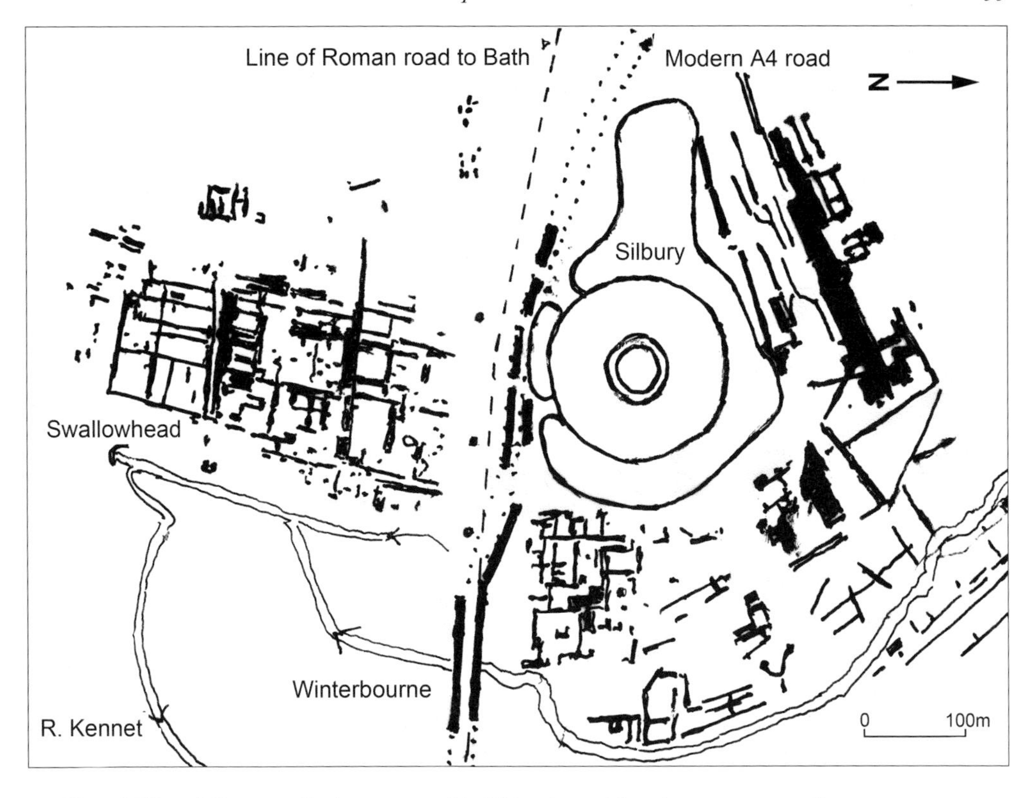

29 Plan of Silbury's Roman pilgrimage township. This substantial settlement grew up from AD 50 to AD 400, and was detected by magnetometer surveys of sub-soil features between 1998 and 2008. The typical 'gridiron' pattern of a planned Roman settlement is particularly strong between Silbury and Swallowhead, the sacred spring.

Town or Village?

No discernible traces of a defensive bank or wall surround Silbury's extensive Roman remains. Therefore they do not constitute a town, say those who think that Roman 'towns' must, by definition, be walled or fortified. However, J. Wacher, an authority on the subject, argues that in Roman Britain 'town' described 'everything urban', since 'Greek and Latin authors were equally imprecise in their use of terms'.[6]

In this case, especially to the south of the monument, the 'grid iron' pattern of streets is a sure sign of deliberate planning, far beyond what the English word 'village' suggests. Here, as Dr Bewley believes, was an urban network brought into being by the desire of a foreign army to worship at the shrine of a native Stone Age divinity.

Holy Waters

South of Silbury the rectilinear network of streets and buildings is orientated almost north-to-south, aligned with the River Winterbourne, one of the Kennet's headwater tributaries, as it approaches the Swallowhead spring. The street plan thereby appears to reiterate the same Silbury-Swallowhead connection that inspired the Neolithic community. Dr Bewley notes: 'Given the sacred value we know Romans attached to sites close to water, it seems impossible that they would not be drawn in the wake of their prehistoric forebears to Silbury Hill, which lies so close to the Winterbourne river and the Swallowhead springs.'[7]

Both Swallowhead *and* Silbury attracted Roman interest, for their waters were still viewed as divine gifts from the earth goddess and her attendant nymphs and muses. To the Greeks, the nine muses, daughters of Gaia, were divine mistresses of poetry, song, drama, dance, memory and prophecy. They were believed to emanate from springs and fountains, set around a sacred mountain, such as Helicon in Boeotia, which is depicted and named in a fourth-century mosaic fragment at Aldborough, Yorkshire.[8]

The Romans gladly adopted the muses as inspiring springhead emanations; they may feature in four of Britannia's mosaics. At Swallowhead, so close to Silbury's 'mountain', they presumably granted the full range of their delightful and civilising attributes. In return, as elsewhere, they were offered wheat grains, kneaded with honey and milk – gifts that the Silbury mother was well equipped to provide.[9]

The remarkable match between the Roman worship of harvest deities, as displayed in their temples, rituals, visual art and literature, and the corresponding devotion that inspired Neolithic Silbury, serves to underline the hill's relevance to the newcomers. These entwined affinities will now be explored, for the Romans help us to solve the Silbury enigma.

To a remarkable degree, despite the linear time gap, the Romans seem to have given fresh voice to Silbury's original purpose. This, in turn, strongly suggests that the monument was revered by

30 Springhead allure. (a) Venus and her nymphs at a spring. A third-century Roman low relief from a High Rochester water tank, Northumberland. (b) The Swallowhead water, 500 paces from Silbury. (c) The hot spring at Roman Bath (dedicated to the goddess Sulis), to which the Roman road runs 21 miles west from Silbury.

Britain's indigenous population for 2000 years beyond the end of Neolithic era, throughout the subsequent Bronze and Iron Ages. In their turn, the Romans appeared to have perpetuated this long tradition.

Religious Syncretism

Soon after their arrival in the mid-first century AD, the Romans established a temple within yards of Silbury, 'a religious site ... an unusually important building in provincial terms, which had stone columns, and a group of metal rings made solely as votive objects', writes Robinson. He sees it as a roadside shrine, and notes: 'It is tempting to link it [the shrine] directly to prehistoric Silbury Hill, though why, of all the prehistoric monuments in Wiltshire it should have been singled out for continued or resumed veneration in the Roman period is difficult to guess at.'[10]

The answer may be that Silbury (unlike monuments to individuals) stands for the fulfilment of a basic need, shared by every race and generation. Food, regarded as a divine gift, was perhaps the common denominator that stopped the Romans in their tracks here. Accordingly, they were more interested in Silbury than in any other Wiltshire monument, including Stonehenge.

In matters of religion, the Romans invariably sought to correlate their own beliefs with those of the natives. 'One of the most mature features of Roman government was the ability to accommodate provincial beliefs and customs [involving] ... the merging of existing cults with classical gods.'[11]

This empire-wide propensity may now be coupled with a growing body of *local* evidence. As will be outlined below, there are sound archaeological reasons to believe that the Romans modified Silbury Hill itself to accommodate their own icons of the Harvest Goddess, so complementing the gigantic Neolithic prototype, while probably casting thousands of their coin offerings (of which Atkinson retrieved over 100) into the Silbury moat-image.[12]

It now seems probable that the Romans engaged directly both with Silbury *and* with the other Avebury monuments, regarding them *in toto* as a ready-made ensemble of sacred architectural venues available for re-use. There they could perform their imported versions of the indigenous mythic cycle, with agrarian deities transplanted from across the empire, as the classically attired leading characters in an annual drama. And this re-enactment involved both lateral and vertical movement.

The Ritual Shafts

Throughout British prehistory, human prosperity was believed to depend on fostering links between the underworld, surface and celestial realms of the gods. With regard to the influence of the subterranean on the upper zones, the Palaeolithic community conducted rites in deep caves. After the introduction of crop growing in the Neolithic, the buried seed placed extra emphasis on the underground region. Hence the 17 Neolithic long 'barrows' built around Avebury, listed by C.T. Barker.[13]

Some of these housed stone chambers were left open to worshippers for hundreds of years, as at the West Kennet long barrow, sited a mere half mile from Silbury. Piggot has described the many Roman coins found close to that barrow's blocked mouth as 'something more than casual losses ... but rather an association between Roman cults and pre-existing native traditions'.[14] Just such a link may have been supplied by the Roman myth, known throughout the empire, of a Harvest Mother's daughter who was trapped in the underworld.

Denied access to the West Kennet barrow, and with the Swallowhead aperture too small for human entry, the Romans felt motivated to dig at least five vertical shafts, arranged in an arc, immediately east and south of Silbury, and within the confines of their new town. When, more than a century ago, two of these were excavated, they were described as 'wells'; but Pollard is

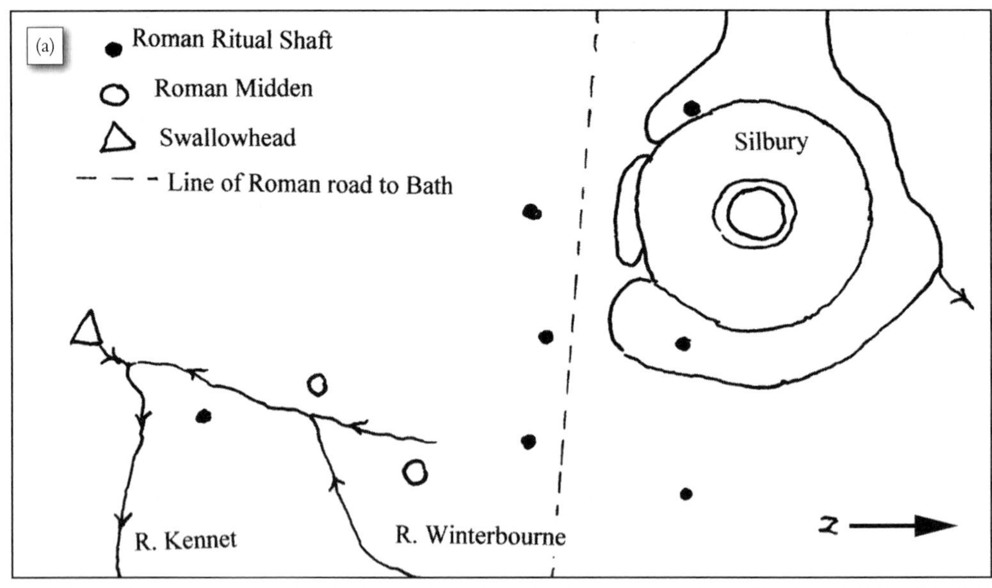

31(a) Roman ritual shafts and middens between Silbury and Swallowhead, based on plan of J.W. Brooke, 1889. (b) Geophysicists surveying the water meadows between Silbury and Swallowhead for prehistoric and Roman buried features in March 2008.

one of several recent writers who interpret them differently: 'A purely domestic function is unlikely, given the proximity of Swallowhead and the Winterbourne. It seems more plausible that a religious function was served by these shafts. It is an engaging possibility that such features encircle the hill',[15] a thought echoed by Corney's: 'Is there a ring of such shafts around the prehistoric monument?'[16]

The compulsion to repeat, as if for the first time, is a of feature mythic rituals. This may partly explain the otherwise 'unnecessary' number of these shafts. Kneeling at the brim, Ceres, the Roman Harvest Mother, or her Greek equivalent Demeter, could cry aloud for a beloved daughter, temporarily lost to the underworld, before eventually witnessing her ascent from the depths.

In essence, the same story involved agrarian goddesses of every era. So if (given the human desire to re-enact sacred events) a human girl was chosen to play the divine daughter's part, she may well have been lowered down one of Silbury's vertical shafts, eventually to be drawn up again as a supernatural 'lost child', now grown to maturity. Myth, shaft and human participants were probably combined in this kind of threshold rite.

The 1896 Dig

Long after they have been dismissed as 'old wives tales', myths tend to leave their mark on surface reality. For instance, in the 1890s a tenant farmer noticed that the soil around a spot 150 yards east of Silbury, close to the modern roadside hedge, subsided every year. His repeated attempts to fill up the hollow with cartloads of refuse had little effect. Sensing that a disused well lay beneath, he asked two local antiquarians, Brooke and Cunnington, to excavate the site.

After removing 6ft of the recently deposited rubbish, they hit layers thickly studded with red and black Roman and Romano-British pottery, mixed with oyster shells. At 8ft they found a bronze finger ring, a bronze balance with its loops intact, bronze coins of Arcadius (AD 383–85) and of Theodosius 2nd (AD 408–50). Sixteen feet below the surface they unearthed 'a beautiful specimen of a red deer horn pick' – the same type of implement used in the building of Silbury Hill! But whatever the shaft's original age, its Roman material was profuse. Three massive pitcher handles, the nether stone of a corn grinding quern, iron meat hooks, horse and pigs teeth, and a section of a Bath stone pillar. Twenty-six feet down they finally hit the 4ft diameter bottom. The entire shaft appeared to have been lined with 'large cut and squared stones'.[17]

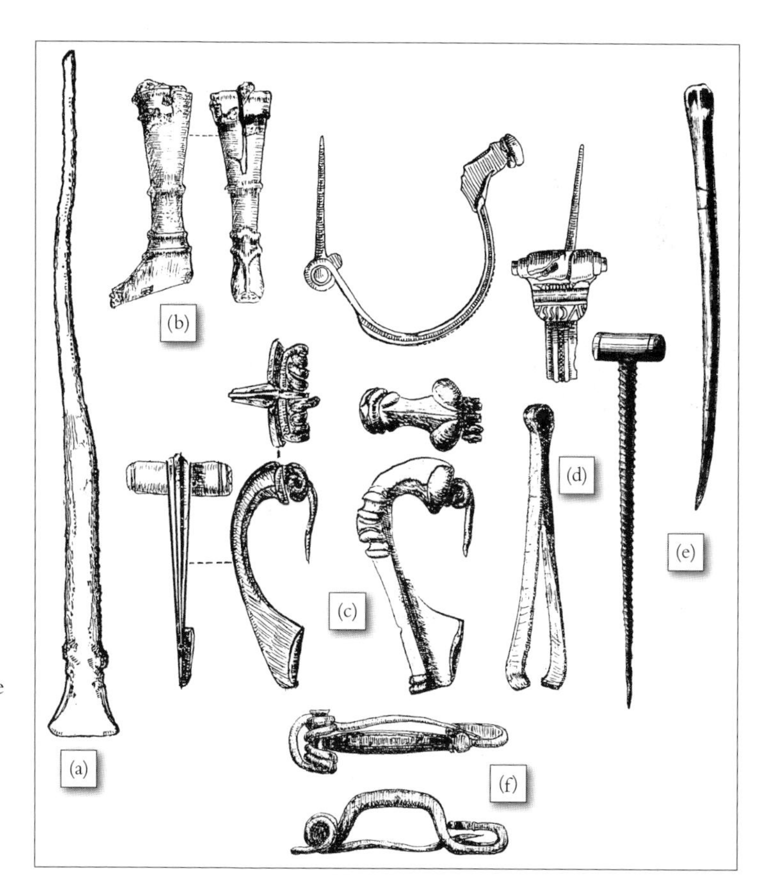

32 Bronze, iron and bone relics from Silbury's Roman town. (a) An iron writing stylus. (b) A bronze knife handle. (c) Three brooches. (d) Tweezers. (e) Two bone pins. (f) A bronze brooch from Silbury; length 2.7cm. (Devizes Museum)

The 1882 and 1908 Digs

Fourteen years previously, in 1882, W. and H. Cunnington had discovered, but only half cleared, another of the five shafts that have since been identified in the immediate vicinity. Eleven coins found there included those of Constantine the Great, AD 306, Magnentius (350), Constantine (337) and the sacred money of Antioch. A bronze beam from a pair of scales (perhaps emblematic of September's harvest in zodiacal form), a bronze ring, one blade of a pair of shears, an iron stylus, a double pot hook, numerous sherds of Roman pottery and a human infant's bones were also found.[18]

In 1908 one of William Arnold's horses was ploughing the same field, turning the sods from the humus-rich underworld towards the sky, in accordance with a 6000-year-old cycle, when its hooves 'sank into soft and yielding ground' over the same 'wellhead' that had been refilled in 1882. Consequently the shaft was re-examined by J.W. Brooke and found to be 12ft in diameter near the surface. At a depth of less than 6ft he came to a sarsen stone weighing half a ton, which took the strength of seven men to lift.

This obstacle had apparently terminated the earlier dig. After its removal, Brooke's later bucket loads were filled with necks, bases and handles of Roman period potsherds, 'in a great variety of shapes, sizes and colours'. In addition, his team unearthed glass and bronze relics, 33 Roman coins, some limestone corbels and column bases, roofing tiles, numerous square-headed nails and a profusion of animal bones, including those of deer, ox, dog, sheep and pig.[19]

Valuable Rubbish

How should this material be interpreted? Professor Green classifies 75 per cent of the Romano-British shafts in lowland Britannia as little more than rubbish pits or 'wells into which rubbish had been thrown after they had ceased to function'.[20] This may accurately describe the fate of the Silbury shafts, following the Romans' departure and collapse of the township in the fifth century AD. But prior to that, rubbish generated by the flourishing town was being dumped in a shallow midden discovered in 1867 close to the south-east fringe of the settlement.[21]

Water was found at the bottom of the ritual shaft emptied in 1896, arising from the same layer of grey clay responsible for the Swallowhead spring and Silbury's moat. To have reached that doubly revered strata and its outpourings again, through such arduous effort, may itself imply a mythic imperative. In any case, ritual and practical needs are often compatible. Water, a particularly hospitable solvent, is able to accommodate both intentions.

Anne Ross has shown that sacred shafts, both dry and wet, played a vital role for British religions in the Bronze Age and throughout the Iron Age[22] – a practice that the Romans in Britain adopted. The cluster of shafts, deliberately sited by them so close to Silbury's ample form and on her Swallowhead southern side, indicate a desire for continuity with native rites, based on the Silbury goddess and the Kennet's inspiring source. A map published in 1897 shows two more ancient 'wells' set *within* Silbury's silt-clogged ditch, in positions corresponding to the moat deity's thigh and breast, thereby physically incorporating the Neolithic harvest deity into later worship, conducted in Latin.[23]

The Farming Goddesses

To the Romans, the time gap between themselves and the Neolithic was no obstacle, since they regarded their own Harvest Goddess, Ceres, as the initiator of farming, even though they had only adopted her by name in 364 BC as their equivalent of the Greek goddess Demeter.[24] In Roman eyes, Silbury and Ceres were interchangeable contemporaries. So Ovid's *Metamorphoses*, composed in Rome during the late first century BC, states:

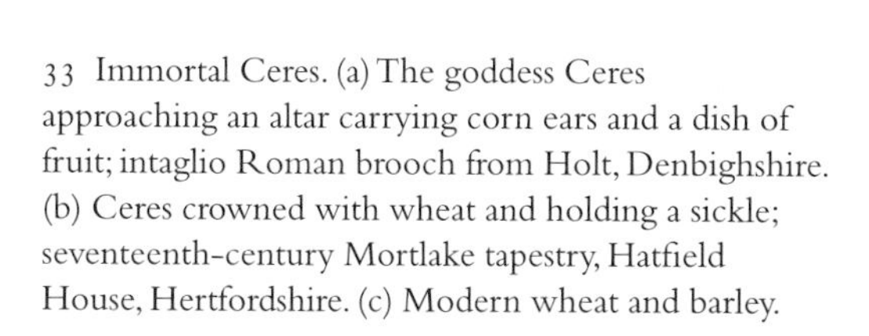
33 Immortal Ceres. (a) The goddess Ceres approaching an altar carrying corn ears and a dish of fruit; intaglio Roman brooch from Holt, Denbighshire. (b) Ceres crowned with wheat and holding a sickle; seventeenth-century Mortlake tapestry, Hatfield House, Hertfordshire. (c) Modern wheat and barley.

> Ceres was the first to break up the sods of earth with the crooked plough, [it was] she first planted corn and cultivated crops, she imposed the first laws in the world. All we have we owe to Ceres. Of her must I sing.[25]

He gives these words to Calliope, the muse of eloquence. Her symbol was a stylus, like that found in the 1896 shaft dig.

For the polytheistic Romans in Britain, Silbury, Ceres and Demeter synonymously initiated the agrarian revolution *and* wove the world's moral fabric – a joint achievement, annually renewed. Thanks to this syncretism, the Romans could properly settle beside Silbury, to dwell in harmony both with native tradition and their own versions of the story, featuring the loss and recovery of the Corn Mother's child.

Proserpine's Abduction

Ovid describes the abduction of Ceres's daughter, Proserpine. It occurred, he says, near a tree-fringed lake in 'a lush meadow bright with flowers, where it is always spring'. As a fixed state, this location is matched by her ambition to remain a virgin forever. In the meadow she was 'picking violets or shining lilies … with child-like eagerness she gathered the flowers into baskets, or into the folds of her gown'.[26]

Then 'Pluto saw her, and loved her, and bore her off' in his chariot. 'With wailing cries the terrified goddess called to her mother.' But 'Pluto urged on his grim steeds and with his strong arm hurled his royal sceptre into the depths of a pool'; a sexual metaphor, perhaps echoed in Silbury's wells. 'When the sceptre struck the bottom, the ground opened up, to afford a road into Tartarus, and the yawning crater received his chariot as it hurtled down.'[27] So congress with the underworld power was achieved. Perhaps the many horse bones found in the shaft explored in 1882 are the remnants of a horse sacrifice, made to re-enact the god's descending steeds.

If that was where the Silbury shafts led, gathered flowers dropped into them would also help commemorate the yearly occasion. Equally, a chosen maid lowered to the bottom to meet her subterranean 'king' could play Proserpine's role in Hades, re-enacting a key passage in the classical myth. This was essentially an episode from the Neolithic story of the seasons, in a Latin (or Greek) translation.

The tale persisted because agriculture has always involved planting seeds underground to germinate. So Proserpine (like Persephone, her Greek counterpart) *had* to dwell below, however unwillingly. As a result of her marriage to Pluto, she 'germinated' and 'grew up', enabling her to eventually reappear above ground; hence Romans derived her name (incorrectly) from Latin *proserpere*, 'to shoot up'.

The outcome was the eventual arrival of the corn harvest, as expressed in Callimachus's third-century BC *Hymn to Demeter*. 'Lady of much bounty, of many measures of corn. As the Basket comes from the ground ye shall behold it, ye uninitiated.'[28] This 'basket' was skull shaped. Its Roman equivalent was the *vannus*. Both were used for winnowing husks from the first of the new corn, regarded as the sacred essence of the harvest deities. In this joint achievement of daughter and mother they became one, visibly combined. Perhaps a grain-filled *vannus* was ritually hauled each year 'from the ground' at the bottom of the shafts so close to maternal Silbury.

First Fruits

The 'First Fruits' of the new crops of wheat, barley and oats were worshipped in prehistoric and classical times throughout Europe, and continued to be revered in the folk traditions of the British Isles till the twentieth century. In Britain the 'first cut' was made on the night of the full moon, nearest to the 1 August quarter day, the midway point between summer solstice and

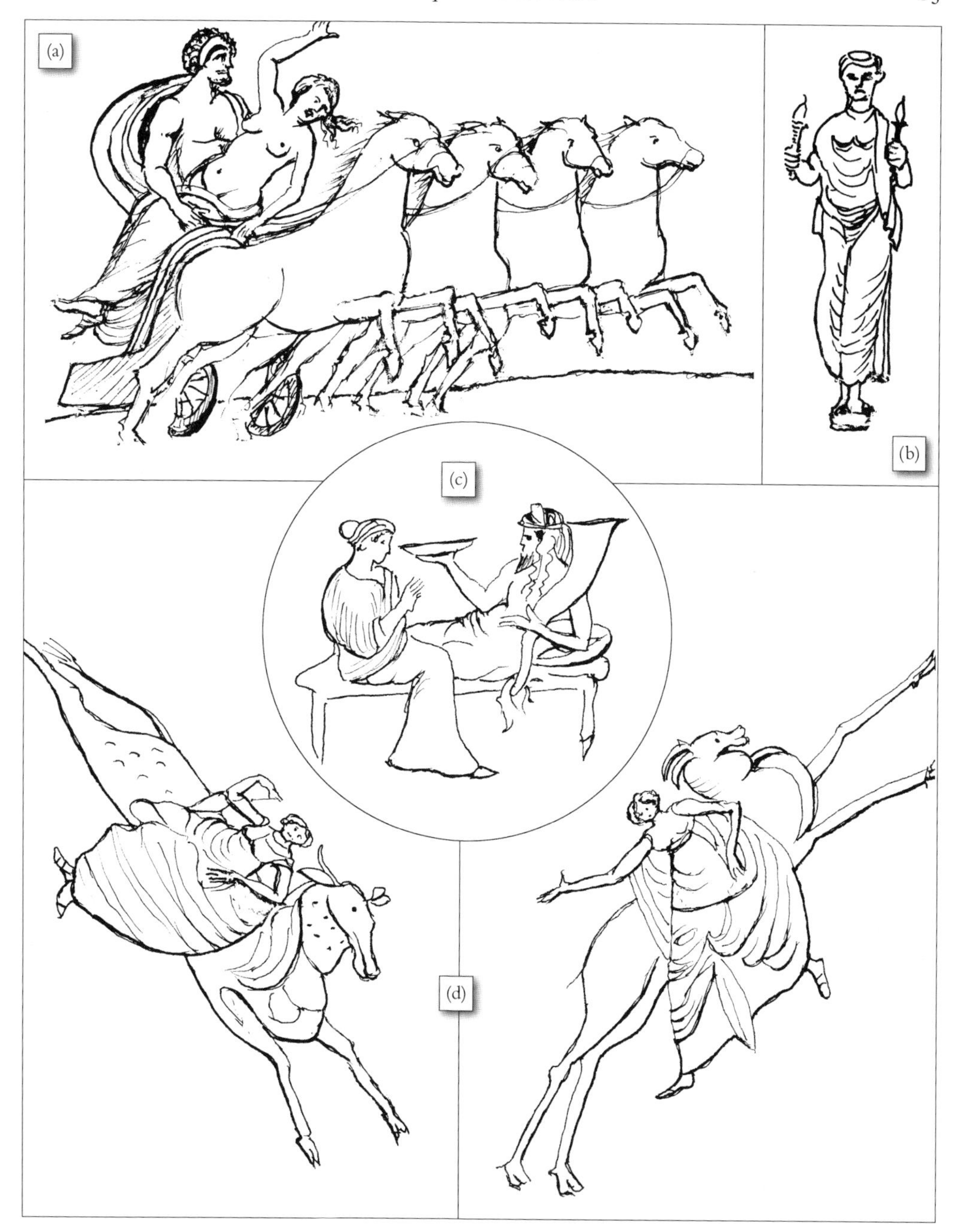

34 The abduction of Proserpine (alias the Greek goddess Persephone) by the underworld god, Hades or Pluto; (a) fragment from the painted tomb of the Nasonii, Rome, *c.*AD 160 (BM). Some scholars relate the 'abduction' to the storage of seed corn in underground granaries. (b) Ceres or Demeter with torches searching the world for her abducted daughter; Roman bronze figurine from Water Newton, Huntingdonshire. (c) Hades with his wife Persephone; Greek dish, third century BC. (d) Persephone (*left*) waves to her mother Demeter (*right*); mosaic beside the River Kennet at Littlecote Park, Wiltshire; fourth century AD.

35 First Fruits. (a) Ceramic model of a winnowing basket containing 'cakes' offered at the Temple of Demeter and Kore-Persephone, Corinth (Corinth Museum). (b) The Roman *Tellus Mater*, 'Mother Earth', with corn measure on her head; mosaic at Newton St Loe, Somerset. (c) Roman terracotta *cernus* or First Fruits 'offering table', 14cm square, from Crookhorn, Hampshire. (drawing by G. Soffe). (d) Demeter instructs Triptolemus to spread the art of agriculture round the world; mosaic from Brading, Isle of Wight. Ceres had three male gods to help with her harvest, (i) Liber, the Italian god of crop fertility, with whom she shared her temple in Rome; (ii) Bacchus, god of wine; (iii) Bonus Eventus, 'Good Outcome', who gathered in the ripe crops. He has carved stone dedications at York and Caerleon, Gwent.

September equinox;[29] hence the Welsh term *Gwyl Awst*, 'the Vigil of August'.[30] The Christian English renamed the feast 'Lammas', a contraction of 'loaf mass', while the Irish termed the 1 August festival 'Lughnasa', after Lugh, their young god of harvest.[31]

In 1867 the Reverend Wilkinson dug into Silbury Hill's south-east side and found a Roman ledge, cut into the Neolithic chalk, on which he discovered among ashes a small whetstone or sharpening stone and an iron knife blade, perhaps used to cut the first corn. Both items are catalogued as 'Roman' by Devizes Museum.[32]

More evidence of the Roman 'First Fruits' ritual comes from Crookhorn, Hampshire, where a *cernus*, a 'vessel for holding offerings' has been unearthed. This little ceramic altar, 14cm square, is of a type known in Crete from *c*.2000 BC. In this example, stylised human figures are drawn onto the sides, their arms raised in worship. The upper surface incorporates eight shallow dishes for grain around a deeper central pot.[33] According to M. Henig this *cernus* was probably 'used for seasonal offerings to Ceres'.[34] Latin *cernus* also means 'inclined forward, nodding position', as with ripening heads of wheat or barley.

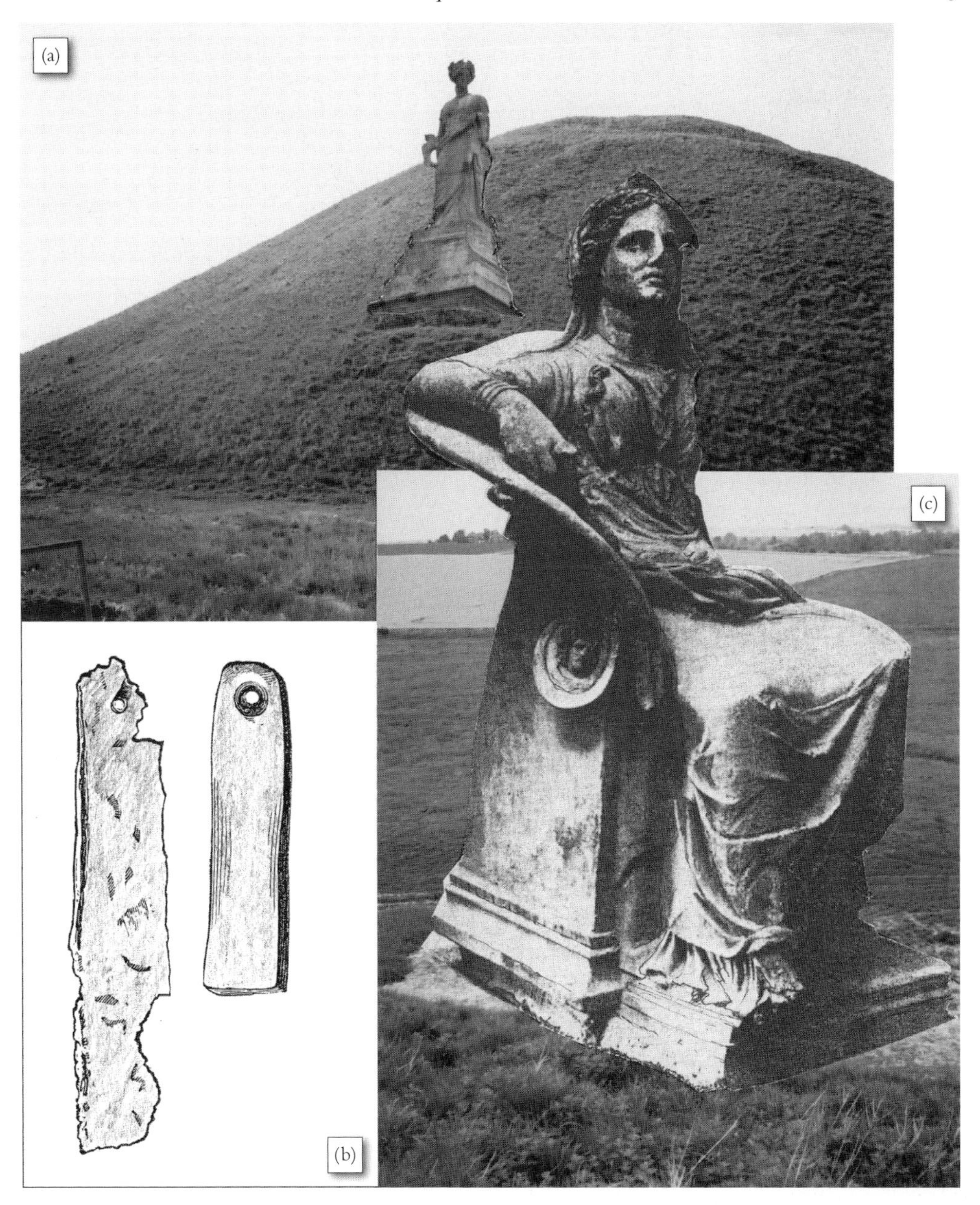

36 Ceres at Silbury. (a) A statue of Ceres by W.H. Hill, AD 1857, here 'borrowed' from Devizes Corn Exchange roof and re-sited on the Roman ledge cut into Silbury's south-east side. (b) A sickle sharpening whetstone and iron knife found concealed in this ledge. (c) Ceres, enthroned and crowned with wheat; terracotta, *c.* 300 BC, from Aticia in Latium, here 're-sited' on the Roman-cut terrace on Silbury Hill's north side, which D. Field thinks was made for a 'Roman monument'.

On its stumpy legs and with nine apertures, the vessel's intimacy contrasts with Silbury's grandeur. Meanwhile, Silbury Hill has been proved by Field's survey to be a *nine-sided* figure at base, rather than a cone.[35] Is it pure coincidence that nine months pass between human conception and birth, winter sowing and August grain harvest? Or should we suppose that the visual arts, including architecture (often called 'mother of the arts'), once aimed to give unified expression to such correspondences?

The Silbury Platforms

In his *Silbury Survey Report* of 2002 David Field draws attention to 'a number of deliberately constructed platforms around the middle and lower slopes of the mound. They cut into the original profile, and therefore post-date its construction'. He attributes them to the Romans, writing: 'It is almost inconceivable that the Romans did not leave their mark on the hill.'[36]

Of the platform cut half way up the hill, facing north towards Avebury, Field adds: 'It may have supported a monument of some kind ... [since the hill] may even have been considered just as sacred in the Roman period as when originally constructed.'[37] For his 'monument', we may safely infer one or more images of the harvest deities, carved in human form. Following the Greeks' achievements in figurative sculpture, that was the Roman way. What better match could there have been for the native Corn Mother than a statue of Ceres, set on the mighty womb of her Neolithic prototype?

As Cicero makes plain, for believers such images often went beyond mere representation of the deity: 'Those who saw the image of Ceres at Henna ... thought of it either as the goddess herself, or as her likeness wrought by no human hand, but fallen from heaven.'[38] This awestruck attitude may also have been the Roman response to Silbury, the goddess.

Whether god-given or not, the Romans needed sacred images. Circa AD 100 Pliny the Younger wrote:

> I am told by the soothsayers that I must rebuild the temple of Ceres that stands on my property; it needs enlarging and improving, for it is certainly very old and too small. Great crowds gather there from the whole district ... and many ceremonies are performed and vows made. We shall also have to make a statue of the goddess, for several pieces are broken off the original one because it is so old ... Please buy me four marble columns and marble for improving the floor and walls.[39]

At Silbury the Roman-cut platform examined by Wilkinson in 1867 is 20ft across, 9ft from front to back at its widest, and plainly visible a third of the way up the hill, on the south-east flank. It directly overlooks the 'groin' of the Neolithic moat goddess, at a point where the light of the full moon, nearest the 'start of harvest' quarter-day (1 August), re-enacts by reflection the annual rebirth of the sacred harvest baby from its mother-hill.[40] So orientated, the platform could have housed statues of Ceres and her harvest progeny, including Proserpine and Bacchus, god of the new vintage. Bacchus is portrayed, along with the Corn Mother, on several Romano-British mosaics.

Lost Daughter

In both classical art and literature, a flaming torch is an attribute of the Mother Goddess during her desperate night search for her daughter, as shown by the bronze figurine from Water Newton, Huntingdonshire. Ovid writes: 'Ceres, with panic in her heart, vainly sought her daughter over all lands and all the sea ... holding in either hand a blazing pine torch, lit from [Mount] Etna's fires ... She searched the whole world – in vain.'[41] (He located the story partly in Sicily because it had been carried there by that island's Greek colonists.)

The goddess's troubled mood was (and is) reflected by the anxiety that farmers feel as they await the germination, sprouting and ripening of the buried seeds. Rome, the world's largest city, lived under the threat of famine caused by unreliable overseas supplies of grain. After advice from the Sibyl of Cumae, Rome's first temple dedicated to Ceres was erected in 493 BC to counter impending starvation. True to the desire for continuity shown at Roman Silbury, in Rome, Ceres, the 'new' deity, was merged with Liber and Libera, the long-established local god and goddess of agriculture. Thus Ceres's temple in that city honoured the trio of Ceres, Liber and Libera.[42] This amounted to a capital precedent for the subsequent adoption by Rome of Neolithic Silbury.

Imperial Ceres

Five decades prior to the Claudian invasion of Britain, the Emperor Augustus had linked the morality and prosperity of his expanding empire to reverence for the traditional deities. Therefore he oversaw the restoration of Ceres's temple in Rome, and encouraged respect for comparable Mother Goddesses in the provinces.[43] This policy had political advantages, for as Catullus says: 'Thy nation, Rome, is fated to rule the earth wherever Ceres looks from heaven upon the fields.'[44] This attitude, maintained for centuries, ensured Silbury's continuing attraction. Her place of honour within the Roman Silbury-side town received imperial approval, in which genuine devotion was coupled with the need for her grain to feed the legions.

As for size, the massive scale of Silbury did not stretch the Roman visual imagination beyond its limits. On the contrary, it was *they* who nominated the entire land of Britain as Britannia, and depicted it (her) as a seated female on their coinage. She is titled 'Holy Britannia' in an inscription from Roman York.[45] This reduces Silbury, in terms of quantity, to a miniature image of the entire 'island-as-deity'. In 2008, Britannia continues to gaze from the reverse of our 50p coins. She illustrates the flexibility of scale inherent in allegorical and sacred art.

In Roman Britannia, the mighty Ceres was also stamped seated onto Claudian coins, and engraved into dozens of men's signet rings and cornelian brooches, worn by farmers' wives throughout the country. There the deity is depicted crowned with a wreath of wheat or barley, with wheatears in one hand and a dish of fruit in the other.[46] She was, in every sense, close to the rural family's heart. On her they pinned their hopes.

Seed corn was Ceres's daughter-in-embryo, destined to be buried beneath the soil in order to germinate. The king of the underworld was therefore helping Ceres's work. Yet she, like Demeter, her Greek namesake, swore that if Pluto would not release Proserpine from his long subterranean embrace, the enraged mother would blast the world with permanent sterility.

To carry out her threat:

> She broke with cruel hands the ploughs that turned up the earth, and in her anger condemned the farmers and the oxen to perish alike by plague. She ordered the fields to betray their trust, and caused seeds to be diseased... Crops perished as soon as their first shoots appeared.

Storms, floods and greedy birds completed the desolation. 'The whole world lay barren.'[47]

Demeter and Persephone

Faced with that dire prospect, several Roman emperors, including Augustus, Hadrian (of wall fame) and Marcus Aurelius, journeyed to Demeter's sanctuary at Eleusis, near Athens, to worship and become initiated into the secret Mysteries of that goddess, from whom the Roman version of the myth derived. (In the first century AD Claudius had contemplated transferring *all* aspects of Demeter's cult to Rome, while Ovid refers to Eleusis as 'the city of Ceres'.)[48]

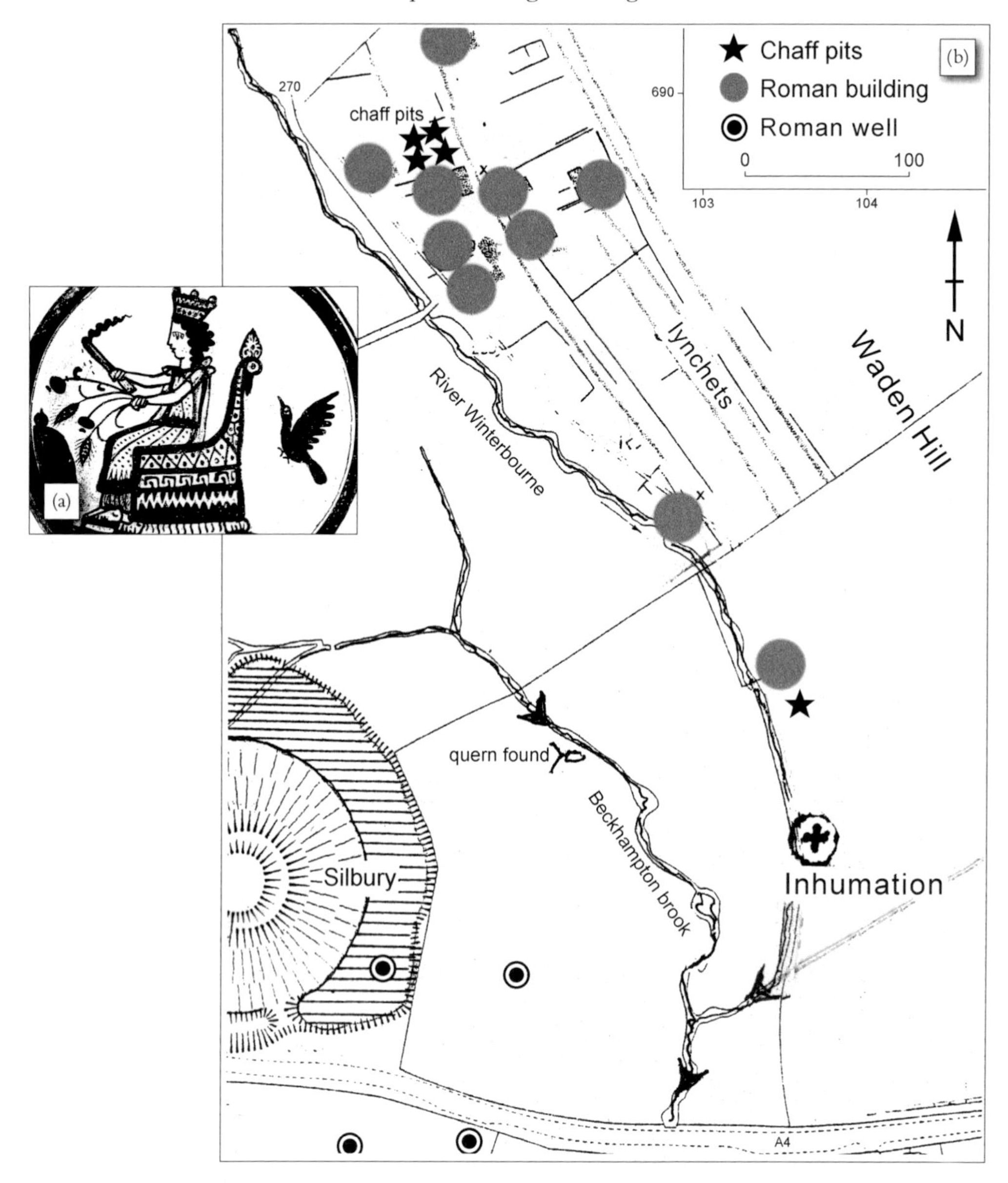

37(a) Demeter, the Greek 'Ceres'. Demeter depicted on a fifth-century BC plate from Corinth. She holds wheatears, poppy heads and a torch to aid her search for Persephone. The pomegranate set before her is a reminder of her daughter's marriage to Hades. The crow wants the grain. (b) Traces of Roman buildings discovered 1993–96, between Silbury and Avebury Henge, east of the Winterbourne. The grave of a Romano-British man has been found by J.G. Evans 250m due east of Silbury, and dug into the Winterbourne's east bank. The corpse lay on its back, head towards Silbury. A cluster of 30 nails from vanished boots lay at its feet. Animal bones of cattle, sheep, goat and horse had been deliberately heaped over the body. Perhaps he addressed Silbury, as 'mother of all life' on behalf of pastoralists as an early version of the *mythic herdsman*, known in Welsh and Irish medieval traditions.

In their pilgrimages to Eleusis (where they added extra buildings to the temple complex), these emperors were seeking good harvests while attempting to engage with the cosmic order, through empathy with a deity who might grant them a share in her immortality.[49] In Britain, this mystical impact of the Demeter-Ceres story was probably attached to Silbury and was also displayed at the fourth-century shrine at Littlecote Park, 14 miles east of Silbury, where a mosaic depicts Demeter waving to Persephone in a mysterious circular drama involving Venus and several wild beasts.[50]

At one stage in the search for her daughter, Demeter turned into an ugly old hag, according to reports from the seventh century BC. She thereby took on winter's year-end character. But when the god Zeus realised that Demeter's threatened famine would cut off his supply of human 'gifts and sacrifices', he sent Hermes to the 'hidden places of the earth' to tell Hades to release Persephone. Hermes found 'the ruler over the dead seated upon a couch, and his shy mate with him, much reluctant, because she yearned for her mother'.[51]

On receiving Zeus's command, Hades 'smiled grimly and obeyed'. Then Persephone 'sprang up for gladness'. But before she could leave he 'secretly gave her sweet pomegranate seed to eat ... against her will'. The pomegranate is a bag of seeds, suggesting buried seed corn. By this gift Hades ensured that she would have to return to him from the surface world to be his wife during the four winter months, every year.[52] Consequently, as his immortal spouse, her Greek name means 'to cause death', a terrible role for a flower maiden to play. But myth is obliged to combine just such extremes in order to match the range of nature's forces, the depths of human experience and agriculture's cyclical needs.

Miller's Tales

Having shot up green and tall from below, and turned to gold in her summer maturity, indistinguishable from her mother's, Persephone's fate was to be cut off at the knee, parched in a kiln, beaten by threshers' flails, winnowed in a basket, sieved and then ground to flour.

Roman corn-grinding querns have been found close to Silbury, and in 1993 a cluster of pits was discovered alongside the Silbury to Avebury Roman road. They were full of dry chaff from spelt wheat, along with some ears of the same variety, 'a popular choice in that period'.[53] So much chaff implies the presence of nearby corn-drying kilns and granaries, yet to be located. Every Roman miller maintained a shrine to Ceres, rather than to Proserpine, in his house and *Ceres*'s name, rather than Proserpine's, was sometimes used as a synonym for 'bread'. At bakeries, the two goddesses were doubtless kneaded together.

Spelt wheat, Latin *ador*, was a grain used in Roman rites. It held mythical significance for them. As a primitive variety of wheat, crossed with wild goat grass, it grew on the borderline between what Roman authors called pre-agrarian 'acorn eating' wanderers and the first agriculturalists. So in Virgil's *Aeneid*, when the hero Aeneas lands at the Tiber's mouth before claiming his right to the country, he and his companions sit on the grass for their first meal in Italy. And there, instead of tables and plates, they find some spelt meal cakes, on which were set 'fruits of the countryside'.

After devouring the fruit, but still being hungry, they are 'forced to eat the plates', the thin meal platters 'provided by Ceres'. As 'they bite this round-shaped crust of destiny', 'Hullo', said Julius jokingly, 'We are even munching our tables!'[54] So the deity who introduced farming also sustained the necessary hero. She was omnipresent. (By the time the Romans had conquered Britain, the god named Christ was also being swallowed in the shape of round, wafer-thin bread.)

Reunion

When Proserpine emerged from the underworld, her mother's sad expression changed instantly to one of joy. With radiant face, 'as when the sun breaks through ... kindly Ceres was restored to cheerfulness'. Despite her misgivings, she then accepted the compromise arrangement with

38 Iron Age milling querns, Powysland Museum; with Silbury Hill in August, as divine flour producer.

Pluto-Hades, and restored the earth's fertility. As a Roman mosaic panel at Brading, Isle of Wight, shows, she then taught the youthful prince Triptolemus how to plough and told him to spread her arable skills around the world, which he did.[55]

In Ovid's treatment of the Ceres myth, Jupiter divides the year precisely into half, allocating six months to Proserpine's confinement.[56] The arrangement exactly matches the Celtic scheme of winter and summer halves, cut along the Beltane to Samhain axis, giving a 1 May–31 October split. This operated in the British Isles before, during and long after the Roman period.

The twinned classical myths of Demeter and Ceres mediate between light and dark, death and rebirth, nature and the supernatural, founded on the integration of spirit and matter. This unity is memorably displayed at Silbury Hill, which was (and is) joined to its inverted 'other world' reflection in the deity's body-moat. The archaeological evidence combines with classical literature to indicate that the Romans were drawn to, and entranced by, that eloquent, yet silently proffered synthesis.

six

CUDA, MATRES, SIL

The Cotswold Mothers

At the time of the Roman invasion, Silbury lay within the south-east border of the British Dobunni tribe's territory, which was centred in the nearby Cotswolds, where Mother Goddess worship was the norm.[1] Thus the Cotswolds themselves are probably named after the native British goddess, Cuda.[2] Throughout her lands, devotion to the Great Mother and her consort (by various titles) is frequently portrayed in Romano-British mosaics, sculpture and carved inscriptions dating from the first to fourth centuries AD.[3]

Like Silbury, these goddesses are often portrayed seated and are mostly dressed in the matronly, ground-length clothes with a veil of the Ceres-Demeter type. However, in deference to local Celtic tradition, the deity is sometimes carved in triplicate, as a threefold group, known by the generic name of Matres or Mothers. They are 'goddesses of fertility in this world and the next', in Toynbee's widely accepted opinion.[4]

The Matres trios represent the Neolithic and classical trinity of Maiden-Mother-Hag, but with all three modes displaying the underlying maternal form, emphasised as the culminating phase of their life cycles. Consequently, each member of these sculpted groups holds an apple, bread loaves or an infant on her lap. (Fruit, wheat and children are all seen as goddess-born gifts, following Silbury's broad maternal scope.)

Again, like Silbury, the Cotswold Mothers are often associated with water; most obviously at Bath, where Sul, the native goddess of the hot spring, probably reclined on a stone couch over her spring, accompanied by statues of the Suleviae, the same goddess in her triple form. Another aquatic connection appears in a trio of fishtailed creatures, doubling as drapery, between the thighs of a Corinium Matres group, interpreted as the Syrian fish-tailed goddess, Atgartis.[5] She is a reminder that sacred fish may also have swam in Silbury's moat.

As for Silbury's enormous size, since the British goddess named Cud (or Cuda) is thought to have embodied the Cotswolds as a whole,[6] Silbury is tiny by comparison. However, since a chain of Neolithic long barrows and other monuments of that period surround an extensive area of the Marlborough Downs, centred on Swallowhead-Silbury, a similarly wide topographic claim seems to be intended there.[7]

Just as Swallowhead's Kennet source became the focus of a sacrosanct region, so in the Cotswolds Cud's worship is often connected to her rivers.[8] Perhaps for that reason the Thames received a temple at Hailey Wood, at what was then (prior to a drop in the water table) the source of that great river. The Hailey Wood sacred enclosure is 80 yards across and contains the footings of a temple of the same square shape.[9] For the Thames' 'birthplace' and the Cotswolds in general, the building completes a super-nature-culture alliance, comparable

39(a) A Romano-Celtic Matres or Triple Mothers group from Cirencester; second–third century AD. The central mother holds a child. (b) Another Matres group from Corinium (Cirencester); limestone, 73cm high. From left to right, they hold bread, apples, beans and other vegetables. Between their legs, the folds of cloth are said to evoke Atgartis, a Syrian fish goddess. Corinium is only 21 miles from Silbury.

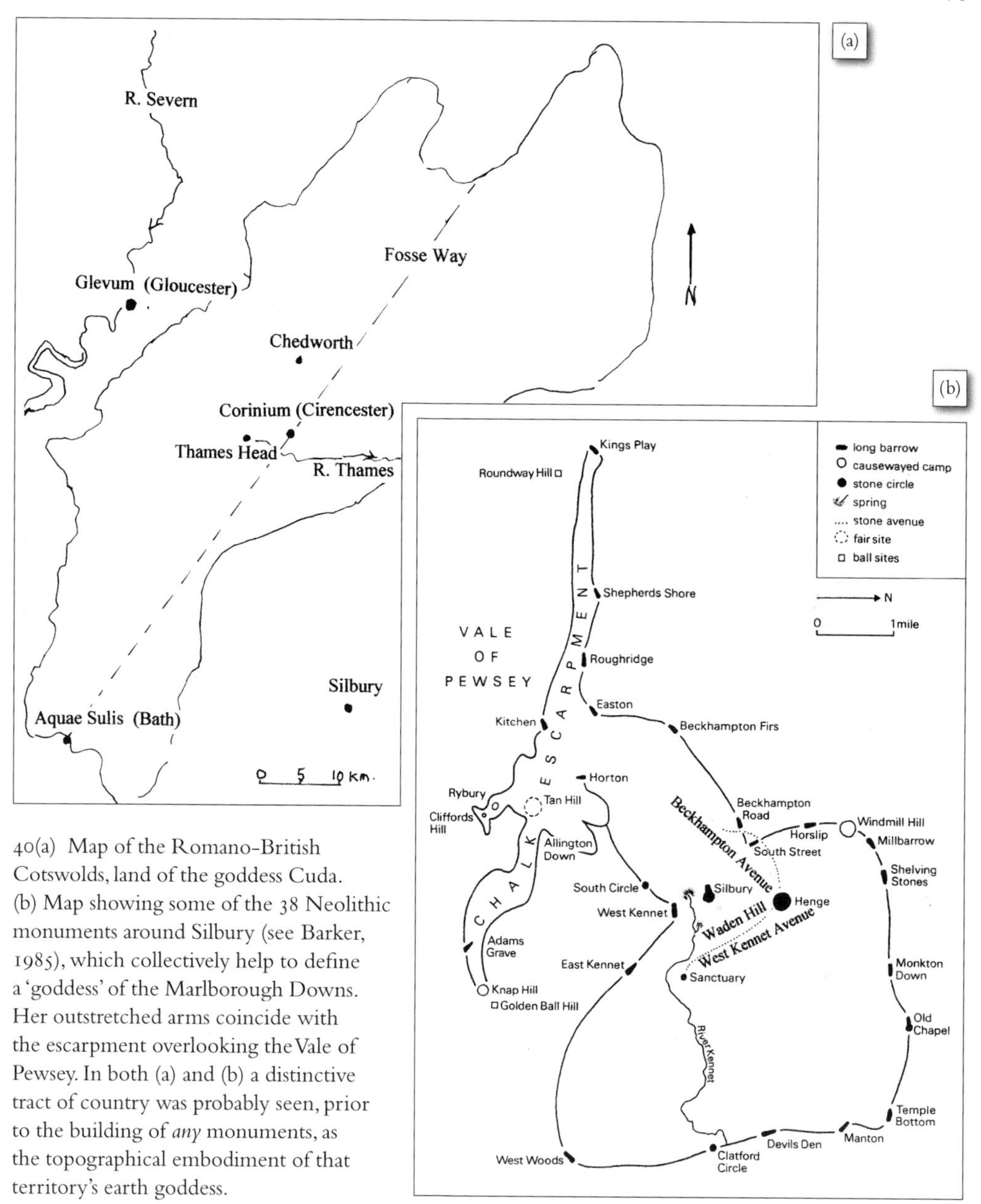

40(a) Map of the Romano-British Cotswolds, land of the goddess Cuda. (b) Map showing some of the 38 Neolithic monuments around Silbury (see Barker, 1985), which collectively help to define a 'goddess' of the Marlborough Downs. Her outstretched arms coincide with the escarpment overlooking the Vale of Pewsey. In both (a) and (b) a distinctive tract of country was probably seen, prior to the building of *any* monuments, as the topographical embodiment of that territory's earth goddess.

to the 'Silbury-Swallowhead – down land' fusion, 'a system in which the landscape itself played a defining role'.[10]

On a smaller scale, and reminiscent of Silbury Hill's shape, are the remains of the circular Cotswold temples or *tholoi*, round in plan. Several Matres sculpts have been found at or near these shrines which, by architectural means, evoke the primal womb. At both Corinium (Cirencester) and Glevum (Gloucester), the round temple was given a place of honour, adjoining the forum, while in Aquae Sulis (Bath) a similar *tholos*, recently discovered beneath the abbey, aligns with the goddess Sulis' springhead temple.[11]

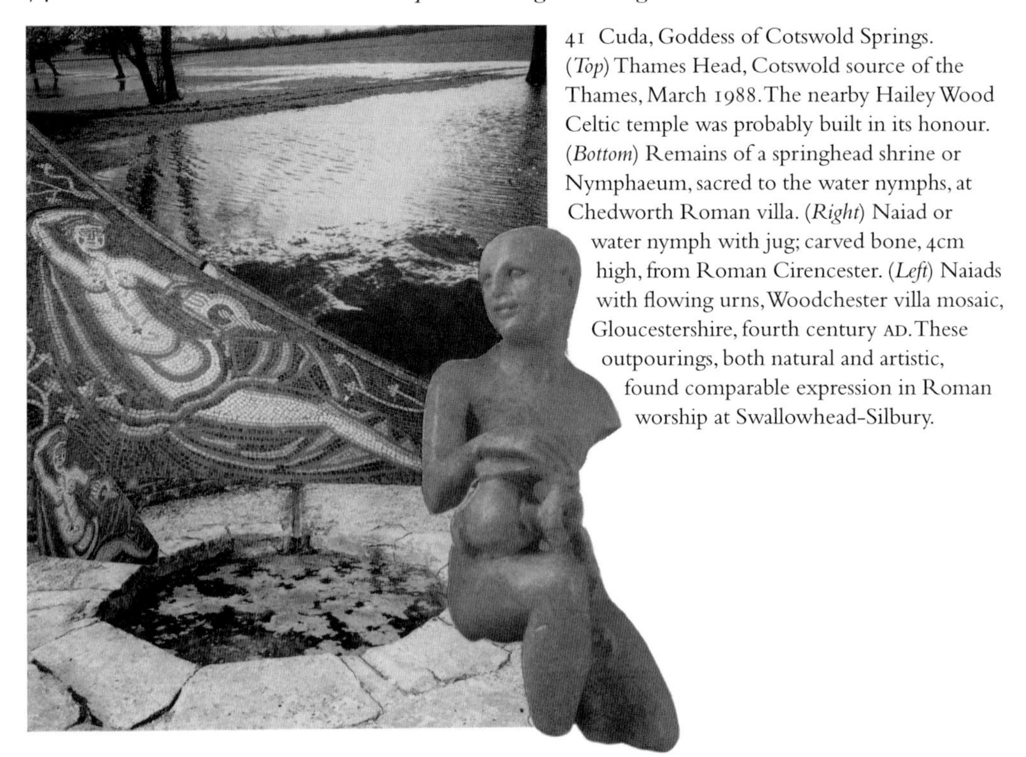

41 Cuda, Goddess of Cotswold Springs. (*Top*) Thames Head, Cotswold source of the Thames, March 1988. The nearby Hailey Wood Celtic temple was probably built in its honour. (*Bottom*) Remains of a springhead shrine or Nymphaeum, sacred to the water nymphs, at Chedworth Roman villa. (*Right*) Naiad or water nymph with jug; carved bone, 4cm high, from Roman Cirencester. (*Left*) Naiads with flowing urns, Woodchester villa mosaic, Gloucestershire, fourth century AD. These outpourings, both natural and artistic, found comparable expression in Roman worship at Swallowhead-Silbury.

Posset, Bowl and Bucket

Silbury folklore, in common with Iron Age and Roman Cotswold practice, attached importance to ritual containers. In the seventeenth century John Aubrey recorded the Wiltshire belief that the Silbury monument was built 'while a posset of milk was seething', presumably in a pot or bowl.[12] Posset is milk, curdled by ale, with honey and spices added. While the milk and maternity link is obvious, in 'seething' the drink swells up in readiness to the pot's lip as a white 'Silbury Hill'.

Cotswold goddess sculpts often portray her with a bucket or bowl, and sometimes with a ladle for dipping. These vessels contained her liquid gift to gods and world. Similarly, the medieval Welsh nature goddess Ceridwen, whose name means the 'Beloved White One', stirs an entire year's plants into her cauldron's stew, from which three drops of wisdom are distilled. The cauldron is her external 'womb of knowledge'.[13]

Under a cairn on the crest of the Cotswold escarpment at Birdlip, a pre-Roman female grave was found to contain an exquisite golden-bronze cauldron, placed directly over the buried woman's face. She wore a sumptuous necklace of amber, a fossilised resin used during childbirth rites in European folk custom that probably dates from the Stone Age. The Birdlip woman also had a bronze mirror.[14] Engraved with interwoven curvilinear shapes, the mirror depicted ceaseless interchange between a myriad of life forms, evoking Silbury's volatility, conveyed by the ever-changing reflections on her moat.

The ability to accept such metamorphosis as 'true to life' is not yet defunct. For example, the place-name expert Margaret Gelling spoke of the view from the Cotswold crest across the Severn Valley to the Malvern Hills as a bowl: steep-sided and flat-bottomed. She did not invent the propensity to make 'far-fetched' comparisons between utensil and landscape or between topography and the human body. Rather, it has always been an innate feature of human expression. In modern English we speak of headland, brow of the hill, cliff foot or cliff face and river mouth. Thus Silbury, (in Cleary's words of 2008) is sited on 'the toe of Beckhampton Down'.[15]

Male Consorts

Cotswold iconography throws a sidelight on yet another aspect of the likely Romano-British attitude towards Silbury in its depiction of the Mother Goddess's male consorts. Of these, Mercury, Rome's version of the Greek messenger god Hermes, features several times on Cotswold carvings.[16] One of his recorded tasks involved corn distribution – necessary following the annual harvest. He served as a go-between, linking Ceres to corn merchants, while remaining a powerful figure in his own right and eager to take over from his Neolithic counterparts.

His equivalent in Irish myth is Lugh, the young god of harvest who gave his name to Ireland's August hilltop First Fruits festival, Lughnasa. In medieval Welsh legend Mercury lives on as Lleu Llaw Gyffes, or 'Lleu Silver Hand'.[17] He likewise dwells in a number of isolated Silbury-type hillocks, for example Dinas Dinlle, in Carnarvonshire, and the Wrekin, Shropshire, which are to be further explored in Chapter 8. (Perhaps Lleu's hand was silver maybe because it ritually cut the first Welsh Gwyl Awst sheaf by the full moon's silvery light.)

The cloaked Genii Cucullati trios who, in the Cotswolds, so often attend the seated Mother Goddess, may be seen both as farmers, muffled up against the winter's cold, and as demigod spirits of the sprouting seeds that their sharp profiles bring to mind.[18] They are her growing boys, protectors, worshippers and sacrificial victims, resembling the English folk song character John Barleycorn. He was fated to be milled and malted into beer.[19]

Just below the Cotswold edge at Gloucester lies another long-lived 'goddess and son' pairing known to the Romano-Britons and then incorporated into a thousand-year-old Welsh tale, *Culhwch and Olwen*. It describes how Mabon, son of the goddess Modron, was imprisoned beneath that city, until released by Arthur's warriors with the assistance of an owl, eagle and salmon.[20] All the world's creatures, men included, were probably regarded as Modron's inter-dependent offspring. She was good at ecology.

The youthful wine god Bacchus was another major Cotswold figure. In the Corinium Seasons mosaic he and Ceres share the work. Perhaps because he personified the October grape harvest, he became closely connected to the underworld and with humanity's hopes of an afterlife there.[21] At Aquae Sulis, Bacchus and the Mother Goddess Sul are presented side by side. Their carved images flank the main altar of that springhead temple. She is shown seated, like Silbury. On one arm she balances a cornucopia and with her left hand pours 'water' from a large ewer. Looking at her, Swallowhead-Silbury fecundity comes to mind. At Bath the sacred liquids are water and alcohol, honoured together.[22]

Cuda, Name and Meaning

The name of the Cotswold Mother Goddess was Cuda according to Professors Green and Henig. Cuda is carved under a Romano-British low-relief panel found at Daglingworth.[23] There the goddess is carved sitting, attended by three Cucullati, one of whom offers her a cake. Beneath her, the letters 'CUDE … LO … V' are inscribed and also embedded in the place name 'Cotswolds', which contains an Anglo-Saxon corruption of her British Cuda name. Her Saxon wolds (Old English 'high, open land') still run 80 miles north-east from Bath towards Banbury, and from the Severn Valley to within sight of Silbury's chalk downs. Cuda is found again in the Cotswold place names Cutsdean and Cudnall, as well as in the old river name Codeswellan.[24]

Cuda's role apparently matched that of Silbury and of many Mother Goddesses through the ages, if one may judge from clues left in the Cornish, Welsh and Irish languages. And what are these languages if not orally derived stores of communal wisdom, assembled over countless generations? We should trust what the Celtic peoples of these islands had, and have, to say of both Cud and Sil. As words, they encapsulate authentic, enduring truths.

In Welsh and Cornish several Cuda-derivatives emphasise the veiled, hidden aspect of the deity. Thus, Welsh *cudd* and Cornish *cuth* mean 'secrecy, veil, and concealment'.[25] Though Cuda

42(a) A goddess with her staff, tub and ladle, accompanied by Mercury, her consort (he has his purse, snake-entwined caduceus and cock.) This is a Roman low-relief carving from Glevum (Gloucester). (b) Cuda and her Cucullati. Cuda, who gave her name to the Cotswolds, is shown seated offering a 'baby' or seed corn to her hooded male consorts; stone relief. Her name is incised below this Romano-British carving from Daglingworth, Gloucestershire (Corinium Museum). (c) The Matres with their infants; limestone relief, 80cm wide (Corinium Museum).

is immanent within the material world, most of the time she lies hidden by its superficial ordinariness, under the mundane surface of things. Yet she emerges during the heightened mood engendered at her festivals. 'To cover or conceal' also describes her full matronly garb, displayed by the Cuda effigies in the Roman city of Corinium. Even there 'the preponderance of local Celtic gods and goddesses is only to be expected', states Toynbee.[26] In addition, as with Cud, the pre-Roman deities' names, along with their meanings, were sometimes retained as words.

Related to Welsh *cudd*, the Irish word *cudnod* combines notions of 'keeping, guarding' with that of 'succour', perhaps coming from the soil, serving as both cloak and seed bed.[27] Irish *cudnod* links to the benevolent quality of other Welsh Cud words, including *cuder*, *cudaf*, 'fondness, affection, dear-ness', and *cudeg*, 'amiable'.[28] Likewise, Cornish has *cuf*, 'dear, beloved, kind, friendly'. At root, despite outward reserve, Cuda was what her name, place names, statues and fertile topography show – a maternally generous, idolised being, corresponding to her Silbury neighbour's inclusive outlook.

Romano-British ritual pit deposits, discovered in towns such as Silchester and Corinium, display a religious sensibility of a prehistoric rural kind, mingling animal and human bones on equal terms. This attitude was maintained throughout four centuries of urbanism in Roman Britain.

Speaking of Sel

On turning to *Sil*bury's name, it is a *male* character rather than a female who first leaps into view. In seventeenth-century Wiltshire folklore a King Sel was rumoured to lie buried beneath Silbury.[29] ('Bury', an Anglo-Saxon word meaning 'hill or mound', was locally spelt 'burgh' – hence 'Seleburgh' in the thirteenth century – and in 1540 as *buri*, giving Selburi.)

King Sel was delivered anew from beneath the hill, whose first syllable he shared, during each Anglo-Saxon '*hay sel, barley sel* and *wheat sel*'. In English, such terms (now obsolete) merge 'King Sel' with the *sel*, or 'season for harvesting' these crops. Accordingly, as a royal 'harvest monarch' he lived, the he was cut down, turned over, desiccated and killed in the seasonal events of June and July's hay-making, followed by a second death during the August and September barley and wheat harvests.

Year after year Sel epitomised the communal toil and joy of successful ingathering. Consequently, he can be discovered in the related (obsolete) English word *sele*. *Sele* is 'season, proper time, opportune moment'. Therefore, *sele* also embodied these connotations: 'happiness, prosperity, favourable and good fortune'. In King Sel's ideal year, fine quality and abundant quantity came together at his funeral feast.

In Middle English, *sel* and *sele* combine with the legendary Sel and the architectural Seleburgh in a fusion of word, demigod and monument. Here sight and sound merge as one. Such a compound is present in the complementary English expressions: 'I say! Look at that!' and 'I *see* what you mean'. So it is at our *Sel*bury, alias *Sil*bury, where archaeology and etymology make perfect, if unrecognised, partners. Just as the hill has physically survived for more than 4000 years because it was built to last, so its associated words have endured because they are so deeply ingrained in the family of tongues that includes Celtic, English and Latin. (Latin *sellisternium* is 'a seat for a goddess to sit on during a religious festival').

The Celtic languages of the British Isles (both 'P' and 'Q') have undoubtedly inherited verbal clues as to *Silbury*'s likely value in the first centuries AD. These vestiges have passed into Irish, Welsh and Scottish Gaelic dictionaries. They all make big claims for the word *sil*, focussed on notions of procreation and abundance, tying human, animal and vegetable realms together. In fact, the surviving cluster of Celtic *sil* meanings amounts to a veritable Silbury manifesto, probably echoing the original Neolithic purposes of the monument.

The Indo-European *Sil* Legacy

Is this mere coincidence or a predictable demonstration of the unity long recognised by the entire Indo-European group of languages? For well over two centuries etymologists have studied this linguistic 'family tree'. Its branches stretch from India to Ireland. Their roots are as old, if not older, than Silbury Hill and so enable that monument's first significance to be traced, in a word, across two continents and over at least four millennia.

Indian Sanskrit is the oldest written Indo-European script, and in that language *sil* means 'to glean or gather corn'. As at *Sil*bury, this practical act carries sacred connotations, since Sanskrit *sil* is also 'to meditate, serve, honour and worship'. The related word s*ila* adds 'good nature, amiability, virtue, shape, beauty, morality', and also (returning to work) 'a grindstone'.[30]

43(a) 'Summer'; one of four roundels from a Roman mosaic of the seasons, second century AD, found beneath Dyer Street, Cirencester (Corinium Museum). Here 'Summer' carries the sickle by which she has cut the 'umbilical' straws, enabling her to hold and be crowned by the harvest wheat child. (b) A traditional staddle barn granary; Alton Priors, Wiltshire, 2008.

The annual repetition of agricultural labour may be sensed further in Sanskrit *silana*, 'repeated practice', while the dynamic nature of the Silbury event may reverberate to this day in *sila-ja*, 'rock-born'. Equally evocative of Sibury's festival is Sanskrit *silpa*, 'any art', such as 'dancing, and acting', involved with 'creation and procreation'. Another meaning of *silpa* is 'a spoon or ladle used in sacrifices to throw butter into the fire' (*vide* the Gloucester panel). Bringing these aspects together is *silpaka*, 'a drama exhibiting magical or mystical rites'. These Sanskrit words show how ritual act and visual symbol unite with speech to reveal the sacred foundations of agrarian society.

Today, many other living languages of the Indian sub-continent lend outspoken support to Silbury's agrarian function. *Sila* means 'an ear of corn' in Kashmiri; 'gleaning' and 'a lower mill stone' in Pakrit. Bengal and Bihar have *sili* as 'grain and husks on a threshing floor, prior to winnowing' and then as 'a heap of grain'.

In short, Silbury reminds us of the well-travelled Rudyard Kipling's words: 'What do they know of England, that only England know?'

From his intercontinental perspective, the *sil* of Silbury appears as an indestructible pollen grain, blown to Britain from the East. *Sil* was carried from voice to voice on a variety of related tongues and eventually arrived in Britain, together with the art of cultivation, to name and inspire the Silbury temple.

Sil in Britain and Ireland

The *sil* evidence from the British Isles (which lay on the north-west extremity of the Indo-European language range) is just as strong, and is compatible with south Asian usage. For instance, Welsh *sil* is 'seed, spawn, newly hatched salmon; young (such as bees), produced in great numbers, hull of grain, offspring, progeny, descendants, the common people'.[31] In one word, inherited from pre-Celtic sources, we are given a condensed summary of Mother Silbury's output.

In the same vein, Irish *sil* yields 'seed of plants and animals; sperm, race, progeny, descendants; cause, origin'. This list brings another echo from Neolithic roots, outlining Silbury's role as the presumed *initiator* and symbolic birthplace of everything in the cosmos. Irish *siul*, 'before', may be another hint that Sil *pre-dated* the universe in believers' minds and existed before she made her planetary earth into a 'bed' (Irish *suil*) and kept her 'eye', *suil*, in 'hope' and 'expectation', *suil*, on the crops as they emerged. Then, on her 'weaving loom' (Irish *siul*), she began to weave the fabric of Neolithic civilisation.[32]

The cognate Scots Gaelic word *siol* concurs with Welsh and Irish, while carrying the additional meanings: 'corn, or oats', *plus* 'poet or bard'. So, in the Scottish Isles (as in India) the perpetuation of a Silbury-type abundance depended on spinners of Sil'*s* myth and poems sung in her praise.[33]

Gaelic *siol* creates a beneficial circuit, running between acolyte and deity, as shown by the Cucullati-Cuda Cotswold panels, and by the accumulating evidence left by Roman worshippers around Silbury. There, Latin *siligo*, 'a soft variety of wheat', much favoured by those making religious offerings, fits both Roman and native impulses, as does Latin *siliqua*, a 'seed pod'.

The maternal shape of the Silbury monument epitomises all these, her many *sil* gifts. She nurtured them from underground by means of her chalky waters, seen as milk when passed through the English word *sile*, 'a milk strainer'. And milk comes again in the 'seething posset of milk' that rose in time to feed the 'child' who emerged from Silbury's hill-womb, as seventeenth-century Wiltshire folklore implies.

With the *sil* syllable now re-attached to *Sil*bury we might ask again: 'What does the monument mean?' and can reply: 'It *says* what it means and *means* what it says.'

seven

SILBURY'S ROMAN AUGUST

'Neolithic' Ceres

With their evident enthusiasm for Silbury the Romans provide a ventriloquist's voice for a silent Stone Age. Yet this is no mere deception, for they, in common with the native Britons, had the Neolithic goddess in their bones. *Ecco La Prima Madre*, 'Behold The First Mother', runs a headline in a recent Italian archaeological journal over a picture of a 'pregnant goddess' stone figurine from Vicofertile, near Parma. She was carved in 5000 BC, which is 2500 years before Silbury was built.[1] Throughout Italy and across Europe, the goddess and agriculture worked together.

After focussing on the corn-giving aspect of the Neolithic Great Goddess, by 364 BC the Romans had, in that specialised role, renamed her 'Ceres' from the Latin word *cerealis*, 'of wheat, its growing and preparation' and 'bread, food in general'. But in Latin these necessary things are inseparable for the same Latin word means 'of, belonging to the goddess Ceres'. For Romans, Ceres was the sacred essence *and* the mundane reality of bread.

This double usage appears to ignore the distinction between 'sacred' and 'profane' often observed by religions. Yet just as Christ identifies his divine body at the Last Supper with ordinary bread, so the point of Ceres's temple (and of the Silbury image into which she infiltrated) may have been to re-sanctify the world *as a whole*. If so, *cerealis* announces that possibility in one word.

Moreover, by the first century AD, Ceres had also broken the historical time barrier, for by then the Romans had back-projected her arrival to cover *all* the centuries from the early Neolithic! Consequently Apuleius described her as: 'the original Harvest Mother, who abolished the rude acorn diet of our forefathers, and gave them bread'.[2] As a deity, she had moved beyond history altogether (where she never really belonged), into the cyclical and endless time of myth. Consequently, when the Romans brought Ceres to Silbury, they could readily regard *that* monument as a gigantic image of Ceres, their own 'originator of farming', and thereby assimilate the British temple into a combined liturgy of Romano-British worship.

Coins stamped with the image of Ceres on the reverse, inscribed *Ceres Augusta* (Latin *augusta*, 'consecrated'), entered Britain with the invasion of AD 43, and were soon 'being extensively and skilfully reproduced by the native inhabitants'.[3] (By then Claudius had enhanced Rome's precarious grain supply by improving the docks at Ostia. Ceres was on his mind, for she brought religion, economics, social justice and politics together. Therefore, 'By the Emperor's favour the cultivator can give to Ceres the first corn ears', wrote Calpurnius Siculus, his contemporary.)[4]

With at least 30,000 troops to feed in Britain, the incoming army's surveyor who stood on Overton Hill, gazing west towards Silbury Hill, chose to aim the line of his new road at Silbury's 'corn-baby', *southern*, side.[5]

As described in Chapter 5, during the next 350 years the purpose of the ancient Silbury effigy was also suggested, if on a smaller scale, by the portrayals of Ceres carved onto numerous intaglio brooches, popular among the country's native farmers.[6]

Ceres in Roman Literature

The proliferating images of Ceres in Roman Britain are matched by frequent references to her in Latin literature, as the following examples indicate:

> Ceres of the yellow hair, from my farm comes a spiky wreath to hang before thy temple door.
> Catullus, *Poem lxiii*, ll. 1–6, First Century BC

> Ceres, to whom we make our prayers, so she might rise on lofty stalk.
> Horace, *Satires*, viii, l. 14, First Century BC

> I will forbid the man who has divulged the sacred rites of Ceres to abide beneath the same roof.
> Horace, *Odes III, ii*, 26

> Ceres ... the rites of whose worship ... are beyond all others mysterious and exalted
> Cicero, *Verrine Orations*, v. 72, 187, First Century BC

44 (*Top*) Silbury in the wheat, July 2007. Agriculture began here before 4000 BC. (*Top inset*) A pregnant Neolithic clay figurine, 20cm tall, from Vicofertile, Italy, made *c.*5000 BC. Romans built a township around Silbury in the first century AD, having inherited worship of a Neolithic goddess similar to Silbury in their homeland. (*Bottom*) Silbury and ripening barley seen from Swallowhead, July 2007. Beneath this field lies a recently discovered gridiron pattern of Roman streets. (*Bottom inset*) A late Neolithic beer beaker, *c.*2500 BC, from the nearby West Kennet long barrow. A barley beer, *cerea* (named after the deity Ceres), was also brewed in Roman Britain.

Well into the fourth century AD, Ausonius was writing of 'the gifts of Ceres' while looking in the reverse direction. Romans did not hesitate to identify her with the earlier established Greek Mother Goddess Demeter, the subject of Callimachus's *Hymn to Demeter*, composed in the third century BC: 'Hail, goddess, and save this people in harmony and prosperity, and in the fields bring us all pleasant things! Feed our kine, bring us flocks, bring us the corn-ear; bring us harvest! And nurse Peace, that he who sows may also reap'.[7]

What is now termed the Neolithic, the Greeks and Romans defined as the 'Silver Age' – the era when agriculture began. Ovid makes this clear. He describes how the preceding period of the berry gatherers when 'the earth … untouched by the hoe, un-furrowed by any share, produced all things spontaneously' was followed by the Silver Age: 'Then corn, the gift of Ceres, first began to be sown in long furrows, and the straining bullocks groaned beneath the yoke.' In Roman parlance, Silbury is an outstanding depiction of Britain's 'Silver Age' Ceres. (Here, as in Italy, her worship continued through the more warlike ages of Bronze and Iron.) When facing Silbury, the Romans beheld the world's earth-bound agrarian roots. In that great Hill, Tellus, their goddess of earth, and Ceres, deity of the corn, were merged in perpetuity, as their poet Ovid described: 'Ceres and Tellus discharge a common function; the one lends to the corn a vital force, the other lends it room'. He adds that the pair had been 'partners in labour' since the onset of agriculture: 'Ye who reformed the days of old and replaced the acorns of the oak with food more palatable'.[8]

Whether prehistoric or classical, the Mother Goddess, as mistress of earth, vegetation and human births, also provided a model for social equity and law. Thus Ceres's temple in Rome was both a place of food distribution to the poor *and* where all the laws passed by the Senate were housed, guarded by the Plebeian *aediles* (magistrates) and available for inspection by the proletariat.[9]

Further, in the Roman calendar the entire month of August was dedicated to Ceres. This perfectly matched Britain's own island-wide August harvesting, which followed the Silbury 1 August First Fruits ceremony. Under the month-long supervision of Ceres, the Romans also introduced a number of other festivals, many of them harvest related, as indicated below.

1 August: Spes, 'Hope'

The Romans celebrate a goddess named Spes, 'Hope', on 1 August. (By chance, 1 August was also the birthday of the deified Emperor Claudius who had brought Ceres to Britain.) Spes had three temples in Rome. One was sited in the Forum Holitorium and was a vegetable market.[10] The Latin word *spes* means (1) 'a feeling or state of hope or expectation of something desired; (2) the divine basis or repository of one's hopes; (3) anticipation; (4) the prospect of future achievements.

However, for *Italy*'s agriculture Spes's feast day came too late, since the wheat harvest had already begun there in July. Yet by coincidence her celebration exactly fitted the climatically cooler 1 August 'start of harvest' quarter day in Britain. This followed the previous night's 'vigil' over the goddess-in-labour for her fruits, known in Welsh as *Gwyl Awst*.[11] For the inhabitants of the British Isles, this was indeed the time to hope. Similarly, on that day in eighteenth-century Midlothian, Scotland, the young men of each parish were busy constructing a conical 'Lammas tower' of soil and turf as the central point of their start of harvest rites.[12]

In Ireland early August was called 'Bron Trogain' (Irish *bron*, 'burden' with *trog*, 'parturition' and *trogan*, 'earth'). Mother Earth was then in labour, hoping to give birth to her crops. There, on 31 July–1 August, it was an obligatory pre-Christian tradition to offer the first of the new corn or potatoes in recognition of her achievement. This usually involved ascending an isolated hillock, hill or mountain to make the necessary presentation. In 1962 Maire MacNeill recorded dozens of such Irish 'Silburys', still representing the annual embodiment of harvest hope for the farming community.[13]

The young goddess Spes first appeared on Roman coins in AD 41, when a *sestertius* of the Emperor Claudius was struck to celebrate the birth of his son Britannicus, who was named in anticipation of his father's conquest of Britain.[14]

45(a) Wheat on a gold stater of King Cunobelinus of Britain, AD 10–40. (b) R. Ling's drawing of wheatears, painted on wall plaster in the Roman town of Calleva Atrebatum (now Silchester, Hampshire), 34 miles east of Silbury. This 'plan' shows corn emanating from a tiered 'harvest hill' and the eight-fold subdivision of the British year is also suggested. (c) Ceres, with red poppies; mosaic from Calleva (Reading Museum). (d) Ceres, with corn, poppies and serpents; low-relief sculpt (Terme Museum, Rome).

Hope Delayed

The Romans chose 1 August for the Spes feast because: 'Though the offering of 'First Fruits' [in July] was common if not universal in rural Italy, the growth of the city had pushed agriculture some distance away.'[15] For the million citizens of Rome whose grain supplies came from far-off districts (and increasingly from Sicily, North Africa and Egypt) there was a considerable time lag between reaping and the arrival of grain. On 1 August they were eagerly awaiting these new supplies.

Consequently the feast days of Rome's principal agrarian deities are clustered, with only one exception, in August, rather than July. And because Rome conveyed its own religious traditions across the empire, her urban 'time slippage' brought that city's August calendar into a chance alignment with Britain's *climatically* retarded harvest ceremonies, including those held at Neolithic Silbury.

As for Spes, the Britons soon had reason to shout 'Some Hope!' Even judging by Roman accounts, abuses by their soldiers and first-century officials amounted to little less than theft of the natives' crops. The Caledonian Calgacus testifies: 'Our goods and fortunes are ground down to pay tribute, our land and its harvest to supply corn … all under blows and insults.'[16] Queen Boudica's rebellion and the destruction of Roman London, Colchester and St Albans was the British response in the south.

Thereafter relations improved. By AD 100 Tacitus could even assert that 'the Britons submit to the levy, the tribute and the other charges of Empire with cheerful readiness'.[17] But whether under British or Roman control, Britannia's grain lands required the propitiation of harvest deities, both native and foreign.

3 August: Supplicia Canum

On this day dogs were crucified on crosses made of elder wood and paraded round Rome's Circus Maximus.[18] (Latin *supplicium* is 'a thing offered'.) The event may be seen as a crueller version of the first-century AD British dog sacrifices that occurred in a cave at Alveston, Gloucestershire. These in turn have been linked to the 'dog god' Nodens who was subsequently worshipped in his temple at nearby Lydney.[19]

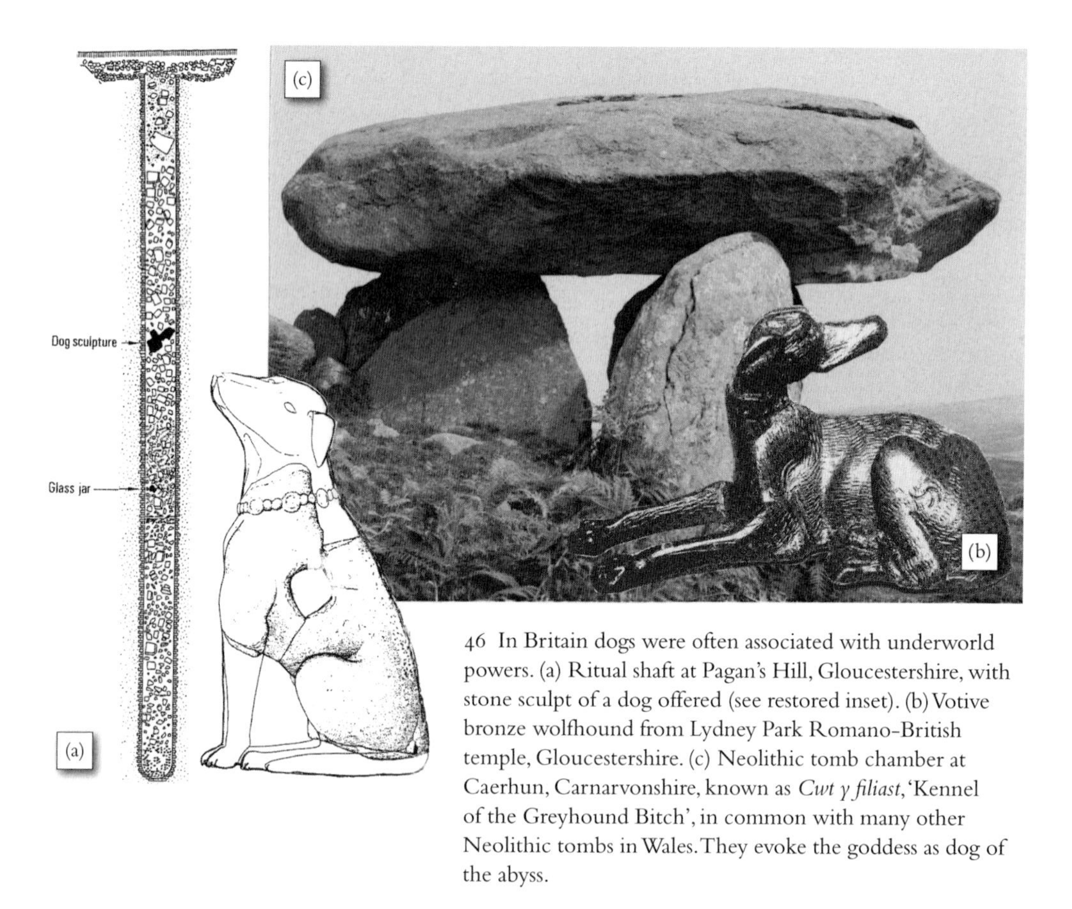

46 In Britain dogs were often associated with underworld powers. (a) Ritual shaft at Pagan's Hill, Gloucestershire, with stone sculpt of a dog offered (see restored inset). (b) Votive bronze wolfhound from Lydney Park Romano-British temple, Gloucestershire. (c) Neolithic tomb chamber at Caerhun, Carnarvonshire, known as *Cwt y filiast*, 'Kennel of the Greyhound Bitch', in common with many other Neolithic tombs in Wales. They evoke the goddess as dog of the abyss.

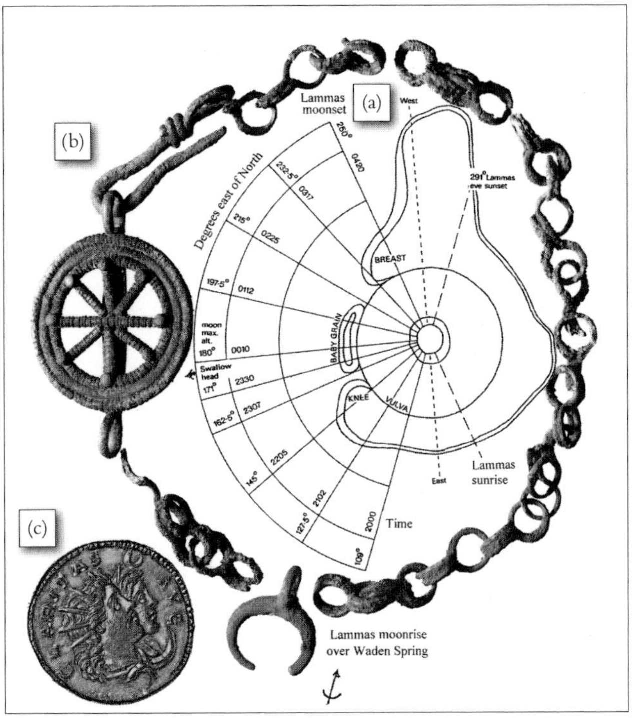

47 Silbury, sun and moon.
(a) Plan of Silbury showing passage of moonlight on the moat, from groin to breast, as cast by the full moon nearest 1 August.
(b) Romano-British gold necklace from Backworth, Co. Durham, with solar wheel and lunar crescent, found with five gold rings inscribed to the *Deae Matres*, *c.*AD 150. (c) Sol and Luna together on a Roman gold *aureus*, AD 267, Koln. As now, so in Roman and Neolithic times, light and heat interacting with earth and water provide the conditions for the generation of new life.

Alternatively the *Supplicia* was intended to confront all underworld canine powers, symbolised by Greek hound Cerberus. Such dogs might otherwise have blocked the harvesting of crops. (Because all cereals are sown and rooted below ground they arguably belonged to the subterranean hounds, still known to Welsh folklore.)

5 August: Salus

The Roman goddess Salus protected 'the safety of material things' and 'physical health', both individual and communal. Her emblem was the serpent of renewal, able to slough off its old skin. Salus shares this device with Ceres who is often depicted holding snakes amongst her ears of wheat.[20] For Romans at Silbury, the nearby Neolithic stone avenues that run to the Avebury Henge from West Kennet and Beckhampton offered two monumental serpentine reminders of both deities. Similarly, the plaited 'grass snakes' found by Merewether, radiating at Neolithic ground level from Silbury's core, establish the same motif in miniature within the founding nucleus of the harvest Hill long before the Romans came.

9 August: Sol and Luna

Given the Roman fondness for subdivision and the specialised, when they saw solar and lunar reflections thrown onto the Silbury moat, they probably wished to name and credit both types as distinct performers in the harvest success story. By contrast, the natives, as shown in our Iron Age art, preferred an ambiguous interweaving of categories. For instance, the Irish goddess Aine functioned as the earth personified, emanating from Cnoc Aine, her hilltop sanctuary in Co. Limerick, but *also* as an ocean-born female sun – hence her by-name: 'She who travels regularly'.[21]

48 A reconstructed Nymphaeum, dedicated to the naiads, sited over a spring at Roman Vindolanda, Northumberland, 2006. (a) The interior. (b) Temple and spring. Forty-five Roman coins have been found in the immediate vicinity of Swallowhead and 95 more, including a gold *aureus* of Nero, in the Silbury moat. (c) Euterpe, the Graeco-Roman muse of lyric poetry and wind instruments, playing her flute; bronze, 20cm tall, found at Silchester. The muses emanated from springs rising around sacred mountains. (d) The deified Empress Sabrina, Hadrian's wife, known as 'Our Mother, the New Goddess Ceres'. She carries poppy and wheat heads in this statue from Ostia, Rome's grain port. Sabina came to Britannia in AD 122.

This difference of outlook should not, however, be overemphasised. A temple in Rome, jointly dedicated to *Sol* and *Luna*, showed collaboration between the two major heavenly bodies. This sun-moon shrine overlooked the Circus Maximus.[22] Since both those deities were portrayed as charioteers, they implicitly 'came to earth' as quasi-participants at the city's chief chariot racing track, in the serious sport of elemental interplay, to 'join' the four human teams of charioteers who represented the four seasons. Therefore, the Romans could readily appreciate prehistoric Silbury's comparable mixture of elemental and human participants in that temple's drama.

For Roman and Briton alike, the August quarter-day sun at Silbury continued to work marvels. Viewed from the hill's sub-summit terrace on that day, the sun appears to rise (and ride like a charioteer) along the back of the nearby Waden Hill.

In addition, the first sunbeam of 1 August aligns Swallowhead with the Waden Hill spring, which rises half a mile to its north-east. Thus, with one flash, the first ray penetrates the mouths of both the two underground watercourses, as if to illuminate the Acheron and Styx rivers of Hades' kingdom with a shared glint of reaper's gold.

As for the moon, in *The Silbury Treasure* I argued that the full moon nearest the 1 August quarter day illuminated the Silbury moat from thigh to breast during the course of the night, thereby enacting the birth of the 'harvest child', represented by the gigantic, 240ft-long 'grain' or 'infant-shaped' hollow that lies pressed against the maternal belly between the two Neolithic 'causeways' of undisturbed chalk. The last moonlight before dawn then gave the 'milk' of its silver reflection to the reclining deity's moat-breast for the newborn harvest child to drink.[23] The Romans could enjoy that sight, but today, with silt now 3m thick clogging the moat, we can't.

12 August: Hercules Invicto

On 12 August Hercules the 'invincible' hero revealed his generous side. At his archaic round temple close to the entrance of the Circus Maximus he entertained the poor of the city to a feast of meat, bread and wine. These tithes represented the trace of a First Fruits ritual, in which vanished generations of farm workers had become a city's proletariat, grateful for charity.[24]

13 August: Camenae, Diana and Vortumnus

Homesick Roman visitors to Swallowhead may have recalled the Camenae water nymphs that inhabited a fountain on the city's Caelian Hill. There they offered libations of milk on 13 August.[25] (As already noted, Wiltshire folklore says that Silbury 'was built while a posset of milk was seething', and the 'pouring of milk upon hills as oblations' is recorded in seventeenth-century Scotland.)

The three Camenae were named from Latin *carmen*, 'charm, song, poem, magic formula, prayer', and were considered to be muses as well as protectors of women in childbirth. Swallowhead, as the Kennet's birthplace (where chalky silt lends a milky appearance to the outflow), would suit the Camenaes' British counterparts perfectly.

In Britain the Romans offered coins and engraved dedications to the nymphs. Nymphs and springs were inseparable. The newly discovered Roman streets running from Silbury almost to the Kennet's source speak of *Swallowhead*'s continuing appeal as a fountain of supernatural inspiration; a role that probably began with the earliest human presence in the valley. The conflation of nymphs with muses, known to Homer in the seventh century BC and accepted by the Romans, reaffirmed the age-old association of spring water with intellectual, spiritual and artistic worth. In Homer's words: 'The Muses are goddesses and know all things.' (*Iliad*, II, l. 484.) A Roman bronze figurine of the muse of lyric verse was found at nearby Silchester.

Diana

To Romans, 13 August was also the feast day of Diana, mistress of nymphs. She had a temple founded in the sixth century BC on the Aventine.[25] (This place name may be derived from Latin *avena*, 'oats'.) Originally an Italian wood sprite, Diana became a goddess of the chase, akin to Greek Artemis, before achieving a broadly defined 'fertility' role. Her duties included presiding over the lunar cycle and women's affairs. Votive offerings made to her include models of reproductive organs and nursing mothers. Her affinity with Silbury as a functioning maternal image is clear.

Diana's temple in Rome was especially beloved of plebs and slaves.[26] This non-patrician flavour is echoed by the Wiltshire peasantry's adherence to the Silbury rites well into the nineteenth century AD. By their very design, Silbury and the Avebury Henge display an 'open-to-all' quality, inviting everyone to a place at the banqueting table.

Vortumnus

The god of orchards and gardens was also worshipped at an Aventine temple in Rome on 13 August. His name, Vortumnus or Vertumnus, is from Latin *vertere*, 'to turn' 'because I receive the First Fruits of the year as it turns round', so he claims in a first-century BC poem by Propertius. The god boasts: 'For me the grape first changes colour with darkening cluster and the spiked ear of corn swells with its milky fruit.'[27] Ovid says the god often appeared as 'a rough harvester' with 'ears of corn'.

Many months earlier Vortumnus had fallen in love with Pomona, the fruit goddess. He wooed her unsuccessfully as ploughman and as her tree pruner. Then, in guise of an old woman, he tried again. Finally, as Pomona's pears and plums hung on the bough, balanced between perfect ripeness and immanent rot, she accepted him. She hoped that the 'crone' would protect the next year's pips beneath her wintry mud-caked cloak.[28]

49 (*Clockwise from top left*) Pomona, goddess of fruits; pictured with pruning hook, from the Roman 'Seasons' mosaic, Corinium (Cirencester); Romano-British seated goddess with apples; limestone sculpt, Corinium Museum; Portrait of Rudolf II as Vortumnus, Roman god of orchards and gardens; painting by G. Arcimboldo, AD 1592.

17 August: The Portunalia

Portunas was an ancient Roman deity who survives in calendars only. Some scholars believe that he was the god of gates and keys who secured the newly gathered stocks of corn in their granaries.[29]

19 August: The Vinalia Rustica

In Italy on this day the first of the new grapes were picked and sacrificed for the sake of the whole crop. 'The new wine shall not be carried into the city until the Vinalia has been proclaimed' was inscribed over the gates of Tusculum.[30] On the same occasion, the previous autumn's vintage was first brought into Rome and ceremonially drunk amidst scenes of rejoicing. After that, all the country growers, or *rustica*, were allowed to bring their liquor to sell on the urban markets.

The Romans imported wine and established vineyards in Britain, as has been proved around Gloucester and Boxmoor, Sussex.[31] They also depicted Bacchus and his two-handled drinking vessel on Britain's mosaic pavements. Was the *vinalia* part of Silbury's Roman August celebrations? The link between Ceres and Bacchus as personifications of bread and wine, as seen for instance on Corinium's Dyer Street mosaic where they occupy adjoining roundels, implies that the wine god's approaching autumn maturity may well have featured in Ceres's high-summer rites. Perhaps a newly brewed barley beer (Latin *cerea*) corresponding to that which filled the elegant bell beakers, made during the period of Silbury's construction, continued to provide the alcoholic mainstream down which the wine god sailed, to join that monument's intoxicated August throng, where piety and pleasure mingled.

21 August: The Consualia

Consus was the god of the stored harvest. His name is from *condere*, 'to hide away, to store'. Smith calls him 'an infernal deity, the hidden or mysterious god of the lower regions'.[32] The most ancient focus of his worship was an underground altar, reputedly discovered by Romulus, Rome's legendary founder. It had been erected in a grain pit beneath the Circus Maximus at the south-east end of the central *spina* and was only uncovered on Consus' feast days. The earliest of these was 7 July, when priests offered him 'First Fruits' of the Italian corn harvest. Then, on 21 August the priest, accompanied by the Vestal Virgins, again uncovered the Consus altar. To mark the end of a successful harvest they burned the First Fruits offerings and then supervised the ritual filling of the god's subterranean granary. After that, the Circus Maximus' games, of which Consus was the founding god, could begin.[33]

Cunliffe has shown in his excavations of the Iron Age village at Danebury, Hampshire, that many prehistoric British granaries also took the form of deep, narrow-mouthed pits. When filled to the brim in September they returned the precious grain to the earth, its mother, for safekeeping.[34]

Because the Romans involved a male guardian god in the same process, we might look to him when considering the Romano-British shafts dug around Silbury. The Proserpine legend and Consus' hoarding instinct might share some of the same holes. However, the two shafts sunk directly into the maternal moat effigy, which might have been dug to contain 'First Fruits' offerings to the Corn Mother, were much too damp for grain stores, though Warde-Fowler is surely correct to claim that Consus (and his British counterpart?) carries us back to the most primitive agricultural society; in other words, to the Neolithic.[35]

The Irish harvest god Crom Dubh may be regarded as a Consus double, and a survivor from remote antiquity. Every year at Lughnasa his dark shape stumbled, stooping, to the surface, carrying sheaves of corn on his bent back, brought from a rumoured subterranean store.[36]

50 Grape harvest. (a) Bacchus, the wine god, with Ceres; fragment of painted plaster from the tomb of the Nasonii in Via Flaminia, Rome; second century AD (BM). (b) The Roman fertility god Liber (later identified with Bacchus) depicted on a silver denarius, *c.*90 BC. In Rome he shared a temple with Ceres. (c) Bacchus with his wine cup, surrounded by deities; Roman mosaic from Pitney, Somerset.

23 August: The Volcanalia

Volcanus and his wife Maia were honoured at a rock-hewn altar at the foot of the capitol in Rome. 'He was originally a favouring nature spirit, embodying the warmth and fertilising spirit of the earth.' But after Rome had suffered a number of disastrous fires he was invoked to prevent future conflagrations.[37] Silbury's truncated cone may have reminded Romans of the fire god who inhabited Italian volcanoes such as Etna and Vesuvius.

24 August: Mundus Pater

The *mundus* was a hemispherical pit dug on the Palatine Hill at the right-angled intersection of Rome's first roads, and attributed in legend to Romulus, the city's founding father. The pit was said to contain his staff, bronze plough and ox yoke. According to J. Bachofen the *mundus* was acknowledged as Rome's birthplace, 'the *locus genitalis* from which all blessings spring'. It was a feminine cavity identified with the goddesses Tellus or 'earth', Vesta, guardian of the sacred flame, and Ceres.[38]

From that pit Ceres produced an egg made of cereal, representing the universe in microcosm, while into the same hole Rome's founders 'threw the first of every variety of fruit', together with seed corn, pot sherds and soil from other cities. Then it was covered over by a stone. But on 24 August, a holy day, the stone was pushed aside, allowing the spirits of the underworld to emerge and roam the city.[39]

Plutarch confirms that the *mundus* was dug *before* the main roads were laid to run east–west and north–south to the horizons, as linear elements in a cosmic mandala, emanating from the pit to produce *Dea Roma*, the city of Rome as a goddess; while Ovid describes Jove's palace, built directly above, as 'the Palatine district of high heaven'.[40]

With the stone temporarily removed, the underworld and the celestial vault were briefly reunited to embrace the surface plane in a holistic revelation of a truth that people were normally too busy to notice. Latin *mundus* means 'ready, in store, earth, world, the heavens' *and* 'the subterranean vault'. Thus a simple crater welded together all vertical and horizontal space, married past times to the future and re-embedded culture into nature, to produce a harmonious present. Just such a role may have been attributed to the Neolithic foundation pit dug under Silbury's core, and also to the hill, when seen united with its inverted reflection.[41]

As for the Silbury monument's orientation, long before any Roman cities were planned by her auger priests to address the cardinal points, the long axis of the Silbury moat was arranged precisely on an east–west line, honouring all equinoctial sunrises and sunsets. To complement this, a north–south axis at right angles joins Swallowhead to Silbury's 'vulva' and runs on to meet the west entrance of the Avebury Henge. Looking south from there, every noonday sun exactly tops this vital axis.

Considering these arrangements, the Romans had reason to respect those responsible for the Neolithic layout. The two axes intersect at the east base of Silbury Hill, corresponding to the spot where the harvest child's birth begins. In Latin this point is a *locus genitalis* (*locus*, 'a place, a spot, a part of the body', with *genitalis*, 'of, or concerned with creation, procreation, reproduction, birth or birthday').

25 August: Opiconsivia

Ops is a Roman goddess esteemed even before Republican times. She was often referred to as *Opifera*, 'The Bearer of Abundance' and equated with yet another deity, Abundantia, 'Abundance'.[42] Ops is a divinity of fertility and plenty. Her second name, Consiva, is from Latin *consero*, 'to plant, to sow'. Her August rites fell only three days after those of Consus. They made a complementary harvesting couple. (Their December 'sowing' festivals were also held only a few days apart.)[43]

In early Rome Ops was patroness of that sacred portion of the harvest stored in a small shrine within the *Regia* or king's house. This shrine held the earth's edible treasures on which the royal family subsisted. The monarch (like later emperors) was the intermediary between divinities and humankind. The daughters of his house always acted as Ops' handmaidens, just as the Vestal Virgins attended to Consus.[44]

'Ops' abode was the ground', according to Macrobius, writing in the fourth century AD; 'therefore those who made vows to her touched the ground'. Ovid says that she was the mother of Ceres. He emphasises Ops' fertility – 'because the earth distributes all goods to the human *genus*'. Latin *ops*, 'riches, goods, abundance, gifts, plenty', strikes the same chord. In August AD 7 the Emperor Augustus erected an altar to *Ceres Mater et Ops Augusta*, for the earth's promise had again been fulfilled.[45]

Quintus Ennius declares that 'Ops is named Mother because earth is mother to all races on earth and takes them back again. She is also Ceres because she begets us crops.'[46]

51 Ops, alias Tellus, and the workers. (a) The goddess Ops enthroned and holding corn; gold *aurea*, Rome, AD 193. (b) Ops was identified with Tellus, 'earth', the ground in which Ceres operated; Tellus, embedded in her rock; low relief from Carthage (Louvre Museum). (c) Neolithic worked flint sickle blade, found set into Silbury's summit in 2007 (EH update, No 14). (d) Neolithic sickle with flints set in wood or bone (Devizes Museum). (e) Bronze Age sickles from Barbury Castle, Wiltshire. (f) Neolithic and Bronze Age corn grinding (after J. Hawkes).

Segesta-Messia-Tutelina (Moveable Feasts)

The Romans saw each farming task personified by an extra minor deity. So when the time came to harvest the new wheat and barley, three more goddesses sprang into view. They were (i) Segesta, named after Latin *seges*, 'a field or crop of standing corn'; (ii) Messia, from Latin *messio*, 'harvesting'; (iii) Tutelina, from Latin *tutela*, 'guardianship', who protected the hoped-for crops.

These divinities were derided by St Augustine in the fifth century, but the elder Pliny says of Tutelina, a goddess of the fields, 'it is irreverent even to mention her name indoors'.[47] Macrobius adds that those who casually did so had, by way of retribution, to observe a 'rest day' avoiding all work or pay a fine and sacrifice a pig.[48] Pillars and altars honouring both Tutelina and Messia were set up in the Circus Maximus, while the conical *tutulus*, a cap worn by the woman involved in Tutelina's rites, matches Silbury Hill's shape. The cap fits the pregnant earth everywhere.

The Segesta-Messia-Tutelina feast days were moveable, being timed to coincide with the First Fruits. All three might well have been given altars on Silbury's 'Roman' platforms. Writing in the first century AD, Pliny makes it clear that in Rome the populace were by tradition denied any of the freshly cut corn until after the priests had offered up the First Fruits to these three deities.[49] And if this strict practice was starting to fade in the big city, at rural Silbury it could recover its original intensity, for there the Romans probably encountered a 'start of harvest' ritual of a type long established throughout prehistoric Britain, and which persisted in diminished forms to the brink of modernity.

By the day of Ops's August festival, British harvesters had been at work for nearly a month and both Romans and natives could enjoy the sense of abundance surrounding Silbury. What Ops devotee could then fail to notice the overlapping of her functions with those of her Neolithic British prototype? Silbury was also the earth and the producer of earthly crops. So, given their polytheistic outlook and non-racist approach to religion, the Romans flocked to Silbury's side, to merge Tutelina, Ops and Consus with this island's greatest Mother Earth working image.

27 August: The Volturnalia

Volturnas was an ancient river god whose stream enters the sea near Naples. His name, meaning 'snake-like or winding', was also applied to Rome's Tiber.[50] Like the Kennet, the Tiber was involved in harvest. On its serpentine back, small boats carried imported grain from Ostia port to the city granaries, close to Ceres's Aventine Hill temple.

28 August: Sol and Luna

As the month of August came to an end, another acknowledgement of the sun and moon was required of the Romans.[51] Tertullian says that Sol's temple was on the *spina* of the Circus Maximus and that a statue of the god driving his solar chariot was sited there on his temple roof. The charioteers he looked down upon ran earthly versions of *his* heavenly circuit. Therefore, the 'finish line' was aligned with his temple. Though now unacknowledged, the solar deity, careering between the goals of dawn and dusk, similarly inspired the game of football.[52]

Virgil's Golden Age

The poet Virgil, born in 70 BC, was a farmer's son, In his *Georgics*, or 'Poetry of the Farm', he delivered practical advice with devout feeling.[53] For him, the Age of Gold was located in the recurring seasonal round of hard farm labour. 'O farmers, happy beyond measure, could they but know their blessings,' he wrote.[54]

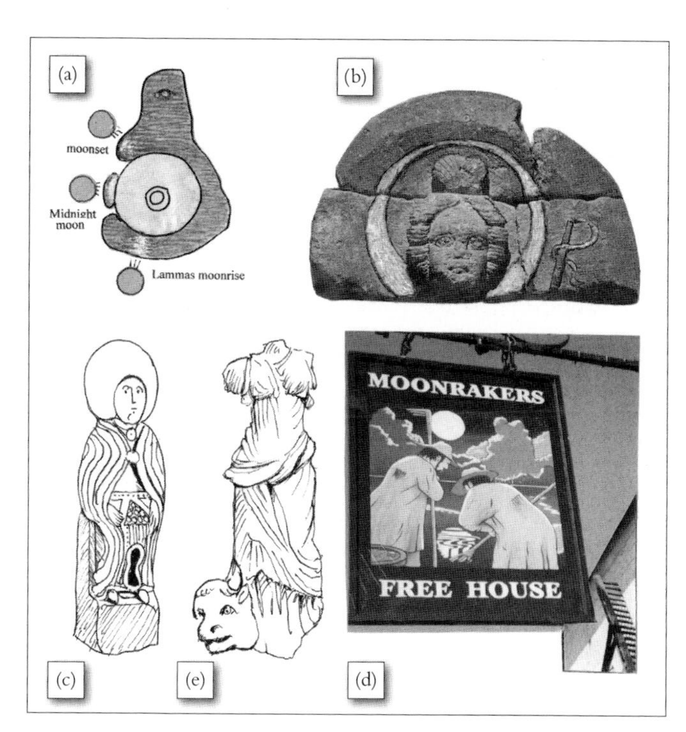

52 Silbury and Luna. (a) Silbury-in-labour. The full moon nearest to 1 August quarter day reflected from her water-groin, via the newborn 'child', to the 'milky' breast. (b) The goddess Luna with crescent moon and whip, from the Aquae Sulis 'Seasons' sculpt. (c) A moon-crowned seated goddess with corn; Roman white paste figurine, from Arrington, Cambridgeshire. (d) Moonrakers Inn, Pewsey, Wiltshire. In Wiltshire folklore, men raked a pond to retrieve the treasured moon. (e) Luna with her chariot bull; a fourth-century marble fragment, 0.44m tall, from Woodchester villa, Gloucestershire.

53 *Dea Nutrix*. (a) The Roman nursing goddess gives suck to two infants; white clay figurine from a grave in Baldock, Hertfordshire (drawing by K. McBarron). (b) A Neolithic 'incense cup' with two 'eye holes' from Windmill Hill, Avebury. In both prehistoric and Romano-British times the deity worked above and below ground. Another possible title for Roman Silbury may have been *Bona Dea*, meaning 'the Good Goddess'. She incorporated a range of female deities, including 'the Original Mother'. Fertility of all kinds was in her gift.

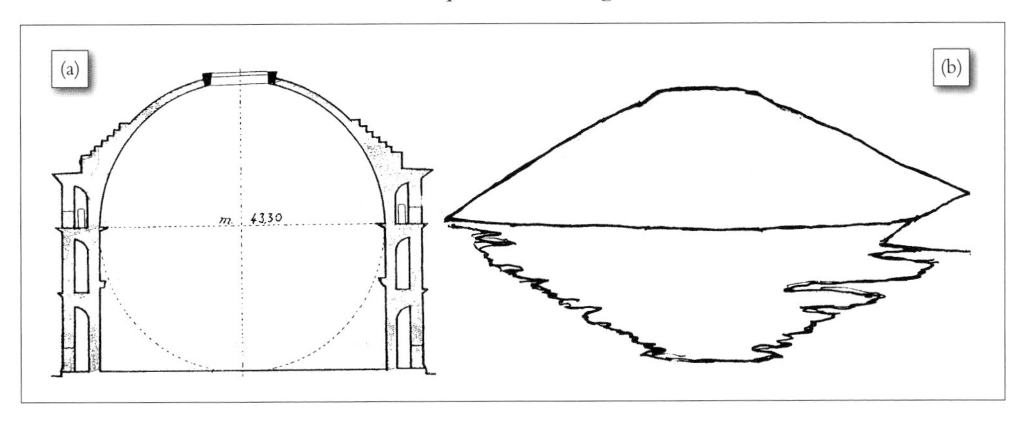

54 Silbury and the Pantheon. (a) Section through the Pantheon, Rome, a temple designed by Emperor Hadrian and built AD 118–125 in honour of 'all the gods'. Like (b) Silbury Hill (which he may have seen and been influenced by on his visit to Britain), the Pantheon is still standing.

With the Emperor Augustus as his patron, Virgil's work was very influential. He promoted the notion of farm work as worship, where human efforts and a cohesive social order were derived from deities such as Ceres, Ops and Consus. Virgil restated the virtuous basis of Rome's culture, grounded on self-disciplined seasonal toil, integral to the mythic tradition from which it had sprung ever since the Neolithic introduction of agriculture to Italy three millennia before Silbury's construction. Virgil believed that the task of poets, artists, architects and emperors was to demonstrate this enduring truth, in fields and in towns.[55]

Accordingly, the Emperor Hadrian who came to Britannia in AD 122 and ordered the construction of its north boundary wall was also largely responsible for the physical renewal of Demeter's sanctuary at Eleusis, Silbury's Greek counterpart.[56] He also designed Rome's Pantheon as a temple to *all* the gods. Its circular dome, still standing after 19 centuries, is in effect a *mundus* on stilts, enclosing a perfect globe of air inside its solid walls as an inhabitable symbol of universal harmony.[57]

There the old belief in a cosmic spirit located *within* matter (which was, and remains, the kernel of Silbury's meaning) is given elegant expression, in keeping with the mood generated by Roman August festivals. Together with Silbury's Roman town, they suggest that the Romans in Britain understood, valued, perpetuated and enhanced the prehistoric harvest-time rites that had been annually conducted at Silbury since Neolithic times. Those Romans who stood before Silbury may have borne in mind the Emperor Augustus' plan for the new Golden Age, which provided the basis for Roman culture for three centuries. It involved 'the renewal of religion and custom, embodied in visual imagery',[58] incorporating 'a deliberate pluralism of traditions' to take account of the empire's expansion. So his Altar of Augustan Peace of 13 BC features images of Pax (Peace), Tellus (Earth) and Ceres as figures welcomed everywhere.[59]

Repeatable Silbury

A Neolithic serrated flint flake, found embedded into Silbury's summit during the repair work done in 2007, is described by J. Cleary as 'of a type often associated with cereal processing'.[60] In other words, the flake is from a Stone Age sickle. At a stroke, it offers tiny yet solid evidence of Silbury's original harvest-birth purpose, maintained for ages thereafter by natives and invaders alike, inspired by devotion to a common need, made visible on the summit's sacred corn field.

Silbury could absorb Roman usage because repeatability was designed into the structure. The alternating bands of light and dark material of which its core was composed suggest a dynamic rhythm of embryonic gestation from humic decay.

55 (*Top*) Ceres departing, August AD 2008, leaving her veil, staff, snakes, poppies, a spray of wheat and a wheaten crown in a barley field, covering the line of the east to west Roman road. In Athens her counterpart Demeter was known as 'the cherisher of children' *and* as 'the travail goddess', a term also applied in Greece to the ripening cornfield (Farnell, lll, p. 81). (*Bottom*) Abundantia, Roman goddess of plenty, with grapes, apples, wheat and a poppy; carved on Londinium's rediscovered ceremonial archway, AD first century. Some grain from Silbury's fields probably went by barge to London for export.

In addition, as Jim Cleary announced at a public meeting in Devizes, held on the day of completion of the monument's restoration, this central deposit 'grew incrementally in small stages, involving hundreds if not thousands of phases'. Memorably, he added that 'Silbury Hill grew like any other living organism, with its regularity of form embodying a regularity of movement'. It was, he concluded, a 'Monument in motion'.[61]

The innumerable little mounds, each composed of flint nodules, river gravel, sub-soil, soil and vegetation, that were placed around the central core in the way that Cleary described may have been deposited, like the eighteenth-century Midlothian Lammas towers, at the start of successive Augusts, with each mound representing a symbolic 'harvest child' born from the centrally sited core. Eventually, all these *Bron Trogain* offspring took shelter under the enormous three-dimensional 'spider's web' of the spirally tiered chalk hill, allowing all future generations to be born from the hill's interior, onto the moonlit waters of the goddess's moat-body. Awe-struck, the Romans gathered round, for the monument aligned with several of their religious obligations.

1 (*Above*) A 'Save Silbury' walk, 29 May 2004, four years after the summit collapse and three years before repairs were undertaken. (*Below*) Silbury's moat-breast and head viewed from the hill. Sky, sun and moon are incorporated into the divine body.

2 Silbury and Swallowhead. (*Top left*) Silbury was inspired by the adjacent Swallowhead spring, source of the River Kennet. (*Bottom left*) Father and daughter at Swallowhead, 2009. (*Bottom right*) Offerings of fruit, flowers and wheat, placed at the spring. (*Top right*) A combine harvester's 'river of wheat', Beckhampton, near Swallowhead, 2008.

3 Harvesting. (*Top and middle*) Combine harvesters cutting, hulling and gathering wheat at Beckhampton Penning, September 2008. (*Bottom*) Safely stowed wheat in a barn at Avebury Trusloe, 2008.

4 Silbury and Waden Hill. (*Top*) Silbury was built close to the sow-back shaped Waden Hill, here seen in shadow, which is as central to the Avebury monuments as the divine sow was to Neolithic religion. (*Left*) Sow with piglets, Worcester Cathedral misericord, AD 1379. (*Right*) An eighteenth-century pigsty from Pontypridd, Mid Glamorgan, re-erected at St Fagans Folk Museum.

5 Palisades Monument and sacred sow (*top*). This massive pair of enclosures (*top right*), defined by close-set oak tree trunks, stood on the Kennet's flood plain between Silbury (*top left*) and the Sanctuary. The river flowed through the middle of Palisade 1. The Palisades was a temple devoted to pig breeding. (*Bottom right*) The sow was regarded as a manifestation of the Great Goddess during the Neolithic era in Europe. (*Bottom left*) Pig roast, Upton on Severn, AD 2008.

6 An Avebury Henge wedding, 2007. The biggest Neolithic henge monument in the world has now recovered its original purpose as a wedding ring. (*Top*) Bride and Groom face the ring stone stump. (*Bottom left*) Bride with corn dolly. (*Right*) Musicians and fairies: the wedding party with Waden Hill beyond.

7 Horse and Serpent. (*Top*) Head of the Uffington Horse, Berkshire, a Bronze Age entrenched image, dug *c.*1000 BC, of the harvest mare (Welsh *Caseg fedi*, alias the horse goddess Rhiannon). The horse overlooks a flat-topped harvest hillock (*centre*), now named Dragon Hill. (*Bottom left*) The snake as embodiment of the life force finds expression in this 12ft-long megalith, erected in the Avebury Henge north circle. (*Bottom right*) A Roman Genius Loci statue, embodying the 'spirit of place'. He feeds a serpent, wrapped around a phallus, and holds a cornucopia; Luckington church, Wiltshire.

8 Silbury's neighbours. (*Clockwise from top left*) Windmill Hill, site of an early Neolithic 'causewayed camp', 2 miles from Silbury. A stone 'head' in the Avebury Henge's outer ring 'gazes' towards Windmill Hill. 'Persephone' returns from the underworld to visit Avebury, disguised as her mother, Demeter. Other versions of the Silbury image crop up worldwide and in many eras. Corn dolly in a willow tree at Swallowhead.

9 Mountainous Henwen. (*Top left*) Mynydd Llwyd regarded as Henwen, the Old White One's sow-backed hill, seen from near the *Black* Sow's well, her wintry equivalent, on the hill's north side. (*Top right*) Triad 26w states that she gave birth to the very first wheat and bee here. (*Bottom left*) A prehistoric 'birthing chair' megalith, 5ft 6in tall, standing erect on Mynydd Llwyd. (*Bottom right*) A prostrate Mother Goddess megalith, over 6ft long, lying within the hill's prehistoric stone circle at ST 439935.

10 The immortal pig in landscape and art. (*Top left, inset*) Bronze boar figurine from Hounslow, Middlesex, found with a solar wheel; third century BC. (*Top left*) Aust Cliff, Gloucestershire, showing alabaster 'tusks' where Henwen, the sow deity, and a legendary boar crossed the Severn. (*Top right*) Wild Boar, sculpted by Sally Matthews; Grizedale Forest, Cumbria, 1990. (*Bottom left*) Bronze goddess figurine with lunar crown, *c.*first century BC; found at Aust Cliff. (*Bottom middle*) Bronze Sow, by Sebastien Boysen; 1994, Newport Market, Gwent. (*Bottom right*) Stuffed boar's head, within the Boar's Head Inn, Aust.

11 Cheese rolling. (*Top*) At Cooper's Hill, Gloucestershire (SO 892418), an annual race is held down the steep escarpment after a double Gloucester cheese (Photographs *Gloucestershire Echo*). (*Bottom*) Llyn Llun Caws, alias 'Moon Cheese Lake' (SH 072318), Berwyn Mountains. Into it a cheese rolled from the apron of Queen Helena. Similarly, a small 'Lammas Cheese', made on Scotland's mountain pastures, was ceremonially presented to children on that day, as J.G. Campbell records.

12 Ground, chair, throne. Images of the Neolithic deity show her sitting to give birth, as at Silbury. (*Anti-clockwise, from top left*) Mother, infant, and oats stook, Lleyn, 1971; Devil's Quoit, Stackpole Warren, Pembrokeshire (SR 9895), is one of many examples of a prehistoric megalith as 'ritual chair'; Demeter of Knidos, Greece, a marble effigy, fourth century BC; Bardic Chair, through which the female muse transmits her inspiring breath to the poet (National Library of Wales).

13 The Newborn, in three traditions. (*Top left*) Baby's christening font at Llangelynin church, near Conwy, North Wales, during harvest festival, September 2004. (*Top right*) Seated Mother of God with Christ and Father's finger above; Inglesham church, Wiltshire; late Saxon. (*Bottom left and middle*) Bengali mother goddess and infant, clay figurine, *c.*AD 1980. (*Bottom right*) The Caerwent Romano-British goddess, with apple and tree.

14(a) Silbury and the parish church. Silbury in harvest, seen from Avebury, 2005.

14(b) A harvest festival worshipper at Avebury's twelfth-century church door, 4 October 2008. By 1861, Silbury, a pagan sacred place, had been integrated into the Christian calendar, as Rev. A.C. Smith reported: 'Silbury Hill is thronged every Palm Sunday afternoon by hundreds from Avebury, Kennet, Overton, and nearby villages.'

15 Midwinter Mummers. (*Top*) The Marshfield Mummers, Boxing Day, 2004. A triumphant King George looks on (left), while the Doctor revives the slain victim. (*Bottom left*) Old Dame Jane, re-named Saucy Jack, carries infants on his back. (*Bottom right*) The Fool, burnt on 6 January at the Haxey village cross, Lincolnshire, during an annual rite known as the Hood.

16(a) Silbury in Winter. The modern A4, which approximately follows the east–west Roman road, here crosses a footpath between West Kennet long barrow and Avebury Henge. Silbury in winter is the dormant hub of their recurring seasonal cycle.

16(b) The Winterbourne brook flows south (right to left), while Silbury stands for all nature, envisaged as supernaturally engendered and endowed.

eight

TRANSFIGURATIONS

The Unifying Core

When Dean Merewether dug into the core of Silbury Hill in 1849 his workmen revealed 'a black peaty substance composed of sods of turf piled together, containing great quantities of moss, still in a state of comparative freshness'. His account continues: 'Above and about this layer was a dense accumulation of black earth ... in which were embedded fragments of small branches of bushes [and] the caudle vertebrae of the ox or perhaps red deer and a very large tooth of the same animal.'[1]

Lying around the circumference of this largely organic deposit he found 'many sarsens [boulders], with their concave surfaces downwards, favouring the line of the heap, casing as it were, the mound'. Other sarsens ringed its circumference. 'On top of some of these were observed fragments of bone, small sticks ... [perhaps] of mistletoe, the ribs of ox or deer, and the tine of a stag's antler ... that may have been specially regarded.'[2]

Silbury Hill, as the womb of the Mother Goddess, was expected to breed much more than corn crops. Therefore, she housed tokens of *all* matter to represent animal, vegetable and mineral aspects of the re-sanctified surface reality, to be engendered from her uterine core. From these hidden 'embryos' all three classes of material could then emerge, fully alive, and imbued with the divine vitality inherited from their supernatural mother.

Engagement of Opposites

Silbury Hill's core meaning is reiterated by the hill's outer shape. For millennia the earthwork stood for stability, but of a kind based on rotational change rather than inertia. The monument functioned through drastic transformations of a repeatable, cyclical kind. So, as the generator of new life, Silbury was founded on deposits bound to decay, death and putrefaction.

As if to emphasise further this life-death interdependence, the pregnant mother temple was built within sight of Britain's most spectacular Neolithic burial chamber, which is contained by the nearby West Kennet long barrow. Silbury and this magnificent barrow flank the Swallowhead spring, and are *equidistant* from it. Swallowhead probably inspired both monuments, since its tunnel mouth is both the Kennet's birthplace *and* an entrance to death's underworld.

56(a) View of Silbury from the Neolithic West Kennet long barrow. At the time of Silbury's construction the barrow's chambers were filled with layers of material comparable to those deposited in Silbury's core. (b) The barrow mound, which is over 100m long, provides a monumental image of the winter goddess, with a megalithic entry to her underworld womb at her eastern end.

Silbury and the Tomb

Long before the first farmers arrived in Britain, Swallowhead offered a paradoxical model for Silbury and West Kennet long barrow to hold in common. Therefore, despite the difference in their ages, the two monuments were destined to act as partners in a 'life and death' dance. Plainly inter-visible across the Kennet, they are closely bound together by human eyesight and by a shared feminine iconography.

Both monuments offer an image of the Neolithic goddess. At Silbury she is portrayed on her right side, reclining on the surface as a 'lady in harvest'. By contrast, the barrow's 'squatting image' is hidden beneath the east end of the 300ft-long chalk mound. Located underground, the goddess' s'body' is composed of four massive sarsen sandstone chambers – two legs and two arms or breasts. These are all made from vertically set megaliths, with a corbelled roof of the same stone, and are arranged in pairs on either side of a 24ft-long 'spinal' corridor that leads to a 'head' cell, which is 8ft high.

The West Kennet barrow chambers are by no means unique in their configuration. Many other Neolithic tombs in Britain and Ireland, such as those at Creevykeel and Deerpark, Co. Sligo, are even more explicitly anthropomorphic in design.[3]

Prior to the advent of abstract written scripts, the main concerns of most societies were embedded in visual symbols. Often, as at West Kennet and Silbury, these were architectural in scale. Together, the West Kennet barrow chambers create a prostrate image of the principal deity, with limbs outspread. She is the queen of the nether regions, pictured giving birth to death, in a reversed act of parturition. As the Destroyer, she draws humanity, and indeed all life, including the farmer's planted seeds, into the subterranean bridal suite of her own stony body.

Thus the West Kennet tomb evokes the Harvest Mother as hag, *and* her own elusive counterpart, her lost winter daughter, whom the Greeks called Persephone. The bones of five adults and a child, along with animal bones, were found in her 'head' chamber, explored by J. Thurnam in

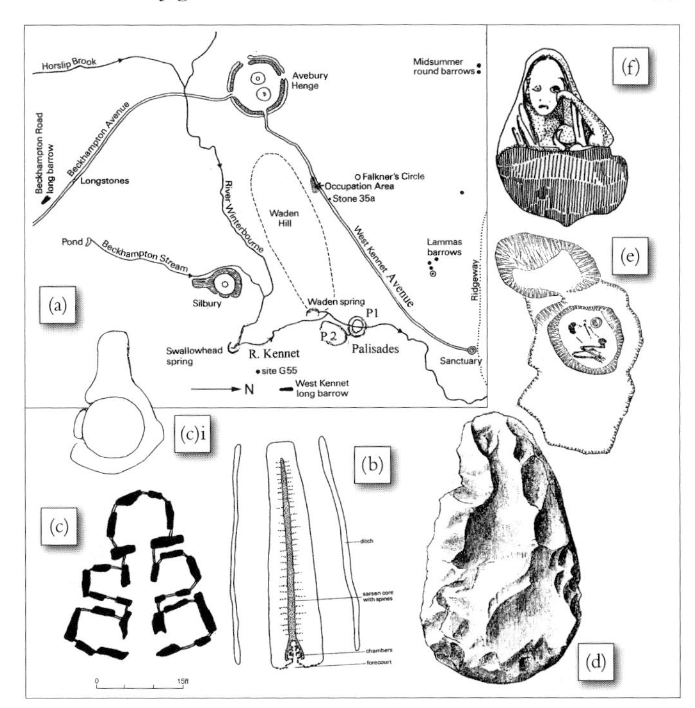

57(a) Map of the Avebury monuments. (b) Plan of the West Kennet long barrow, 340ft long, built *c.*3500 BC. (c) Plan of the barrow's chambers, compared to Silbury. (ci) These chambers are collectively shaped as the squatting goddess of the underworld, giving birth to death. (d) A Neolithic worked flint, depicting a hooded female, found in the barrow's 'head' chamber. (e) Crouched late Neolithic sacrificed girl with ceramic vessel, West Kennet Avenue, Avebury. (f) Ceres, mourning Proserpine; Roman carving, Levens, Cumbria. A seventh-century BC Greek text describes how Demeter turned into a hooded hag when seeking Persephone in Hades.

1860.[4] Dozens of adult skeletons, and those of seven infants and four babies, were discovered in the rest of her 'body' by S. Piggott during his excavation of 1955–56. Some skulls and femurs had been removed in antiquity for ritual use.[5]

In seasonal terms, Silbury's only hope of recovery after harvest was to engineer and endure destruction within death's dark realm, personified both by the loss of her daughter to the underworld and equally by herself in 'old hag' mode. Only then might that daughter, as 'bringer of death', find a way to resurface in the spring as the Maiden (Greek *Kore*) who epitomised the buried corn seed's eventual sprouting.[6] In essence, the three agrarian cultures, Roman, Greek and British, shared and enacted the same mythic drama. Though millennia apart, Romans and Neolithic Britons effectively walked in step as they processed at summer's end between Silbury, Swallowhead and the West Kennet barrow.

In the British Isles, Irish *Samain* and Welsh *Calan Gaeaf*, falling on 31 October (the Celtic year's end), marked the annual threshold between the two monuments. On the *Calan Gaeaf* 'spirit night' in nineteenth-century Wales it was still customary to visit Stone Age tombs with trepidation *and* hope. For example, at Tinkinswood, Glamorgan, the original tomb deity may have been recognised in the hooded, stooping megalith overhanging the chamber entrance.[7] Wishes whispered to her, it was believed, would be granted in the following year. At the nearby Maes-y-Felin Neolithic chambered tomb, a 6ft tall, wide-eyed, open-mouthed megalith that supports its capstone seems to cry 'continuity!' across the ages.[8]

The West Kennet tomb was not a dead end, but rather a vital contributor to an endless dialogue between subterranean and surface realms, regarded as different aspects of a multifaceted deity, revealed also in the act of ploughing. The Silbury and West Kennet figures combine to show the iconic female who gave birth to all life and also received the dead to thereby match human, solar-lunar and cosmic cycles.

That the task involved much sadness is shown by the stone figurine discovered sitting on the domed head chamber of the Neolithic barrow at Notgrove, Gloucestershire. Filled with grief, as when Demeter loses her daughter Persephone to Hades, this 'winter mother' is depicted as an old, stooped woman, hooded and cloaked.[9] A 4in-high carefully worked flint found on the Neolithic

58 (*Top left*) The two-eyed, 12ft-tall 'Hag' Stone in the West Kennet long barrow façade, erected *c.*2500 BC, a thousand years after the main construction. (*Top right*) 'Winter', from the Bignor Roman mosaic, Sussex. 'Ceres of the Underworld' was how Statius (first century AD) referred to her in this condition. At the barrow, Silbury (alias Ceres) seeks her daughter, lost to the underworld. (*Bottom*) Interior of the West Kennet long barrow built *c.*3500 BC from selected natural sarsens and imported rag stone.

59 Silbury into hag. (*Top right*) The seated deity, as bent and hooded 20cm-tall stone figurine, found on the domed stone 'head' chamber in the Notgrove Neolithic long barrow, Gloucestershire (*top left*). (*Bottom left*) A 'shouting goddess' holed megalith, 2m high, supporting the capstone of Maes-y-Felin Neolithic tomb, *c.*4000 BC, Glamorgan. (*Bottom right*) A stooping 'hag deity' megalith at the entrance to Tinkinswood Neolithic barrow, *c.*4000 BC, Glamorgan. Until *c.*1900, requests were whispered to this stone at Hallowe'en.

floor of West Kennet's 'head' chamber shows her in a similar style,[10] as does another worked flint found at the Neolithic site named G55, situated half way between the barrow and Swallowhead.[11]

The supernatural 'Old Mother' of the Neolithic tombs lives on in Gaelic folklore as 'the Cailleach'. She is also seen as old lady winter in one corner of a Romano-British Seasons mosaic, as at Brading, Sussex.

Throughout and beyond the Neolithic era, to Silbury worshippers the adjacent barrow was much more than a lost deposit. Rather, like the Celtic deity Brigit of northern Britain, who was known as the 'Mother of Memory', the West Kennet's female-shaped chambers contained the inherited secrets of agriculture. Similarly, a Greek drama composed in 405 BC and set in the *deepest part of hell*, parades a chorus of the dead, who in life had been initiated into Demeter's mysteries. From the abyss they re-enact her annual procession, staged above ground at Eleusis, and sing: 'O Lady, over our rites presiding, Preserve and succour the choral throng, And grant us all in thy help confiding, To dance and revel the whole day long.' In the black netherworld they chant to 'Demeter, goddess, the harvest queen, the giver of corn'.[12] In Britain the West Kennet barrow and Silbury collaborated in the interest of a comparable resurrection.

Blocking or Linkage?

With Silbury in full view, Romano-Britons scattered coin offerings around the West Kennet barrow's east end, although they found the forecourt, corridor and all the chambers completely blocked. Modern excavation has revealed that over a 500-year period from *c.*2800–2300 BC the barrow had been tightly packed to the roof with chalk rubble, laced with sarsen nodules, and interspersed with up to 10 horizontal black, greasy layers of decomposed, compressed vegetable matter. In addition, the entire deposit had been studded with the bones of deer, ox, pig, sheep and goat, along with numerous Neolithic pottery shards and some undamaged vessels. This composite material rested directly on top of the people (many of whom had been arranged in a foetal or prenatal position) who had lain there since *c.*3600–3700 BC.[13]

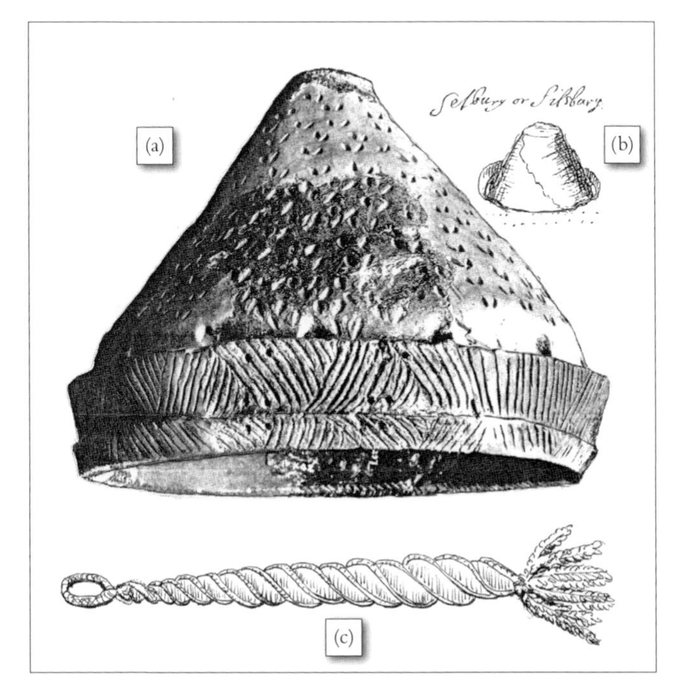

60 Silbury as pot. (a) A 'Silbury Hill'-shaped pot, 8in tall, deliberately broken and scattered in the West Kennet long barrow forecourt and chambers during the period of Silbury's construction. 'Corn grain' dents and a ring of 'eye' impressions are combined with 'plough furrows' on the collar and 'avenues' of paired marks to represent phases in the agrarian cycle. (b) Silbury Hill, drawn by John Aubrey, *c.*1660. (c) An English corn dolly, plaited from the last sheaf of the harvest, and known as 'the Maiden' or 'the Hag', implying their fundamental identity, and spanning the year from 'wedding ring' to underworld.

The superimposed 'filling' was interpreted in the 1950s as a 'blocking', and a rejection of the barrow's original purpose.[14] Today it seems more like an annual cycle of deposition, matching that which occurred during the initial phases of Silbury's construction. According to the latest estimates these twin processes could well have been completed simultaneously. The close resemblance between the layered deposits placed into the barrow and those that formed the core of Silbury Hill is evident, and indicates a ritual interplay between the two sites. That the bones of children were found to predominate in the top layer of barrow material poignantly strengthens the link further still.[15]

Silbury's core was also made from sarsen rocks, subsoil, soil and vegetation, along with animal bones. Together these layered ingredients were the nucleus of the image's procreative powers. Because the Silbury builders believed that flora, fauna and human culture stem from supernatural underworld roots, they may have wished to involve the barrow goddess in their Silbury endeavour to maximise the potency of their new monument. Consequently, the organic stripes and animal bones introduced into the barrow may depict a subterranean promise of future 'above ground' prosperity, year upon year. This made a form of sympathetic magic, conducted between lower and upper worlds, which today's farmers repeat in their own terms.

As if to emphasise the link, Silbury's builders may have transferred *to* the barrow some of the vast quantity of chalk, dug when making their moat image, and reused it as barrow chamber filling. Bedrock, like the Roman earth goddess Tellus, is, after all, the foundation upon which life depends. And this rubble could well have come from the sacred quarry that was to make the Lady of the Lake's head, torso and breast. Moreover, since the barrow chambers were themselves laid out in a 'goddess-in-labour' plan, a symbiotic relationship existed between the two birth acts, namely those of winter and summer seasons, and of netherworld and surface realm respectively.

Ceramic evidence from the barrow proves that the infilling process probably did occur at the period of Silbury's construction; for example, a magnificent bell beaker, incised with lozenge pattern (thought by Gimbutas and other authorities to be a stylised form of the goddess), is of late Neolithic date. Among the broken pots unearthed in 1956 was one *shaped like* Silbury Hill, with conical sides pinched, before firing, into a cascade of 'grain impressions'. Deliberately smashed, the vessel's fragments lay in and between the barrow's 'thigh' chambers, perhaps symbolising harvest's end and winter's onset.[16]

The barrow's packing could also have served as a gesture of protective reverence towards the skeletal remains of the ancestors – those pioneers who had introduced arable and pastoral farming, along with pottery making and weaving, into the district. The organically striped infill offered those ghosts solid evidence that the annual cycle they had enhanced was continuing.

Emerging Maiden

In a further act of identification with the earlier tomb builders, the late Neolithic community erected five mighty forecourt stones across the crescent-shaped West Kennet barrow forecourt. I suggested in *The Avebury Cycle* that these megaliths, viewed together, made a stylised image of the divine ox, embodiment of strength, who pulled the sacred plough.[17] As the bronze statuette from Maiden Castle, Dorset, shows, in Britain it was from the interior of this beast that an incarcerated goddess traditionally re-emerged to initiate the next round of changes. Such a magical freedom of exchange between megaliths, supernatural beings and living animals was accepted, indeed *expected* in prehistory.

Regarding the ox's power of augury, on each Plough Monday, 6 January in nineteenth-century Herefordshire, a cake was stuck onto one of its horns. After the beast had tossed the cake off, the pastry was closely examined for the ox-given signs of prosperity or hardship due in the coming year.[18]

Many re-emergence myths combined experience of winter's death and spring's renewal (involving another agricultural round) with the need to supervise the onset of puberty in the

61 All-life playground. (a) 'Bull Stones', in the West Kennet long barrow forecourt. Two sarsens, 9 and 12ft-tall, serve as the south-pointing head and humped body of a bull or male ox, epitome of strength, from which the goddess of renewal rose after winter's 'death'. (b) Goddesses rising from a sacrificed bull; Romano-British bronze from Maiden Castle, Dorset. (c) Medieval Mummers, as stag, hare and horse. Human-animal transformations played a part in many pre-Christian religions. (d) Neolithic pierced ox phalange bones from West Kennet long barrow.

next generation. The late Neolithic group of monuments built around Silbury was designed to cater for these polyvalent changes. Together the temples made an architectural ensemble in which the divine daughter's gradual re-emergence is combined with dynamic male and animal energies, displayed and contained in a sequence of temples where each stage in the mythic drama could be performed by people of the right age, and in an appropriate setting, thereby uniting with their volatile deity. Moreover, as with Silbury, the surrounding monuments are *visually iconic*, displaying in solid yet inhabitable form the appearance of the characters (protean in variety) as the myth unfolds.

The Sanctuary and Silbury

The Sanctuary stood on the summit of Overton Hill, 2088 yards south-east from Silbury. Today, five concentric rings of concrete pegs mark the Neolithic postholes that held vertical wooden supports for the roof and wattle wall of a circular Neolithic temple. Further rings of markers denote the position of two concentric rings of Neolithic standing stones. Based on the original central point, these megaliths replaced the wooden building and survived into the early eighteenth century AD.[19]

Looking west from the Sanctuary, Silbury Hill appears to rise majestically beyond the rounded south end of the Waden Hill ridge. Generations of Neolithic Sanctuary girls could have seen in that prospect hopes of future maternity. As if to reiterate the fact, the dimensions and probable shape of the Sanctuary building bore a striking resemblance to the hidden conical core of Silbury's chalk womb, the sacred prototype for their own fulfilment.[20]

Most attempts to recreate the shape of the wooden Sanctuary, undertaken since the site was excavated in 1930, have advocated a large truncated cone, with its flat top open to the sky. This shape closely resembles Silbury Hill in profile, with the same 30-degree roof slope. Moreover, the postulated low vertical outer wall of the Sanctuary hut, deduced from a ring of slender stake holes, has a 65ft diameter. This is identical with that of the wattle fence found to have contained Silbury's multi-layered primary mound.[21] It appears that the Sanctuary was Silbury's immature, and therefore hollow, counterpart.

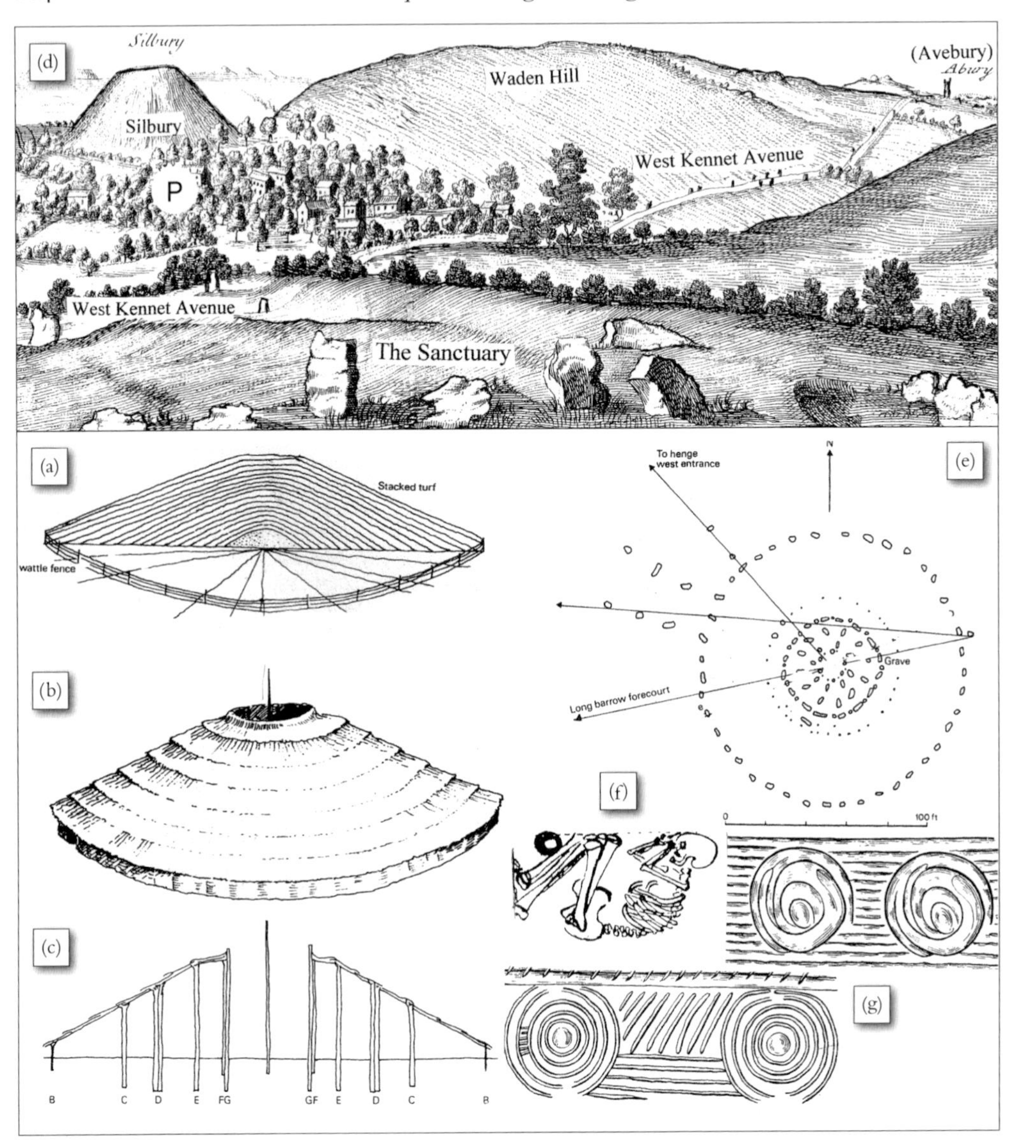

62 Silbury and the Sanctuary. (a) Silbury grew from a wattle-fenced core, 65ft in diameter. (b) The wooden Sanctuary temple on Overton Hill was also 65ft across and was probably built at the same time. (c) Cross section of the Sanctuary's post rings. (d) Stukeley's 1719 drawing of the concentric stone circles that replaced the roofed structure. (e) Plan of the post rings and stone rings. (f) A Sanctuary 'foundation' sacrifice of a young woman, buried in foetal position with pot and pig bones. (g) Neolithic coiled snake and eye motifs on pots from Durrington Walls Neolithic wooden temple, Wiltshire. 'P' marks the area of the recently discovered Palisade Enclosures.

The Sanctuary was a place where girls might follow in the footsteps of the maiden goddess by entering an airy full-scale version of the Silbury mother's solid nucleus. So incarcerated, they could learn the secrets of fertility, symbolised by Silbury's hidden stack of clay, flint, silt, gravel, soil and organic material. By contrast, the Sanctuary was an early spring 'staging post' on the divine *and* human daughters' journey to maturity. Its relative emptiness resembled the virgin state of their wombs.

In terms of the annual cycle, the Sanctuary matches the 1 February quarter day, which was the feast of the pagan goddess Brigit in Ireland and Christianised as *Gwyl Fair*, 'Vigil of Mary', in Wales. The Welsh *Gwyl Fair* rite centred on a young maiden seated beside a wassail bowl. Lighted candles floated on its alcoholic brew. Visiting parties of young men tried to drink the liquor without burning their hair.[22]

Unlike the classic Greek maiden 'Kore' (who emerged each year from her own 'bringer of death' double, Persephone), these human girls could not literally 'die' inside a wintry underworld

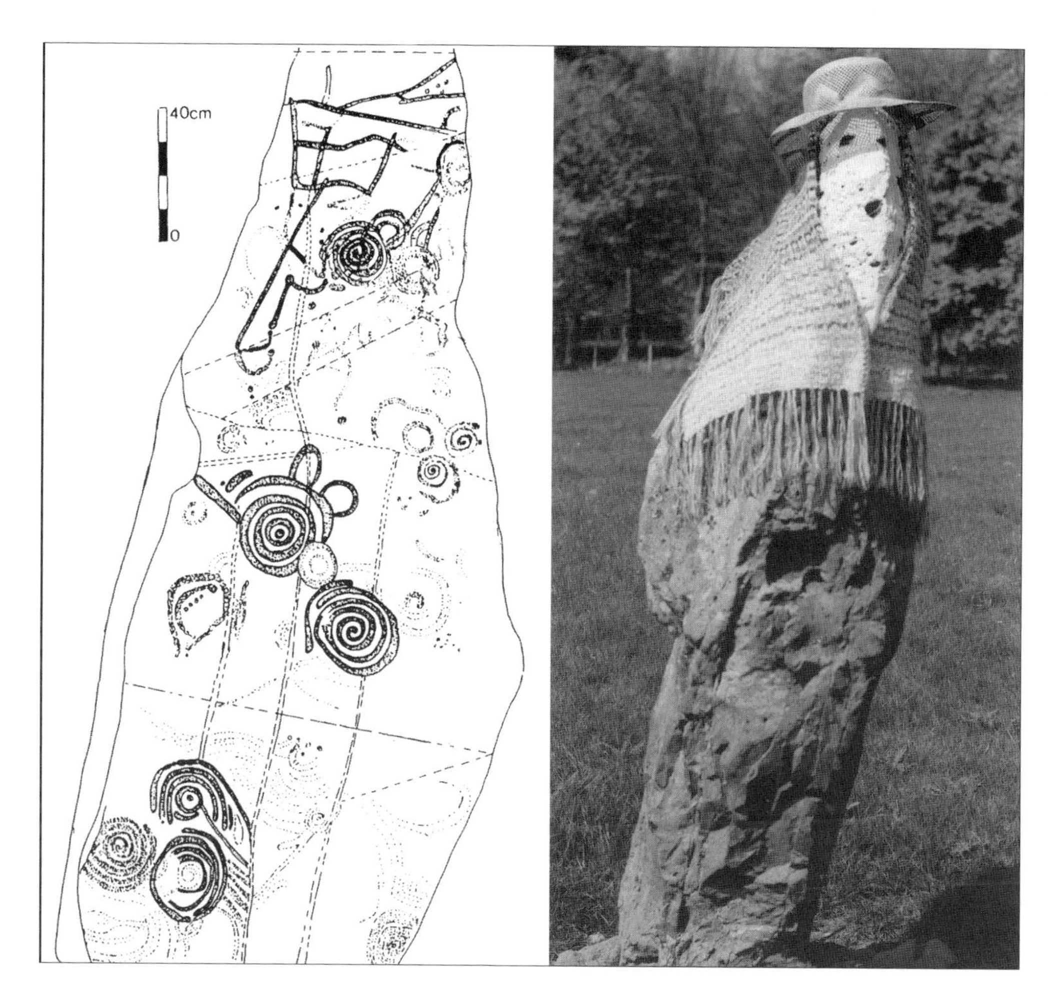

63 (*Left*) Long Meg and her daughters is the name of a Neolithic stone circle at Hunsonby, Cumbria. Mother Meg, 3.7m tall, stands outside the ring of her 'daughters'. She is incised with several coiled circles, comparable to the Sanctuary temple plan and its 'coiled serpent' theme. D. Field believes that Silbury's 'chalk tiers' are in fact arranged as a continuous spiral ramp. This made construction easier *and* created a hidden image of the gigantic coiled, hibernating serpent – the ultimate life force in reptilian mode. (*Right*) Prehistoric megalith at Glasfryn, Carnarvonshire. Until *c.*1900 'she' was dressed once a year and her face whitewashed, as shown, before she was said to hurry to a nearby lake.

barrow. Instead, as Piggott who excavated the West Kennet tomb believed, many of its accumulated vessels and bones were carried to the Sanctuary and stored there, as in a 'museum'.[23] These transferred objects invested the hut with an ancestrally confirmed netherworld power. Given this endowment, the girls could be educated *backward and downwards*, as well as onwards towards a Silbury maternal future.

Further strengthening the Sanctuary's underworld connection, one of the girls was killed and buried there as a foundation sacrifice. She played the abysmal goddess to the full and was interred beneath the Sanctuary in a foetal position, with her head to the south and with a beaker, image of the mother, set between her knees.[24] She lay close to, if not under, her friends' feet as they dreamed and danced in semi-darkness among the rings of posts that were arranged in the pattern of a gigantic snake, coiled up in early spring hibernation. If aroused, the serpent might symbolise the pubescent changes in the young dancers. Gaelic folklore asserts that 'the serpent emerges from his knoll ... on the Brown day of Bride' (Brigit's 1 February quarter day).[25]

The view of the Sanctuary's purpose outlined above has worldwide parallels in which neophytes join together in a serpentine chain to promote the idea of a new birth, via entry into the primordial womb of the Great Mother. In Silbury Hill's case, this theme is represented by the gigantic coiled chalk spiral, of which it is now believed to be constructed.[26]

After the collapse of the Sanctuary wooden temple, the link with Silbury was apparently maintained, for the inner stone ring's 65ft diameter repeats that of Silbury's primary mound, while the outer stone circle, 130ft across, exactly matches the height of Silbury. So, until their demolition *c.*1720, the Sanctuary 'daughter-rings' cried out across the Kennet valley for recognition from their mountainous 'mother'.[27]

In a secular post-mythic age such correspondences might be dismissed as 'pure coincidence', yet even today the panorama from the Sanctuary is rich in significance. It includes two long barrows and Silbury, and links together separate phases of a repeatable round, attuned to the seasons, as well as bringing a heightened sense of shared dwelling on earth.

The Palisades

An air photograph taken in the 1950s gave the first hint of *another* major late Neolithic monument in the Avebury group. Its traces were situated below ground, midway between the Sanctuary and Silbury, close to West Kennet Farm. A pipeline sunk across the area in the 1970s confirmed the presence of two deep prehistoric ditches. The three-year excavation of the site by A. Whittle, begun in 1987, traced the ditches around an almost circular enclosure, 220 yards in diameter, since named Palisade 1. A second enclosure, oval in shape, termed Palisade 2, was then discovered immediately to the south-west and physically joined to Palisade 1.[28]

The concentric ditches of Palisade 1 contained an estimated 800 deep postholes, made to receive vertical oak timbers, each more than a foot across but set only 4–6in apart. After lumps of sarsen rock had been firmly packed around each post base, the trenches were refilled. Whittle estimates that the outer ring of posts rose more than 6 yards high above the unroofed enclosure floor, and the inner ring towered no less than 8 yards above ground level. Narrow entrances, orientated north to south, gave access into the circles. Today, the River Kennet bisects the monument from east to west, as was the likely original intention.[29]

Because the Palisades were built midway between Silbury and Sanctuary and align with them, Whittle believes that these enclosures almost certainly played a part in the overall ritual cycle. His prediction is supported by a possible mid-third millennium BC radiocarbon date for the monument that fits those recently confirmed for Silbury and the Sanctuary.[30]

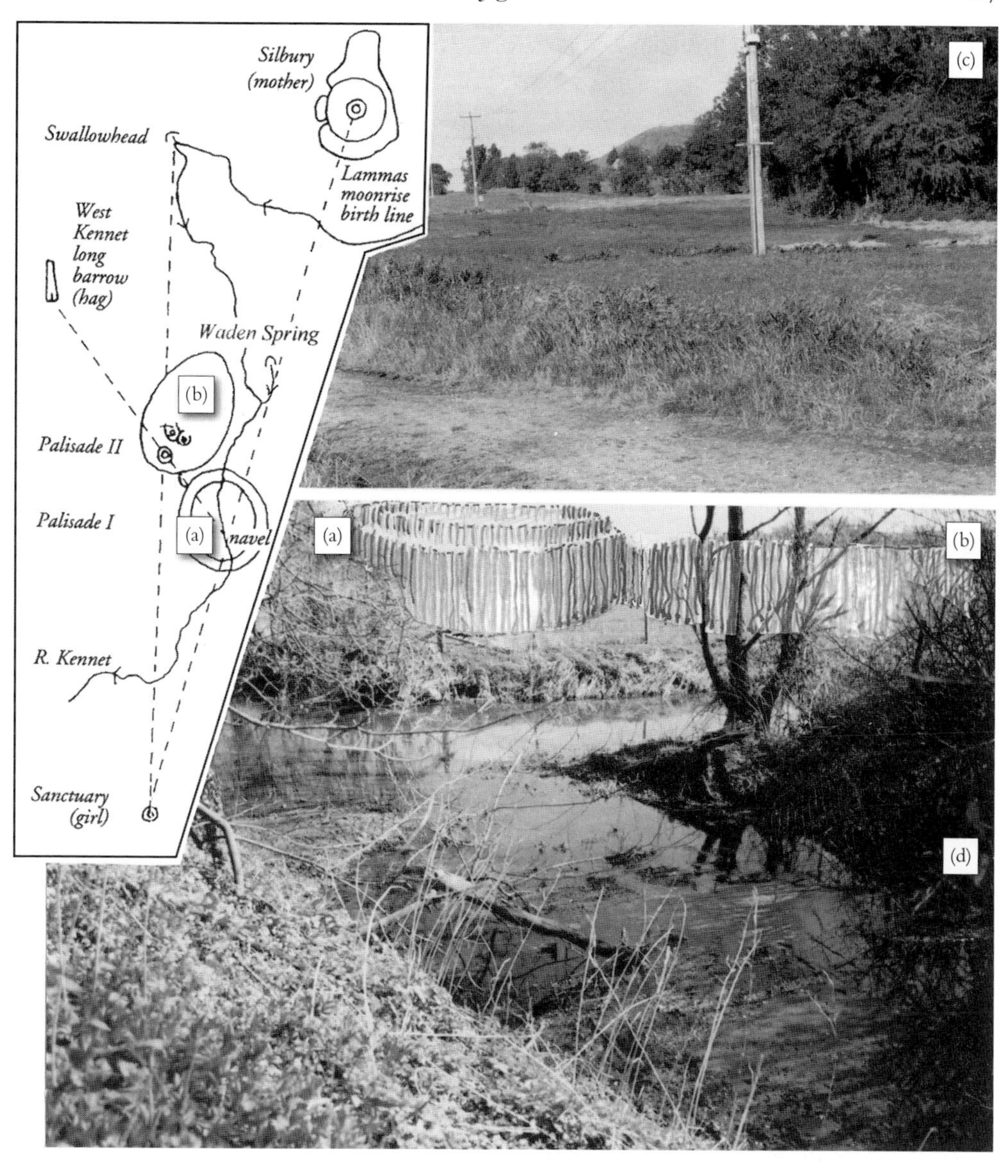

64 Palisade Enclosures at West Kennet, *c.*2500–2300 BC. (The earliest radiocarbon date obtained for the structure was 2602 BC.) (a) Palisade 1 was a double ring of 2800 close-set oak trunks, with the outer ring being 18ft high; inner ring 24ft high. The site aligns with Silbury-Sanctuary and is bisected by the Kennet's 'umbilical cord'. (b) Palisade 2, which is attached to P1, has a long axis of 1109ft. This is the same length as the east–west long axis of Silbury's moat. P2 may be regarded as 'head' to P1's 'body', making Silbury's P1-P2 gigantic 'pig child'. Thousands of pigs were reared in the enclosures. Eighty-seven per cent of the bones from P1 were of pig. (c) The Palisades site, looking west to Silbury. (d) The Palisades, seen near the Waden Hill spring (*bottom right*) at its confluence with the River Kennet.

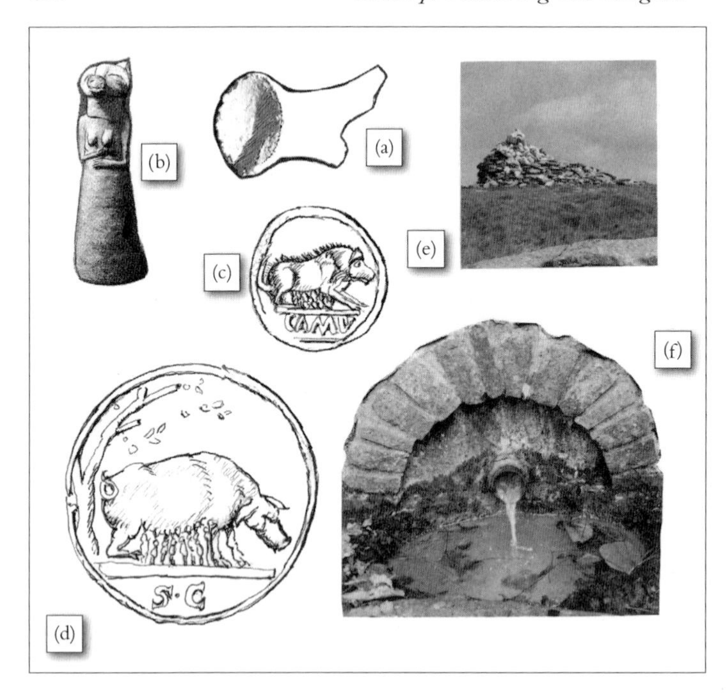

65 The sacred sow.
(a) Pig bone found inside Silbury Hill in 2007.
(b) Pig-headed humanoid deity, Egypt, *c.*3000 BC.
(c) Sow with piglets; coin of British Cunobelinus, AD first century. The sow was worshipped in Europe as a living symbol of fecundity from the early Neolithic and onwards into classical times.
(d) Sow suckling seven of eight piglets; brass *sestertius*, Rome, of Antoninus Pius.
(e) Cadair Bronwen, Berwyn Mountains. Welsh *carnen*, 'cairn' or 'tumulus', also means 'wild sow'.
(f) Ffynnon Cwm Twrch, 'Boar Valley Spring', Glam., famed for cures.

Sacred Pig

The Palisades add pigs to the Silbury story. The large scale breeding of pigs for slaughter was these grandiose enclosures' function, as bones from their scoop and midden deposits prove. The Palisades functioned as an intensive pig farm and slaughterhouse. Nearly 3000 domesticated pig bones from 'thousands of pigs' were found within the enclosures. Some bones were placed around the posts as 'foundation burials' during the building's construction, while other young swine bones were sunk vertically into the ground. To Whittle, these acts denote a sacred pig-centred purpose for the Palisades.[31]

Such deposits are echoed on a smaller scale by the pig bones that Piggott recorded as 'the most striking feature' of the West Kennet long barrow infill.[32] Pig bones were also ceremonially laid over the crouched body of the young female at the Sanctuary, and a pig's scapula was found 50m inside Silbury in 2007. Numerous pig bones were also incorporated into that Hill's summit and were found in Neolithic Pit 1, dug into the West Kennet Avenue.[33]

As a 'pig in the middle', the Palisades were apparently engaged in mythic play with their neighbours who, as architectural images of the mother and daughter, mistresses of change, were willing to identify with and *transform themselves* into pigs for the sake of a trans-species 'commonwealth of being', upon which the world's eco-health has always depended.

Professor Miranda Green points out that the close affinity between goddesses and animals – both wild and domesticated – was also typical of the Celtic world, where 'images of female and beast were intimately associated'. Further, she states that the very identity of the goddesses was 'to some extent dependent on this zoomorphic association', and that there was no rigid boundary between their humanoid and animal modes of representation.[34] In prehistoric art and legend deities could appear as pigs and vice-versa.

White Sow

Around Silbury, the monuments' planners were probably following an early Neolithic tradition found widely across Europe, where, from the seventh millennium onwards, the Mother Goddess is frequently depicted as a white sow. Pregnant goddess figurines, wearing pig masks were placed near effigies of sows. In addition, Neolithic sow-shaped vases are found in Syria, Greece and the Balkans, and sow-masked dancers were painted in ancient Greek shrines.[35] Greek plays of the fifth century BC, like Aristophanes's *Acharnians*, use many 'pig-woman' double meanings.

The sow was the Great Goddess in her typical animal guise. She was depicted in that shape partly because pig domestication occurred simultaneously with the advent of agriculture. Further, the sow's fast-growing, rounded body and her ability to produce litters of a dozen piglets in less than four months emphasised maternal fertility. In the wild, the pregnant female builds herself a miniature 'Silbury Hill' of branches and leaves, beneath which she retires to give birth; hence Welsh *carnen* means both 'small cairn or tumulus' *and* 'wild sow'.

In addition, pigs habitually plough up the ground with tusks and snouts, thereby presaging the arable plough; hence Welsh *swch*, 'plough', derives from Welsh *hwch*, 'sow'. Equally, in rooting beneath the surface world, a Welsh 'young sow', or *gwys*, became synonymous with Welsh *gwys*, 'profound, deep knowledge'. Thus in Celtic Britain the sow retains its status as the embodiment of supernatural wisdom.

The Romans who arrived at Silbury brought with them traces of a Neolithic sow-venerating tradition. For example, when Aeneas, the legendary hero of Virgil's *Aeneid*, first landed in Italy 'a remarkable and imposing sight came into view. On the green river bank was a shining white sow with her white litter of the same colour'. He sacrificed them all on an altar to the goddess who then led him to his new territory.[36]

Here, as so often, mythic 'fiction' is copied by farming fact. Cato's *On Agriculture*, written *c.*200 BC, advises: 'Before harvesting spelt, wheat, barley, beans and rape seed, offer to Ceres a sow as *porca praecidania* ('sow sacrificed in advance'). Then, 'make an offering of *strues* [a heap of little votive cakes] ... and a *fertum*' (a bigger oblation cake). Cato adds that after propitiating Janus and Jupiter, the pig's extracted entrails and a glass of wine are presented to Ceres.[37] At harvest's end another sow was sacrificed to Ceres, while at Roman funerals a sow was offered to Proserpine, the underworld or 'daughter' mode of the same goddess. Likewise, in Greece young pigs, thrown into the abyss '*were* a form of Persephone', Frazer concludes.[38]

The interplay between corn goddess and pig permeated every phase of the ancient agrarian round. As a devotee of Greek Demeter, Hadrian had probably witnessed piglets being thrown down a rocky shaft in her honour. Their putrefied remains were eventually pulled out and used in the following year's rites, so completing a sacred cycle. It was believed that farmers who mixed bits of this rotten flesh with their seed corn 'would have abundant harvests', Lucian reported.[39]

Persephone, as another form of the divine pig, destined for the underworld, smelled of pork: 'Most exalted lady, daughter of Demeter, What a nice aroma of pork wafted over me,' murmurs Xanthias in *The Frogs*, and uses 'piglet' in puns for a 'young woman's pudenda',[40] while the current *Oxford English Dictionary* defines 'in the pig' as 'pregnant woman'. Some of the Palisade pigs were young – no more than 2 years old when dispatched. They echo the Sanctuary's maidenly purpose and are matched by the burnt pig leg bones and teeth found scattered over the girl's body sacrificed and buried there.

In Britain, traces of prehistoric sow worship feature in the Welsh medieval *Triads*. There a divine sow named Henwen (literally 'Old White One') is credited with giving birth to the first grains of wheat and barley in our island.[41] Her counterpart, a ferocious black tail-less sow, appeared annually at the *Calan Gaeaf* (Hallowe'en) bonfire, determined to devour someone, according to Welsh folk belief. In an old Welsh nursery tale this creature 'grew so big that its bristles stood up above the trees in North Wales... It rooted up the earth to such a depth that the sea ran in and made lakes all through the land'.[42] Behold the Great Sow as destructive-creator, credited with creating the entire country.

The pig's importance is also suggested by *Muicinis*, 'Pig Island', a sixteenth-century name for Ireland, connected to the Irish sow deity Banba. Moreover, early Irish literature nominates a huge pig as the main food at other world feasts, given for deities such as Finn and the goddess Anu, alias Aine, who lived within the hills that still bear their names.[43] Similarly, pigs' bones have been found in many of the Neolithic barrows within a few miles of Silbury, including Overton Hill barrow, Cold Kitchen Hill barrow, Millbarrow and also at Knap Hill's Neolithic camp.[44] Whether above ground or below, the Neolithic pig and Mother Goddess are hard to separate; thus Old Irish *crain* meant 'a sow', 'a litter of pigs' *and* 'a woman, especially a mother'.

Although the Palisade enclosures are now invisible on the surface, their buried imprint is part of a pan-European goddess legacy, connected to and interchangeable with a divine maternal image in *human* form; hence the Silbury-Palisades pairing.

Yet because Professor Whittle, who led the Palisades dig, has been unwilling to consider the possibility of Silbury as an orthodox Neolithic pregnant goddess image, created on a grand scale, he struggles to make sense of the Silbury-Palisades relationship. Though he concedes that Silbury's ditch was 'dug to trap water' and that 'the mound could be a metaphor for earth', for him the goddess fails to show up at Silbury, despite the fact that she was displayed on an architectural scale in Neolithic Maltese temples and elsewhere in the British Isles, including Orkney and Shetland. Nevertheless, he concludes that the Palisades *were* inspired by unspecified 'sacred imperatives ... inextricably linked with the context in which Silbury Hill arose'.[45] So far so near!

The Waden Hill Sow

The Neolithic pregnant Mother Goddess in superhuman form, along with her destructive, maidenly and bridal variants, could often change into a pig. Even when below the ground she affirmed her underlying swinish presence by bulging upwards, into a 'sow back-shaped hill' (Welsh *carnen*), such as Waden Hill, which directly overlooks the Palisades site. Waden Hill joins the Palisades 'to the sacred landscape of the area', as Whittle rightly affirms.[46]

Waden Hill is an isolated 1300-yard-long ridge, surrounded by major Neolithic monuments. The bank and stone circles of the Avebury Henge lie at its north-west or 'snout' end. The Neolithic West Kennet Avenue (joining Sanctuary to henge), runs along the hill's east flank, while Silbury rises only 200 yards from Waden's west flank. In addition, Palisade1 and 2 were built at Waden's steep south-east end.

In position and significance, Waden Hill was evidently pivotal to the entire Neolithic design. Its sow-back shape showed Mother Nature as supernatural pig, an epiphany that confirmed a long-held belief in the goddess-as-pig that the first farmers *c.*4000 BC brought with them into the area. In Waden's steep-sided shape they saw her supernatural epiphany on a topographical scale and built a major causewayed enclosure within sight of Waden, 1½ miles north-west, at Windmill Hill.[47] Their successors eventually surrounded Waden Hill with the finest group of late Neolithic temples in the world.

At Waden's south or 'rump' end a copious spring similar to Swallowhead emerges. Its water flows down a 400-yard tributary that joins the Kennet only a few yards upstream of the Palisades site. As a display of the 'sow hill's' innate fecundity, the Waden spring offered an extra incentive to build the pigs' corral here, midway between the maidens' Sanctuary and maternal Silbury. The Waden fount was probably seen as the 'sow-hill's' breaking birth waters and the emergence of a new litter. Palisade 1 was sited so as to enable this sacred 'uterine' emission to run right through the monument. There the divine pigs were housed, overlooked by Silbury, which displayed the same goddess but in human form. (Even now, the English phrase 'in pig' denotes 'a pregnant woman', thereby mixing species in the Neolithic manner.)

The Waden hog's back, together with its stream, appeared to portray the goddess as a topographical sow-in-action. Like the Welsh word for 'badger', *moch daear* (literally 'earth pig'), Waden Hill as 'pig' spanned the underworld-upper world divide and thereby inspired the Palisades temple. What

66 Silbury and Waden Hill. (*Top*) Waden Hill, aligned north-west to south-east, is a mile long and 500 yards wide. Rising 100ft above the Kennet Valley, its sow-backed form is central to the Avebury monuments' purposes. Silbury equals Waden's ridge in height. Waden's south end, viewed from West Kennet. (*Bottom*) Waden Hill (*top left*) seen from Silbury's inter-causeway ditch. Twenty-eight pig bone fragments have been found embedded in Silbury's summit.

is more, when that spring is viewed from Swallowhead at dawn on the critical 1 August quarter day, the rising sun aligns with the two outpourings. This correlation was doubtless interpreted as another divinely granted propitious sign. The *combination* of all these attractive features created the district's numinous allure.

The place name 'Waden' is from a Saxon implant, *weoh-dun*, 'idol hill'. The pagan Anglo-Saxons idolised a fertility goddess, Freyja, also known as *Syr*, 'sow'.[48] In Anglian Scots 'sow' can denote 'a bride's outfit', while English 'sow' is 'a female pig' and *also* a 'a shroud, a fat woman, a large oblong-shaped corn rick or hay stack *and* the main channel along which molten metal runs to make its metal pigs'. The magic sow and her litter have trotted from the Neolithic, through Bronze and Iron Ages and far beyond, carrying their integrating metaphors from language to language. This unbroken inheritance enables us to share archaic perceptions in modern English, as we walk on Waden's fertile back.

The hill's head is 'crowned with barrows of various sorts and sizes', Stukeley wrote in 1743. Faint traces of these are still detectable. Stukeley dug into another Bronze Age barrow at the hill's steep south end (termed the 'Great Bank' on Smith's nineteenth-century map) and found an urn,[49] which in English can be called a 'pig'.

Waden Hill was also the site of an early Neolithic settlement, at least 1000 years older than the Palisades. Pig bones and round-based pottery from a habitation pit on the ridge top were discovered by N. Thomas.[50] Other Neolithic sherds picked up around the Waden spring point to *its* early significance. Four thousand years later, several Roman coins (reminiscent of those offered to the West Kennet long barrow) and quantities of Romano-British pottery were deposited at this springhead, while a massive (as yet undated) vertical shaft sunk into Waden's south end at SU10696840, honouring the Sanctuary-Silbury line, suggests ritual exploration of the Sow-hill's 'uterus', perhaps by enlarging one of the natural vertical 'pipes', caused by chemical solution of the chalk.[51]

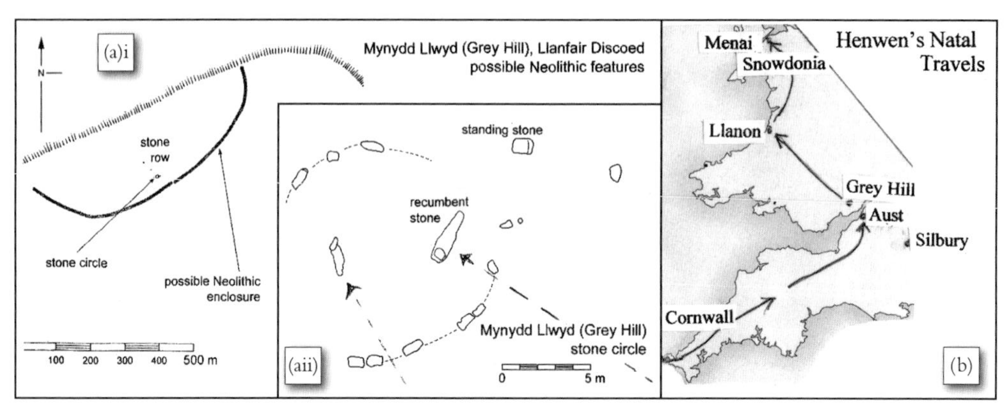

67 Mynydd Llwyd (alias Grey Hill), Gwent. On its sow-back summit are the remains of a Neolithic enclosure and stone circle and stone row; (ai) recorded in 2002. (aii) As drawn in 1868. Henwen, the mythic Welsh sow, 'laid the first grain of wheat' at Maes y Gwent, under the east end of this 265m-high ridge. She came from Cornwall, via Aust, and then toured Wales, giving birth to other things; see map (b). (c) Pig-killing day at Maescar, Brecknockshire, *c.*1900.

Henwen and Gray Hill

The recovery of Silbury's lost meaning depends on the conjunction of visual forms (both natural and human made) with prehistoric tales, passed down and preserved in oral and early written sources, and with the reconstruction of ritual acts. Where, as in Silbury's case, this combination is incomplete, help can be sought from related examples, like that offered by the divine Welsh sow Henwen.

Triad 26w states that Henwen came from Annwn, the Welsh otherworld. When pregnant and 'about to bring forth', she set off from a hideout in Cornwall and crossed the Severn from Gloucestershire into Wales at Aust (Welsh *Awst*, 'August', a start-of-harvest place name). Then 'in the Wheat Field in Gwent she brought forth a grain of wheat and a bee. And therefore from that day it is the best place [for them]'.[52] (See plate 9.)

In Henwen, the Neolithic Great Goddess of Silbury-Palisades reappears as a pig. Moreover, she enjoys far-reaching procreative powers, repeating those displayed in Neolithic art and at classical Eleusis. Henwen, as a medieval extension of the all-life mother, then gives birth to a barley grain and a second bee at Llonion (modern Llanon) in Dyfed, followed by a wolf cub, an eagle and a fierce cat in Snowdonia.[53] Thus her progeny includes wild animals, honey-givers and the staple grains of food and drink, grown here for 6000 years.

Throughout her journey, the swineherd Coll clung to Henwen's back 'with his hand on her bristles, wherever she went, by sea or land', adds *Triad 26*. Welsh *col* means 'embryo, foetus, hillock, peak, and beard of corn'. In a word, Coll is herdsman *and* farmer, operating in the mythic present, *and* as yet unborn. He is Henwen's guardian and her unborn child. As *col*, he is her prenatal foetus *and* the pregnant hilltop under which he gestates prior to his emergence onto the surface as the protective husk around her wheat or barley grain. In this way, mythic characters herd things together.

Henwen's bristles make an animal version of the sacred cornfield's straw, with which Col identifies. This pig bristle-wheat straw metaphor was deeply rooted in early Britain. Thus in *Culhwch and Olwen*, the legendary giant boar, Twrch Trwyth, carries a treasured comb, razor and shears between his ears. These implements may be seen as the boar's 'reaping tools', used to cut the 'straw' of his sow's 'crop' after her 'corn heads' had ripened. But Arthur's men wrest the razor and shears from the boar, so giving to humanity the task of harvesting.[54] Spectacular geological 'tusks' of alabaster, revealed at the foot of Aust Cliff, provide a (super) natural incentive to place the Twrch-Arthur contest there. A prehistoric bronze goddess figurine wearing a moon-shaped crown has also been found at that spot. (See plate 10.)

Coll and Henwen follow a pattern set by Neolithic farmers who stood on the sow-shaped Waden Hill. Now confined to western Britain, Henwen's 'Waden' is the prominent sow-backed ridge, named Gray Hill (ST 438936), that overlooks fertile *Maes y Gwenith*, the very 'Field of Wheat' mentioned in the *Triads*. On top of the Gray Hill ridge (formerly called Mynydd Llwyd, 'holy or blessed mountain') there is an embanked Neolithic enclosure measuring 700 x 225m, with the straight edge formed by the hill's steep north face. This enclosure was 'a place of periodic aggregation for feasting and exchange'.[55] It contains several Bronze Age cairns and the remains of a stone circle, 10m diameter, including a 2m-long fallen megalith resembling a full-breasted goddess image. Five metres to the north-west is an erect 2m-high stone 'chair' or throne facing towards Aust. This megalith suggests human birthing rites that are a known aspect of Irish Lughnasa hilltop ceremonies. The tallest megalith, 2.2m high, stands almost on the crest of the ridge, and may represent Coll, clinging to Henwen's back. Traces of prehistoric field walls indicate that the hill has been cultivated in previous eras.[56]

More divine inferences may flow from Brideswell, a spring and wood at the hill's west end are linked to the pagan goddess Brigit, while Afon Tarogi, or Troggy, the river at the hill's *east* end, is derived from Welsh *torrawc*, 'pregnant, about to give birth'. On the northern 'dark side' of the same hill, the Black Sow's Well, still used in 1990, introduces a counter-balancing ominous note.

At sow-backed Gray Hill, Coll and Henwen bring topography, archaeology, place names and mythic agrarian literature together. In so doing they help to illuminate the comparable Waden Hill-Palisades-Silbury ensemble.

Aine at Keshcorran

In Ireland, the coalescence of goddess in human form with divine sow is seen at Keshcorran, Co. Sligo. This 1188ft-high limestone mountain is a hog-backed eminence named after a sacred sow Caelcheis (Irish 'lean young sow'). She was drawn there by music played by Corann, the harper of the Irish gods. They had given him that *sidh*, but Irish *cheis* means both 'harp' and 'young sow'. Language, myth's storehouse, brings them together and so gives Caelcheis a musical ear.[57]

Folklore affirms that the goddess Aine (known in Munster for her dazzling midsummer beauty) also lived in Keshcorran's caves. When the solar demi-god Finn and his men were lured inside, she appeared to them in her *winter* guise as a trio of hideous hags. 'Three black unsightly mouths, six white eyes never closing, three red bristling heads of hair, six twisting legs under them ... giddiness and faint sickness came over Finn and his men at the sight of them.' They were bound up, and the lusty Finn was reduced to 'a withered quaking ancient' within the hill-sow's entrails. He and his troops became excrement within the year's gut, but were eventually all released, with vigour restored.[58] The supernatural cycle is bound to rotate.

68 Keshcorran, Co. Sligo. This limestone hill is named after Caelcheis (Irish 'lean young sow' and 'harp'). In Keshcorran's caves the solar demi-god Finn was ensnared by three divine hags.

Silbury and Waden Hill

Waden Hill plays a vital role in Silbury's 'start of harvest' birth event. Before dawn on that 1 August quarter day, an observer waiting for the sunrise could stand on the purpose-built terrace just below the 'sacred wheat field' of Silbury's flat summit. By facing east-north-east, with the dark, nearly horizontal ridge of Waden Hill forming the horizon, the rising sun in red-to-orange glory would emerge from within the 'sow-hill', and then appear to roll along her Waden Hill back. A verbal echo of this event can be heard in the English phrase 'on the pig's back', signifying 'in a fortunate position, on top of the world' and 'heading for prosperity'. In Ireland the Gaelic saying 'We shall soon be on the pig's back, for Lughnasa Eve is at hand', specifies an August quarter day usage, because until *c.*AD 1900 the new crops were not supposed to be cut until that festival day came round.[59]

As P. Devereux has shown, it was only through the skilful positioning of Silbury in relation to Waden that enabled this Lammas sunrise event, as seen from Silbury's terrace, to rise *entirely* from Waden Hill's sow-back shape, rather than from the more amorphous Avebury and Overton Downs, which form most of the north-eastern horizon.[60] Silbury's terrace was raised by dint of stupendous effort to 618ft above sea level, in order to match precisely the height of Waden Hill's sunrise 'saddle'. It was, I suggest, the need to annually witness the Lammas sun rising (and riding) on Waden Hill's 'sow's back' that determined the extraordinary height of the Silbury monument *and* its location *vis-à-vis* Waden.

With this achievement, the goddess in superhuman shape described by Silbury was integrated with her alternative swinish mode, seen in Waden Hill. They made a good pair, for the union implicitly merged humanity with all other animals on an equal footing. (Partnership was preferred to dominance.) Moreover, since Silbury's 'birth-act' involved moonlight flickering on moat water, followed by this Waden Hill sunrise, all the elements can be said to have contributed to the birth event.

Like a clown in motley, Silbury's child was made of this and that. How else was overall harmony to be won? As for air, that is the stuff upon which the uttered *sil* and *sel* words floated, conveying,

69 (*Top*) The restored section of the West Kennet Avenue, looking north-west towards the Avebury Henge. (*Bottom left*) WKA stone 37a, east face, displaying 'smile' and broad hips of Piggott's female type. (*Bottom right*) Stone 37a, west face; its 'hog's ears and snout' look towards Waden Hill. A sow was sacrificed annually to Bona Dea, the Romans' 'good goddess'. Pliny recommended 'the grease of a sow that has never furrowed as the most useful of all cosmetics for the female skin' (*Natural History*, Book 28).

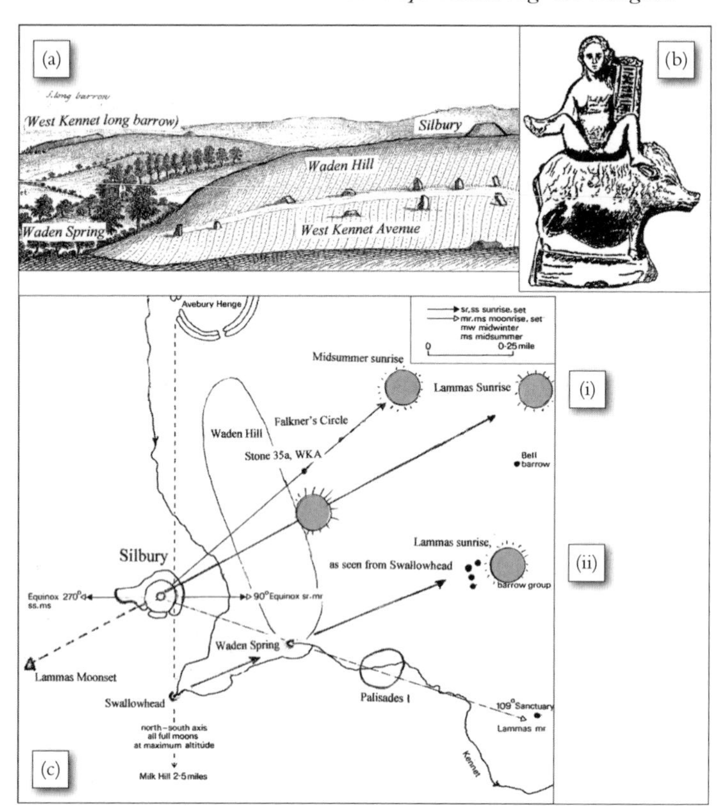

70 Silbury and Waden Hill's 1 August sunrise. (a) Stukeley's drawing, *c.*1720, of Silbury's top, rising above Waden Hill and the West Kennet Avenue, as seen from an Overton Down. (b) Figurine of the goddess Isis giving birth on a pig's back while carrying her sky ladder; *c.*2100 BC. (c) Map showing (i) the Lammas, 1 August sunrise, 62 degrees east of north, apparently riding on Waden Hill's 'sow-backed' horizon, as seen from Silbury's original sub-summit viewing terrace; (ii) 1 August sunrise, as seen from the Swallowhead, over Waden spring and the south end of Waden Hill.

in story form, the message of divine cohesion. Myth's air-borne words summon up the pattern of things and present the marvellous array to human consciousness.

This elemental play was also found in people's games. Modern football, Irish hurling and Scottish shinty began as mythic rites that sought to match and perpetuate the world deity's metabolism. For example, near Silbury, once a year, a springtime game called 'bandy' was played until AD *c.*1860. On the steep sides of the Martinsell and Roundway Hills young men stationed themselves at intervals, obliquely up the slopes, and then hit a ball with their 'hockey sticks' from one to another until it reached the summit. Meanwhile, boys chased after oranges, rolled down from the top. Thus 'sunrise and sunset' were urged on, in miniature. Sport was never more serious.[61]

Equally, the urge to stage, take part in or at least *witness* a divine performance inspired Silbury's construction. That unique civil engineering feat was designed to re-enact the Great Mother's birth of the staple foods, represented as a 'divine child'. Here was an *opera* (Latin 'work, labour') that, by inference, sang everything back to life. Similarly, Irish *muice*, 'daybreak, dawn', also means 'pork, bacon', while Irish *trogain*, the 'painful parturition' by the earth goddess of the First Fruits child, can means 'sunrise', because the goddess delivers both herself-as-sun and smoked pork (herself) from her underworld body.

To understand Silbury is to enjoy just such 'poetics of fusion', which draws sacred and practical life together. In this art, considered indispensable throughout prehistory, the gods took the lead.

By way of preparation for the August quarter day achievement, the *midsummer* sunrise line seen from Silbury across Waden Hill illuminates stone 35a in the West Kennet Avenue. Uniquely, the face of this stone is set at right angles to all its neighbours, as if to honour the Silbury midsummer axis. Moreover, the markedly contrasting shapes of this stone's two sides effectively join the 'slim maiden' and 'hunched hag' aspects of the triple goddess, while the corn-grinding Neidermendig lava, buried at the stone's foot, represents the third member of the trinity – the Harvest Mother, Silbury.[62]

71 (*Top*) 1 August sunrise over Waden Hill, which, seen from the Silbury terrace, forms the horizon without interference from higher downs. (*Bottom*) The 'muddled' 1 August horizon seen from Silbury's summit. The summit was 'out of bounds' since it was still growing the sacred corn crop at dawn on that day.

72 A tale of two springs. (*Left*) Swallowhead's stream giving birth to the Kennet (or Cunnit) from the Earth Goddess. (*Right*) Waden Hill spring, rising half a mile north-east of Swallowhead, sends its tributary stream into the Kennet. Seen from Swallowhead, the two springs align with Lammas sunrise (Ellis, C.J., in *PPS*, 69, 2003, pp. 107–8).

73 Midsummer stones. (*Left*) Stone 35a, south side, West Kennet Avenue. This is the only megalith set at right angles to the avenue. It coincides with the midsummer sunrise line from Silbury. A corn-grinding stone was buried at the stone's foot. (*Right*) Stone 36a, with its crescent moon-shaped 'head', gazes skywards over Waden Hill.

Silbury and Palisades

Just as Greek Demeter was also referred to as Phorcis the Sow,[63] so on the night of the full moon nearest to 1 August, Silbury, squatting in childbirth, was joined to her multiple porcine self at the pig-filled Palisade enclosures, for the rising birth-night moon rose directly over the Palisades. Therefore, a double nativity rite could have been held simultaneously at Silbury and the Palisades, where one of the many sows held there probably gave birth to another litter.

Both parturitions involved water. Silbury's moat provided the surface on which the play of the moon's light could act out the birth of the newborn offspring and provide 'milk' on her water breast. By contrast, the Waden Hill sow's breaking 'birth waters' fed directly from her 'uterine' spring into the Kennet and thence through the middle of the Palisade 1 enclosure. This was deliberately sited to include the *combined* waters of the Swallowhead and Waden springs.

As already noted, when viewed from Swallowhead on 1 August, the Lammas sunrise appears directly over the Waden Hill spring. The two water sources are additionally tied together by one primal sunbeam. This sun-spring alignment touches the former western tip of the Palisade 2 enclosure – an oval shape bounded by a single massive stockade measuring 340 x 200m. Palisades 1 and 2 are contemporaries and their 'ditches were dug in a uniform manner' to receive equally massive close-set posts. Both enclosures were used for intensive pig breeding and are physically connected by a short 'neck' of stout posts.

In terms of monumental image making, Palisade 2 might have been intended as a large 'head', equipped with a pair of 'eye' rings and a double-ringed 'mouth', constructed from the same vertical timbers as the outer fences but on a smaller scale. Whittle found pig bones ritually packed around the bases of these inner features which he did not interpret as roofed huts.[64]

This Palisade 2 'head' is joined to the Palisade 1 'body'. Planned as one, they may have been intended to describe a gigantic, superhuman timber-defined 'water baby' in the act of uttering its first cry after a Lammas delivery from the womb of the Waden Hill 'sow mother', via her fountain's outpoured waters. If so, once again, pig and humanoid prototype are seen to intermingle and exchange roles.

74 Silbury and the quartered spoons. (*Top*) August quarter day sunrise over Waden Hill, seen from Silbury's top terrace, with Overton Down's tree-covered barrows to the right. (*Top inset*) One of a pair of Iron Age bronze spoons from Llanfair, Denbighshire, with 'solar head' and engraved quartered body, 13.5cm long. (*Bottom*) Silbury at the May quarter day, with hawthorn tree in bloom. (*Bottom inset*) A pair of Iron Age bronze spoons, 12cm long, from Penbryn, Dyfed. As 'mother and daughter', the 'mother' (*left*) has one gold-filled nipple (Ashmolean Museum), while her daughter shoots up from below ground imprisonment.

With the outline of a superhuman offspring, the 'Palisades-as-child' is defined by oak trunks, hewn from the wilderness, the source of wild boar pannage; yet the stockades contained innumerable *domesticated* pigs, thereby engaging in an Old to New Stone Age dialogue and requiring a mythic herdsman, such as Welsh Coll. Here, at and *as* the Palisades, his job is to keep the herd of pigs together within his wooden walled body. (The intimate connection between pigs and Ceridwen, the Welsh nature goddess in human form, is reflected in three terms: *meichiaid*, 'swineherds', as her priests were known; *moch*, 'swine', her disciples; and *perchyll*, 'young pigs', her novitiates.)[65]

It should be noted that the long axis of his Palisades 2 'head', measured from top to 'chin', is 1109ft. This exactly equals the long axis of the Silbury mother's moat, which is also 1109ft in length. If, as Professor Whittle advises, we should expect to find Silbury-Palisades connections, here may be measurable evidence of an intended family link, inherited and passed directly between two monumental beings.

Thus for centuries, as long as the Palisades stood, Silbury bore two August children; firstly the new corn harvest child, ripened from her womb-hill; secondly the 'Palisades child', who became her divine swineherd. By this double parturition the Mother Goddess could claim to have initiated both arable farming *and* animal husbandry or pastoralism.

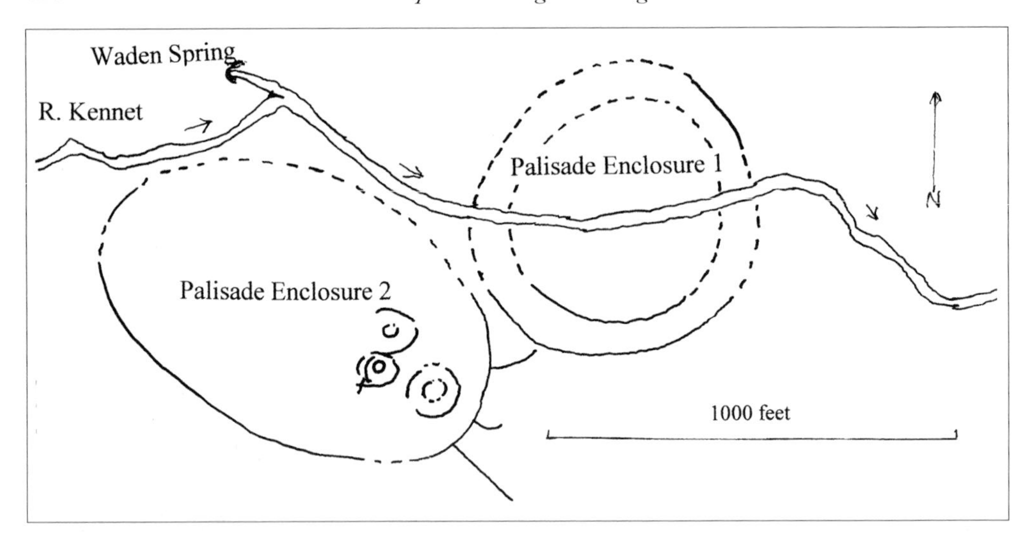

75 Plan of the Palisade Enclosures (after Whittle). Physically linked, they made the head, neck and body of a gigantic 'water baby', nourished by both Swallowhead and Waden spring waters. Palisade 2, the 'head' of this 'child' is 1109ft long, which exactly equals the long axis of Silbury's moat. The massive pigs pens were probably seen as Silbury's humanoid 'son', who acted as her mythic herdsman. He penned thousands of pigs within his wooden frame. The swine were 'born' from the topographical Waden Hill sow. Such collaboration between Silbury, Waden Hill, and Palisades displayed and encouraged metamorphosis between pigs and superhuman deities.

76 The Salisbury Giant with Hobnob (Salisbury Museum). This 13ft-tall civic giant, known to have existed in the fifteenth century, paraded annually through Salisbury on 1 August until 1869. Before the Reformation (and in the folk mind well after that), gigantic beings were accepted as 'real' and often attached to Neolithic monuments. Four long barrows are still named 'Giant's Grave', while 'Giant's Cave, Frying Pan, and Quoit' are other examples of their superhuman scale at work. In 1600 Sion Dafydd Rhys listed more than 50 Welsh giants and where they dwelled. The Palisades and Silbury were living beings in an age of giants, too big for us to see.

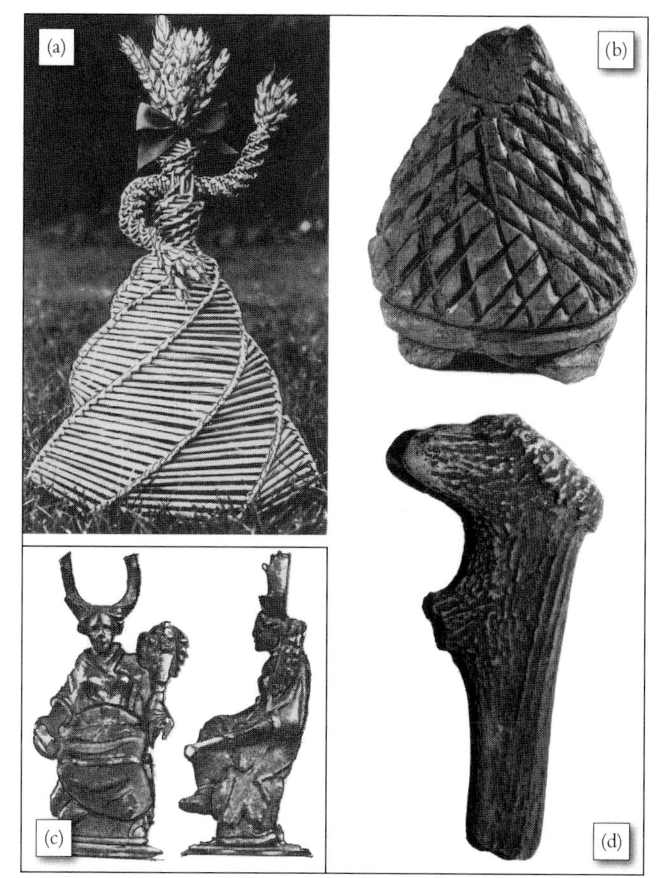

77(a) 'Mother Earth' corn dolly, by Mrs G. Henley of Lower Sands Farm, near Avebury, 1976. Each year Silbury may have given birth to herself as a corn dolly (idol), plaited from wheat grown on her summit. (b) Ceramic pinecone, symbol of renewal, associated with Bacchus; from a Roman shrine at Great Witcombe, Gloucestershire. (c) A Romano-British bronze deer goddess with cornucopia and bread on a platter (BM). (d) Deer antler pick, found in 1849, placed on a sarsen stone at Silbury's core. 'It may have been specially regarded', wrote Merewether. (An antler fragment buried in Silbury's top has been dated 2490–2340 BC, as has an antler pick found in the base of Avebury's Henge ditch. The two monuments were designed and dug together.) In the Scottish Highlands J.G. McKay found traces of a pre-Celtic deer goddess cult. As in the Stone Age, wild roe deer still browse the fields around Silbury.

Silbury and the Snakes

A creature frequently selected to symbolise the ecosphere's sacred life-with-death totality was the serpent. 'Throughout the Neolithic the snake is 'clearly a benevolent creature [and] a manifestation of the Goddess'.[66] In classical times, paired snakes were painted in Roman household shrines as the male and female spirit of the family, and of its individual members. Air-borne, the winged serpent or dragon could represent the tribal life force (and still does in Wales), while rivers and meandering streams like the Kennet, which flows east from the Palisades and wraps itself around the base of the Sanctuary hill, have been seen as the substance and spirit of a divine snake.

From the Sanctuary, a snake emerged at the start of spring, after a coiled up winter hibernation, to resuscitate and 'become' the West Kennet Avenue. This late Neolithic processional way, 50ft wide and 1½ miles long, was made from 100 pairs of megaliths, many of which were re-erected in the 1930s. It linked the Sanctuary to the Avebury Henge by *c.*2400 BC.[67]

There the avenue met its 'partner', the now largely destroyed Beckhampton Avenue, approaching from the south-west. It was originally of similar length, as proved by the location of buried megaliths along the former route. (This avenue is comparable to Shesha, mythic king of India's snakes, who holds a plough and a grain-crushing pestle as a symbol of bread making.) The 'mating' of Avebury's two monumental 'snakes', and of the young men and women processing within their respective avenue 'bodies', gave the Avebury circle its Beltaine or May quarter-day purpose, as a communal wedding ring.

In *The Avebury Cycle* of 1977, I showed that the henge's central arena is equal in diameter to the long axis of the Silbury moat, and that Silbury's summit is plainly visible from the spot in the henge's south circle where the tallest megalith formerly stood. This inter-visibility, together with the horizontal match, offer reminders that May and August, like lovemaking, pregnancy and childbirth, are inter-connected, as are seed planting, germination and harvest.[68]

To express and encourage the cycle of regeneration, the Neolithic builders laid on the ground beneath Silbury's primary core a radiating pattern of 'snakes', 'a sort of string, of two strands, each twisted and composed of grass', as Merewether reported in 1849.[69] These 'grass snakes' extended outwards from the very centre of Silbury Hill, protected by the 'coiled serpent' shape of the overlying spiral of chalk walls. Thus the Great Mother-as-snake bred in her womb a new generation of serpents, tokens of renewed life, and uncannily prescient of the twinned barbed serpents in the DNA helix.

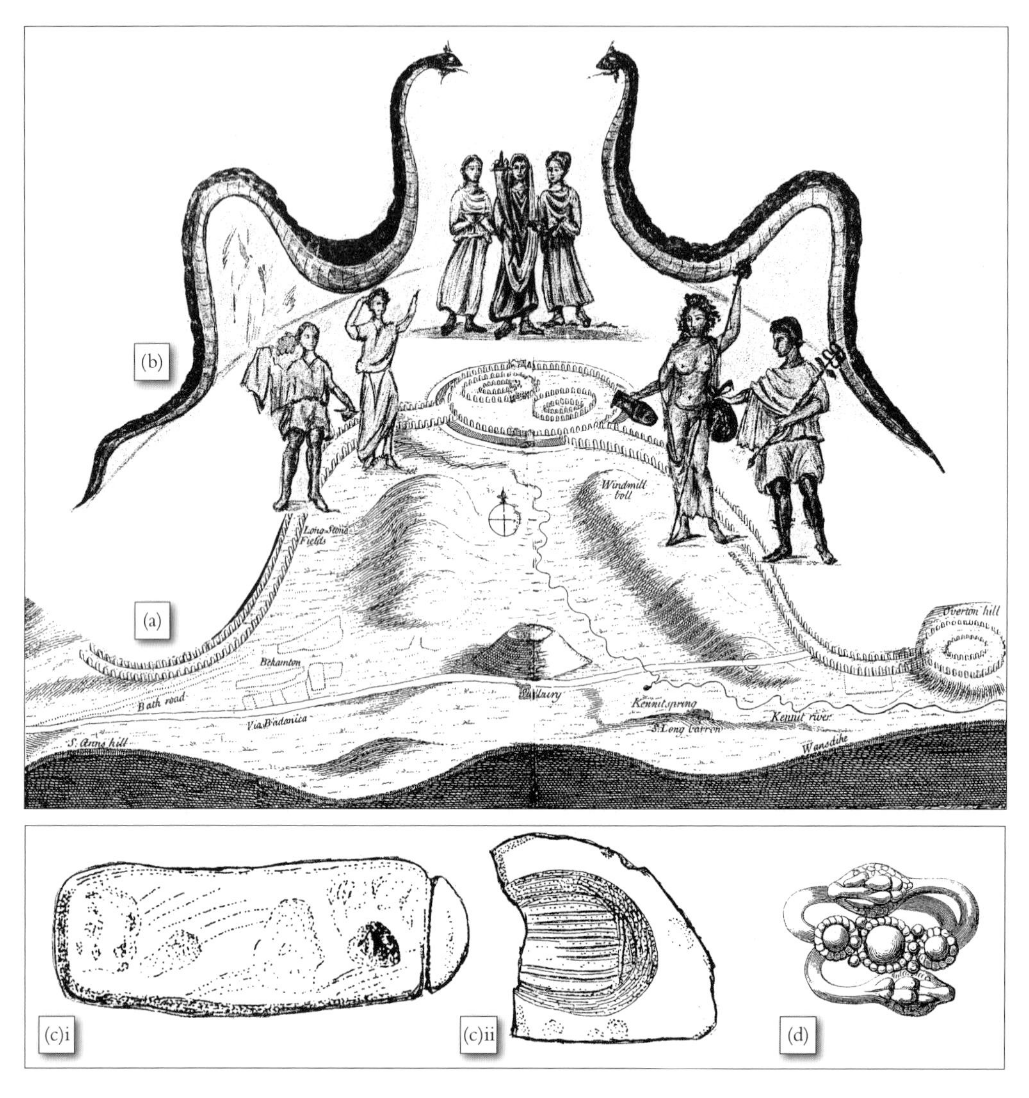

78 Avenues of Continuity. (a) Stukeley's drawing of the West Kennet Avenue, the Avebury Henge and the Beckhampton Avenue; 1724. (b) Roman household Lararia mural, in Casa di Polibio, Pompeii, first century AD, showing Deae Matres, Mercury and a young married man and woman (*left*); protected by the benign male and female serpents, symbolic of family continuity. (c) Carved chalk phallus and 'female' cup; both from Windmill Hill, Avebury; fourth millennium BC. (d) Entwined serpents; gold ring from the AD second century Backworth hoard, Co. Durham, dedicated to the Deae Matres.

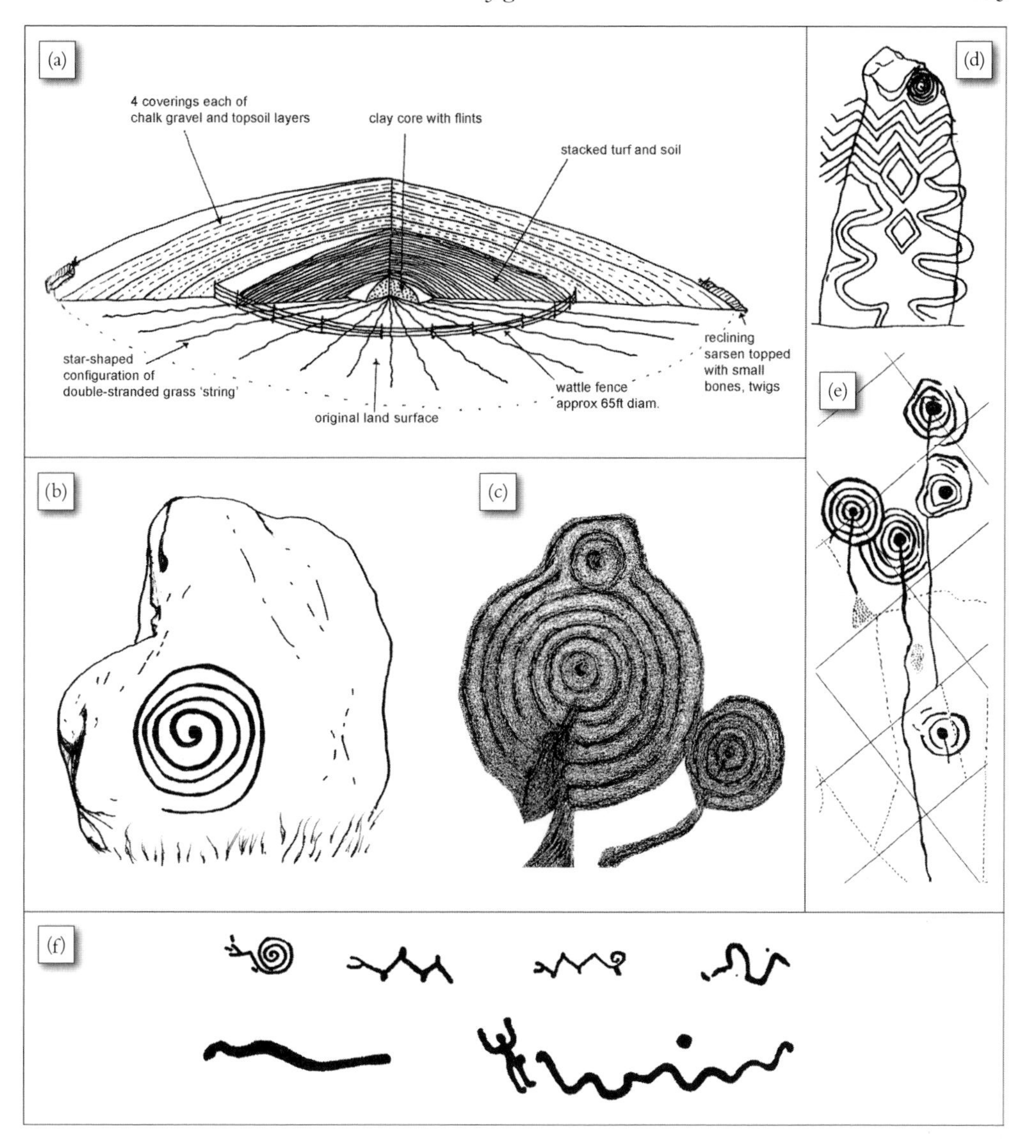

79 Silbury and the snakes. (a) In 1849 Merewether found that Silbury's core sits on a radiating pattern of 'a sort of string, of two twisted strands composed of grass'. Silbury bred 'snakes', a well-known Stone Age symbol of renewal. (b) A 'mother' megalith, with coiled serpent engraved; Castlerigg stone circle, Cumbria, 5ft tall. (c) Prehistoric rock engraving, Chatton Law, Northumberland, as 'mother and child' with serpentine channels running from each. (d) Incised Neolithic megalith, in Barclodiad y Gawres ('Giantess' Apron-load') chambered tomb, Anglesey. (e) Circles and snakes rock carving, Achnabreck, Argyllshire. (f) Bronze Age rock engravings of serpents from Scania, Bohuslan and Ostergotland, Sweden.

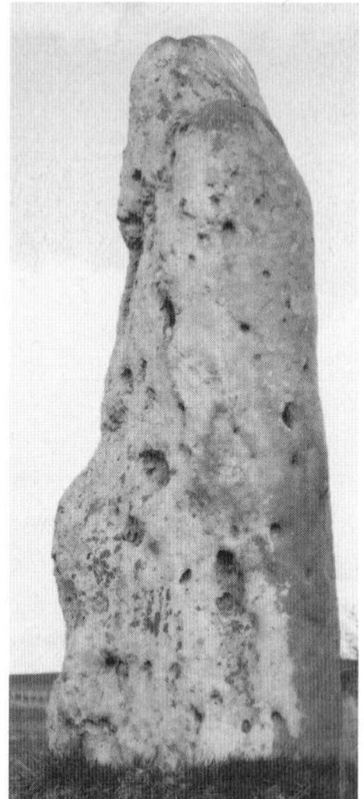

80 Imagining Silbury. (*Top*) Silbury is here hidden behind the north or 'snout' end of Waden Hill's long shape. Likewise, the Romans 'esteemed breeding sows that are very long in shape', wrote Columella, *c.*AD 40. A sow, termed *praecidanea*, was ritually offered to Ceres before harvesting the new crops, states Aullus Gellius, *c.*AD 150. 'Silbury Hill' as phantom pregnancy suggested by stones 36a (*bottom left*) and 24b (*bottom right*), in the West Kennet Avenue. Their prophetic shapes became reality *after* the Avebury Henge's May-Day wedding ring was entered and marriages consummated.

Silbury's double, as a benevolent snake goddess envisaged in a squatting position may be seen in the coiled serpent engraved megalith at the Castlerigg stone circle, Cumbria, and in Scotland's numerous rock engravings, such as those in Argyllshire.[70] Since many Neolithic snake goddess images occur in continental Europe, the serpentine motif that runs throughout the Avebury monuments appears entirely orthodox.

At a later period, Lucian wrote of Demeter's Eleusis that the rites involved creating 'certain unmentionable holy objects made of dough, as imitations of serpents and men's phalluses', while in her vaults living snakes gorged on sacrificed pigs and offerings of grain.[71] This readiness to identify a human organ with a reptilian form as conjoined attributes of the Corn Mother is wholly typical of the inherited Neolithic outlook, as demonstrated around Silbury.

The serpent symbol, essential to Silbury's comprehensive purpose, drew all life together, both in Neolithic and classical times. This may account for the revulsion felt towards it by Judeo-Christian monotheism, wherein the omnipresent serpent has become the embodiment of evil, bringing the Devil himself to the middle of Silbury Hill.

81 Transformations at the Avebury Henge. (a) On May Day, by folk tradition, the May Queen was enthroned on the ledge seat of the henge portal stone, facing the West Kennet Avenue. This marked the arrival of the young goddess into her wedding ring, described architecturally by the henge, as the 'Renewed Land' of the summer half of the year rose into view. (b) A pre-Roman bronze goddess from the Henley Wood Celtic temple, Somerset, 7.5cm high. (c) A 'Venus' clay figurine from London, AD first century. (d) The length of Silbury's moat, as the mother-to-be, exactly matches the long axis of the henge enclosure. (e) The flat top of Silbury is visible above the henge bank and Waden Hill. Thus an amalgam of serpent avenue and hog hill, with maiden, bride and future mother, was secured.

nine

A BEVY OF SILBURIES

Multiple Epiphanies

Silbury is unique. From the outset the monument may have attracted island-wide attention, as indicated by the Neolithic stone axes found in the vicinity, some made in Cornwall, North Wales and Cumbria.[1] Yet because Silbury embodied a commonly held perception of the earth as an active, harvest-giving deity, that belief found physical expression in many other places.

Throughout Britain and Ireland people were drawn to evocative features in the natural landscape, such as isolated hills, that were seen to embody the same procreative theme. Alternatively, as at Silbury, they *constructed* a 'pregnant' mound *or* artificially modified an existing hill to enhance its suitability for 'First Fruits' ritual performances. Examples of these three approaches will now be given, since they each throw additional light on the meaning of Silbury and demonstrate the persistence of Silbury-type behaviour and belief. Silbury invites us to renew an acquaintance with many other former harvest hill ritual sites, scattered throughout the land.

Paviland

In his 1998 study of the Palaeolithic goddess figurines, carved *c.*22,000 BC, that were found in Paviland cave, Gower, Aldhouse-Greene remarked upon 'the numinous quality of the site – a sensation experienced by many at the present day who are able at low tide to view the cave as its prehistoric occupants did, from below on the plain, now drowned by the Bristol Channel'.[2]

Seen from there, a 50m-tall truncated cone of white limestone rears skywards as 'a natural landmark ... sacred or imbued with mythic importance, [an attitude] widespread in the ancient and pre-industrial world'.[3] Carved entirely by nature, the cone head displays 'eyes' set beneath a beetling brow and a gaping mouth, with the lower cave serving as her uterus. Paviland offers an enduring example of topographical imagery, pre-dating Silbury Hill in its goddess-orientated appearance and usage. The ceremonially buried dead, both human and mammoth, along with goddess images of carved bone, were laid in her 'womb' 17,000 years before agriculture came to Britain.

Llyn y Fan Fach

Continuity between Neolithic and early modern times is evident in 'Celtic' western Britain. There the population, which retains traces of a *pre*-Celtic inheritance, were, until recently, well

82(a) Paviland, Gower (SS 437859). The Old Stone Age goddess figurines found here in Goat's Hole Cave were overlaid by Mesolithic flints of *c.*9000 BC, a Neolithic axe and Roman offerings of coins and pottery, *c.*AD 300. To our ancestors, humanoid-shaped cliffs were sacred. Since 2500 BC rising sea levels have provided a 'mirror', reflecting this gigantic cliff effigy. (b) Worm's Head, Gower, South Wales. [SS 387877]. The worm, winged serpent or dragon continues to stand for Wales, as the Welsh flag shows. Topographical images, confirmed by place names, speak of a living landscape involving animals formerly regarded as supernatural in origin.

disposed towards 'Harvest Lady' legends, centred on memorable natural features. Such was the case at Llyn y Fan Fach, a small lake set below the Welsh Brecon Beacons.

Oral accounts of 1861 tell of a widow who sent her grown up and only son to graze her cattle near that lake.[4] There he saw a beautiful lady sitting on the smooth water, which she used as a mirror, while combing her long ringlets. He offered her some of his barley bread and tried to touch her. Eluding him, she cried: 'Hard baked is thy bread. It is not so easy to catch me!' Then she dived, disappearing under the water. When he came home, his mother told him to try unbaked bread. The next morning, before sunrise, he returned to the lake with raw dough to give the phantom. On reappearing she rejected it, saying: 'Unbaked is thy bread. I will not have thee', and submerged again.

Throughout a third day, now carrying the *slightly* baked bread that his mother had cooked for him, he waited by the *llyn* from dawn till dusk. Eventually he saw several cows moving across the water, followed by the lady. She approached, took his hand, and agreed to be his bride, but would break off their marriage if she received three causeless blows from him.

By the following spring, to his chagrin, he *had* struck her three times, albeit only slightly. The blows fell at a christening, a wedding and a funeral whereupon the lady called the cattle to join her and both she and the herd sank back beneath the lake.

83 (*Main image*) Llyn y Fan Fach, Mynydd Ddu, Brecknockshire [SN 803218]. (*Inset*) The supernatural *Gwyl Awst* or 'Harvest Vigil': lady greets the youth (after Sikes, 1880).

'The lady' was the goddess of the annual cycle, owner of the first domesticated cattle and the world's first baker. Having overseen the three mortal thresholds of birth, marriage and death, she and her animals retired to the netherworld. Yet future generations were eager to witness a repeat performance for themselves. Accordingly, as an old woman from the nearby village of Myddvai recalled in 1881, in her youth 'thousands and thousands of people visited the lake on the first Sunday or Monday in August' when 'a commotion took place' on its waters. They 'boiled' and this was a sign that the lady and her oxen were about to reappear.[5] Both the calendar date and the 'boiling' (Welsh *berwi*) are reminders of Silbury and *its* posset of milk, which by repute seethed as that hill arose.

In 1858 it was reported that both sexes visited Llyn y Fan Fach on the night before the first Sunday in August. 'Sunday' represents a Christian variant on the pagan Welsh *Gwyl Awst*, 'August Vigil' or night watch, held at full moon nearest to the 1 August quarter day, when the goddess was in labour, as reflected by the 'moon-on-water' Silbury birth event. At Llyn y Fan Fach the pilgrims also expected to 'see a host of fairies', the lady's lake-born offspring. They were supposed to emerge from rocky crevices at the lake edge and skim their 'mazy dances across its surface'.[6] Beneath them swam eels, plentiful there in August, according to a Llandovery fishwife.[7]

Other people spoke of an ancient town under the water that could only be glimpsed at sunrise on 1 August. (Apparently the other world could take an urban form, comparable to Roman Caerwent in Gwent built for the Silures tribe in the first century and still inhabited today.) A red sandstone mountain wall, over 220m high, rises above the tiny lake. Across its sparkling water the August lady came. Dressed in white, her long yellow hair gilded by sunbeams, she sometimes arrived paddling a golden boat with a golden oar.[8]

After she and her cattle had disappeared again, it was believed that her son guarded the herd on the adjoining Black Mountains, where the rivers Twrch ('Boar'), Gwys Fach and Gwys Fawr ('Little and Big Sow') meander southwards through those rough pastures. As at Silbury, swine and goddess are often found in close proximity.

Another version of the Llyn y Fan Fach event was located in the Glamorgan parish of Ystradyfodwg and centred on a pool and farm named Dyffryn Safwch. This place name is a corruption of 'Valley of the Sow's Mouth'.[9] There the lady-as-pig spoke for all animals and brought them to the surface as her other world progeny. The same archaic idea finds echoes in the medieval Welsh *Mabinogion* tales, in which the mistress of the underworld entertains Pwyll, Prince of Dyfed, for a year. His son Pryderi is then given her pigs, which are subsequently stolen by Gwydion the magician.[10]

Madron and Carn Fadrun

The tallest mountain on the Lleyn peninsular in North Wales is the 371m (1217ft) high Carn Fadrun. This steep-sided igneous mass is named after the Welsh Mother Goddess Madron, alias Modron. Her name is derived from Celtic *Matrona*, the 'Great Mother'.[11] The clouds on the mountain's summit are said to make her hat. Madron-Matrona is also related to the Romano-British Matres trio of mothers; and when approached from the north-east, Carn Fadrun *does* seem to have three rocky 'heads'.

Clustered on the mountain's summit plateau are the remains of numerous stone huts. Often called *Cyttiau'r Gwyddelod*, 'Irishmen's Houses', they were probably occupied at start of harvest ceremonial gatherings that were held on both sides of the Irish Sea.[12] (Lleyn is named after Irish settlers from Leinster.)

Like the seasons, Madron was always on the move. According to medieval Welsh sources, she journeyed from Garth Madrun in South Wales, via Trawsfynydd in Merioneth (where the church is dedicated to a *St* Madrun), before arriving at Carn Fadrun with her infant daughter Annun. From there she crossed the turbulent waters that swirl around Lleyn's western tip, to reach Ynys

84 (*Top left*) Carn Fadrun, Lleyn Penninsula, Carnarvonshire 1217ft, 371m (SH280352). This mountain is named after the Mother Goddess Madron. (*Top right*) Statue of Madron fleeing with her daughter Annun, formerly in Broom Hall, Lleyn. (*Bottom left*) Maen Melyn, the 'Yellow Stone' megalith (SH138252). Positioned on Lleyn's western tip, it evokes Madron's legendary journey to the Isle of Bardsey. (*Bottom right*) Bardsey, alias Ynys Enlli (SH120218). This 'Otherworld Isle' has the Silbury shape of a pregnant deity and a Christian dedication to Mary, mother of Christ.

Enlli (Bardsey), an island dominated by a hog-backed mountain.[13] Thus Madron linked mainland reality to an oceanic dream state.

Bardsey is a Welsh 'other world', and a fabled *Caer Sidi* (Irish *sid*, a word meaning 'a hill of deities and fairies; enchanting, delightful' *and* 'a woman of a wondrous form'; also 'peace, goodwill, conciliation, forgiveness'). Madron shared and suited this blessed isle. The demi-god Taliesin sang of it: 'The disease of old age afflicts none who is there … three organs play before it… And above it is a fruitful fountain; sweeter than white wine is the liquor therein.'[14]

As a *Caer Sidi*, Bardsey is also a 'Turning Castle', connected to the Welsh word *sydydd*, 'zodiac', and all *its* revolving constellations, of which Madron is mistress.

Welsh *madron* means 'spinning, or giddy'. Even when stationary, Madron was the cosmic dynamo. In this sense Bardsey, like Carn Fadrun and Silbury, might be described as 'stills' advertising the Great Mother's action movie. All three sites served to project a maternal image of perpetuity, encompassing everything.

Madron had a son, the divine hero Mabon (Welsh *mabon*, 'boy') who gave his name to the medieval *Mabinogion* tales. The earliest of these, *Culhwch and Olwen*, describes how only three days after Madron bore him, Mabon was 'imprisoned' underground at Gloucester, like the sun at night. However, thanks to the assistance of a salmon and an eagle (representing submarine and celestial realms), he was found and released.[15] In Scotland, Mabon occurs in the place name Lochmaben, Dumfriesshire, and as a large glacial boulder, the Clochmabenstane, on the Solway estuary near Gretna.

Mabon is a Welsh version of Celtic Matrona's son, Maponos. (In Roman Britain he was identified with the Greek god Apollo.) The effigies and inscriptions of all these deities appear together on a Roman altar at Ribchester, Lancashire.[16] At Carn Fadrun Madron re-absorbed all their fire and air into her own stony gut prior to labouring over Mabon's next rebirth. He was the male aspect of her annual 'new fruits'.

Moel Famau, Hill of the Mothers

According to the Welsh *Triads*, Madron also bore a daughter and another son at Llanferres in north-east Wales. Llanferres lies at the foot of the tallest mountain in the Clwydian range. This is the 1820ft-high Moel Famau, or 'Hill of the Mothers', a name highly suggestive of the triple Matres, beloved in Romano-British times.

A folk tale places Madron at the Llanferres river ford in the role of a washerwoman, surrounded by barking dogs from the underworld. Here the river Alun (in Welsh 'holy') often vanishes beneath its porous limestone bed. 'I am daughter of the King of Annwfn … fated to wash here until I conceive a son by a Christian,' Madron tells Urien Rheged, the legendary founder of Wales. She promises him a son if he returns in a year's time. Her triple functions as cleanser of filth, loving mistress *and* future mother are the three classic tasks of the Neolithic deity.[17] The Alun, like the Kennet, is involved in threshold events.

Moel Famau's summit was crowned in 1820 with an obelisk, set on a tower, both designed in the newly fashionable Egyptian style to celebrate George III's 50-year reign. It collapsed in 1862, leaving only a stone podium behind. Even more shrunken is the previously strong belief in the *Bend Y Mamau*, or 'Mothers' Blessings', associated with the mountain. They were the now-vanished host of the Matres' offspring, known in English as fairies.

Moel Famau, like many other hills, could sometimes be heard groaning in labour. The *Annual Register* reported in 1773: 'You will scarce meet a peasant, or even a manufacturer who does not pretend to have heard the groan or sigh of a voice, rushing like a sudden wind from out of the earth.'[18] This assertion probably echoed an earlier belief in the birth pangs of the earth-in-labour (called *Bron Trogain* in Irish) as she was delivered of the first agrarian fruits and her fairy infants. As recently as 1872 a *Bye-Gones* enquirer wrote to ask: 'Are these groanings heard anywhere in Wales nowadays?' He received no reply.

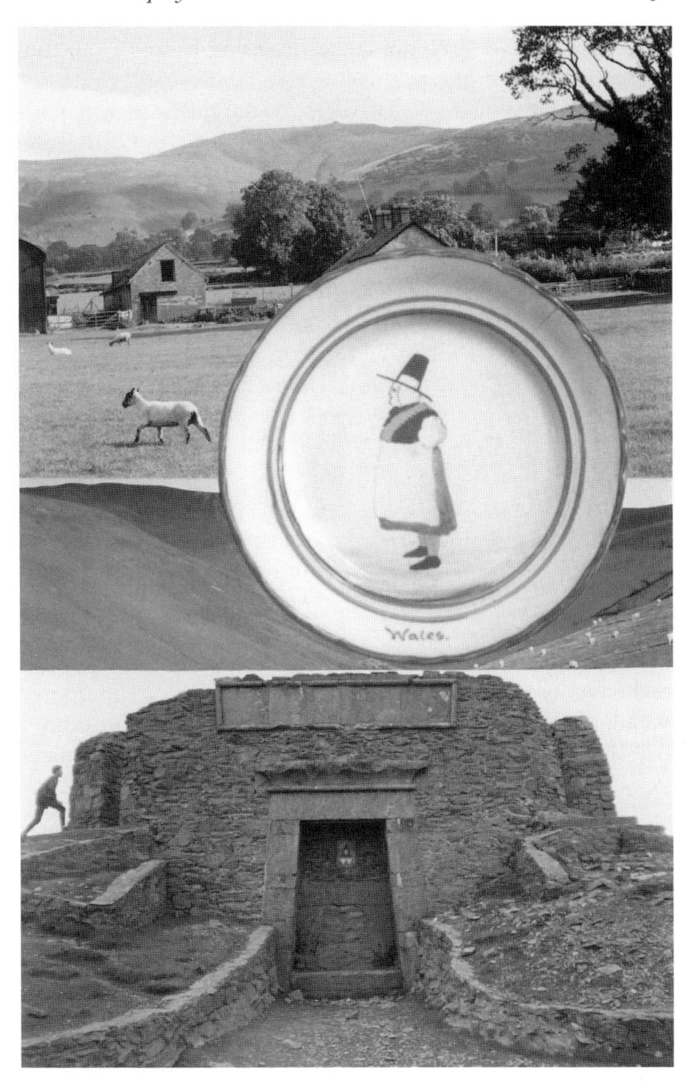

85 (*Top and middle*) Moel Famau, 'Hill of the Mothers', Denbighshire, 1820ft-high (SJ 160626). (*Bottom*) Stump of the collapsed Jubilee Tower, built 1810, on Moel Famau's top. (*Inset*) *Mam Cymru*, 'Mother Wales'; plate by Mari Jones, *c.*1910, Llanelly Pottery.

The fairies were considered 'blessings' (despite also being known as mischievous nuisances, involved in switching babies, demanding food and trapping the unwary within their all-night dancing rings), because they acted as valued intermediaries between the current human generation, the ancestral and the supernatural realms. With fairies (sometimes termed *Y Tylwyth Teg*, 'The Fair Folk', in Wales), divinity arrived in a timeless, low-powered mode, small enough to enter people's homes at night for exchanges of goods or services.[19]

During six months of every year Moel Famau produced nutritious (if rough) grazing for flocks of sheep, goats and herds of cattle. Young people from the surrounding vales drove them up at the start of May. Living in primitive huts, or *hafodtai*, they remained on the heights, milking and cheese making, before returning to the valleys in late October.[20] This 'summer half' tradition, which continued into the nineteenth century, combined common sense with respect for the ultimate 'landlady', the pregnant earth as provider, a figure enlarged nationwide as *Mam Cymru*, 'Mother Wales'.

Equally broad in scope, the *mam* of Moel Mamau (Welsh m's and f's mutate) means 'mother, ancestress, queen bee, a source of sustenance and protection, origin, cause, root, uterus and womb'. Moel Famau, Madron and Mam Cymru together perpetuate some of Silbury's original meaning.

In Wales *and* England, traces of the 'Silbury outlook' survived into the twentieth century. For example, only 4 miles south of, and visible *from*, Silbury, a 6–7 August assembly of shepherds took place at Tan Hill, on the escarpment of the Marlborough Downs. This lofty gathering was a market and a celebration, held on the feast of St Anne. (Drayton names it St Ann's Hill in 1620.) Within that saint dwelt the pagan British goddess Anu.[21]

The Tan Hill fair site was abandoned after 1932 because lorries could not manage the climb up in wet weather. From then until 1939 (when the Second World War finally killed it off), the fair was moved to the field between Silbury and Swallowhead![22] But what has gone might still be understood, if not recovered, through an appreciation of Britain's evocative landforms. By their scale and latent imagery, they inspired innumerable Tan Hill-type gatherings *and* the construction of Silbury Hill.

Mam Tor, Derbyshire

Mam Tor is the 1696ft-high 'mother hill' of Derbyshire. It commands a prospect over the whole Peak District and into four counties. In prehistory, the summit was embanked and seasonally occupied from *c.*1200 BC, if not earlier, as more than 100 platforms, dug for round huts and two Bronze Age cairns indicate. Numerous potsherds and other artefacts of that and later periods have been excavated from the site.[23]

Though parts of the enclosure have disappeared due to subsequent landslips, enough survives of its outline to justify nominating Mam Tor as a topographical image, reclining in a 'birth giving' position, emphasised by the perimeter bank's outline. If this *was* the intention, as the British *Mam* name suggests, the two cairns were perhaps positioned to correspond to 'foetuses' carried in her womb.

'The vulgar theory', recorded by Camden, was that despite the tor's many 'shivering' landslips, it never diminished in size.[24] Instead, like a living being, it (she) was able to retain her bulk. Place names extend this superhuman metabolism to the nearby Peak Cavern (the mouth of an underground limestone watercourse), known in 1636 as Peak's Ars, or the Devil's Arse Hole.

Lady Low, Derbyshire

The entirely natural grit stone outcrop named Lady Low reclines at SK 0678, 6 miles south-west of Mam Tor. It was named 'the Ladie Loe' on a map of 1640, and on the ground, to this day, we can see why. The configuration looks like a giantess. Her rugged head points south-east, while her 8ft-tall 'child' (or phallic 'consort') inclines towards the mother. The Anglian fertility goddess Freyja, wife of Freyr, was often referred to as 'the Lady'.[25] (Anglians had settled in this area by the seventh century AD.) Here their 'lady' discards her blanket of peaty soil and sunbathes naked.

Another outcrop, half a mile south-west, is named Hob Tor, after Hob (alias Robin Goodfellow or Puck), the hobgoblin. Supernatural male spirits apparently attended to the Lady's needs. The 'Bull Ring' Neolithic henge monument, 72m in diameter, which once had an internal circle of standing stones, lies only a mile north of Lady Low and suggests that she may have drawn Stone Age worshippers.[26]

The Wrekin, Shropshire

The Wrekin is an isolated 407m (1335ft) high sow-back granite mountain. Although it lies near the edge of their large county, Shropshire people regard it as their defining 'central place', as in the Salopian toast 'to all friends round the Wrekin's circle, may our love resound'. The Wrekin provides a collective sense of identity. An expatriate, G.H. Ralphs asks: 'Why is the Wrekin so potent

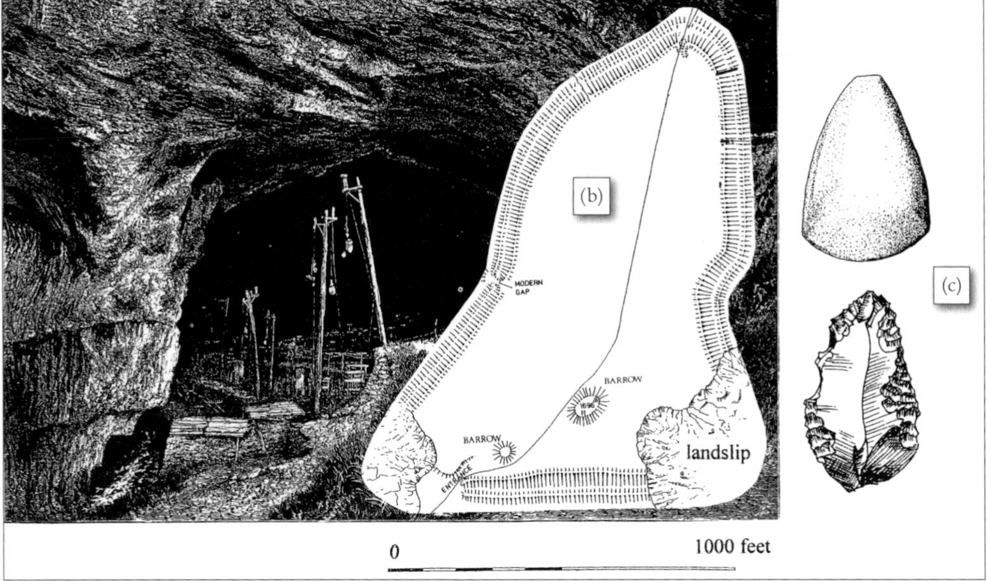

86(a) Mam Tor, Derbyshire (SK128835), 1696ft. (Welsh *tor* means 'belly' or 'breast of a mountain'.) (b) Plan of the banked Mam Tor enclosure. This 'mother' hill of the Peak District has been seasonally inhabited since 1200 BC (Coombs). (c) Prehistoric polished stone axe and flint scraper from Mam Tor. (d) Peak Cavern, alias 'the Devil's Arse', beneath Mam Tor, with rope works of 1876. In prehistory this nearby cave system was probably seen as Mam's guts, but after Christianity demonised the subterranean realm they passed to the devil.

87 Lady Low, Chapel-en-le-Frith, Derbyshire (SK065783). Formerly known as the Ladie Low, this is an anthropomorphically shaped natural grit stone outcrop with its 'phallus-partner'. She overlooks the remains of the Neolithic Bull Ring henge monument.

88 The Wrekin, Shropshire, 1335ft, 407m, (SJ 629082). (*Top left*) Viewed from the north-west, with the Ercall (265m) forming the head of a 'reclining figure'. (*Top right*) The Wrekin from the south-west, with the River Severn. (*Bottom left*) A 'reclining mother' granite rock stack on the Wrekin's summit, showing the narrow gap through which maidens passed at the May Wakes. (*Bottom right*) The Raven's or Cuckoo's bowl on Wrekin's summit.

a symbol in the minds of Salopians? For those born around it, or who view it with the eye of the imagination, it will always hold a certain magic.'[27]

Towards the south end of its summit crest is a granite outcrop named the 'Needle's Eye', comparable in form to the Lady Low feature. Here, by long-established custom, young women contemplating matrimony would crawl through the narrow gap between the huge stone 'needle' and the adjacent rocky image of the 'reclining mother'.[28] This they did from the south-west to the north-eastern, or 'sunrise', side of the gap, thereby mimicking birth in both celestial and earthly terms.

Then the girls were required to drink from the Raven's Bowl, a tiny pool in a nearby rock, said never to be dry.[29] In doing so, they were swallowing the dark winter half of the Celtic year, which ended on May Day. After that the pool could become the 'Cuckoo's Bowl', a title it retained for the next six months. This division was matched by an annual May Day battle on the summit between local coal miners and farm workers, representing subterranean and surface powers. This fight was suppressed after 1826.[30]

The Wrekin May Wakes had been immensely popular. 'The top of the hill was covered with a multitude of pleasure-seekers, with ale booths and gingerbread stands, gaming tables, swing boats, merry-go-rounds, three sticks-a-penny, and all the etceteras of an old English fair.'[31]

Professor Rhys derives the Wrekin's name from Old Welsh *gurcon*, which incorporates Irish *gur*, 'labour pains', plus *con*, 'a cone'. He adds that the prehistoric Cornovii tribe who lived in the region, and had adopted Roman habits at nearby Uriconium (now Wroxeter), located their origins in an ancestress named Gurcon.[32]

Some medieval Welsh sources enlarge the hill's name into Dinlle Ureconn, with Dinlle signifying 'Fort of Lleu'. Lleu is the Welsh form of Irish Lugh, the young god who arrives on 1 August, the start of harvest.[33] Thanks to the pairing of Gurcon and Lleu, the Wrekin (which remained in Welsh hands until the eighth century) has etymologically convincing 'Mother Goddess and Son' credentials. Moreover, as we have seen, Gurcon displays on her hog's back profile the monumental image of herself as a superhuman goddess-in-labour, carved by nature out of granite, with a passageway offering the means for young women to identify with her annual travail.

Pontesford Hill and the Golden Arrow

Seventeen miles west of the Wrekin, the 520m high Pontesford Hill rises 'like a crouching lion', writes Burne[34] (or, in a county without lions, perhaps a pregnant giantess?) Lleu may also have left a trace of his former presence on Pontesford Hill in the traditional 'Golden Arrow Hunt', even after this rite had been switched to a Christian Palm Sunday date. As Burne reported:

> People believed that the golden arrow had been dropped in days gone by, and that the search for it was ordained by a good fairy, as the condition on which she would undo some unknown injury, curse, or spell, inflicted by a demon. But to be successful the quest had to be undertaken at midnight by a young maiden under twenty, who was the seventh daughter of a seventh son. That would ensure good fortune for a year.[35]

Was this elusive 'arrow' originally intended as the first sunbeam of the year's May Day 'summer half', and a precursor of the first ripe corn stalk, which was Lleu's staff and emblem? A seasonal reference seems probable, since after villagers had gathered on the hill for dancing and drinking, there was a race to pluck the first spray from an ancient and reputedly haunted yew tree growing nearby, perhaps as a token of the dark 'winter half' that was about to end.

The second race was down the very steep east end of the hill to the Lyde Hole, where a brook falls into a crater which was believed to be bottomless. Whoever could run at full speed into the

89 Pontesford Hill, east side, Pontesbury, Shropshire, 320m-high (SJ 409 049); with 'golden arrows' of ripe wheat in the foreground.

hole from the hilltop and dip the fourth finger of the right hand into the water was *bound* to marry the first person seen thereafter.[36] This resembles the Wrekin's Needle and Raven's Pool ceremony, but with a dangerous underworld dimension.

Prior to the spread of Protestant distaste for Britain's erotic landscapes, Lyde Hole may have served as Pontesford Hill's 'vulva'. From an Indo-European perspective, the golden arrow finds an equivalent in the god Siva's fiery arrow of ultimate energy, which can only be stabilised within the vulva of his voluptuous wife Parvati, the Lady of the Mountain and daughter of the world's central mountain.[36A] Without that union, Siva's arrow would have turned the world to ash (a fate now rapidly approaching).

Is this Siva-Parvati comparison with Pontesford far fetched? Pontesford and India are much closer than is Paviland from Siberia, whose Palaeolithic figurines Aldouse-Greene so convincingly links together.[37] Ever since then Eurasia has shared a pool of myth deeper than Lyde Hole.

The Banbury Stone, Worcestershire

In a hollow on the 997ft top of Bredon Hill, an outlier of the Cotswolds, sits an enormous honey coloured limestone boulder named the Banbury Stone. It is roughly 10ft high and 60ft long, yet people believed that at midnight the stone travelled a mile downhill to drink from the river Avon, and then returned.[38]

As with Derbyshire's 'Lady' and the Wrekin's 'Needle's Eye', a 2ft-wide gap, through which initiates could pass, separates the Banbury Stone's 'groin' from her eastern 'child', so offering another version of the goddess in labour. A landslip that occurred *c.*1800 close to the stone's foot exposed a large quantity of stored wheat, 'perfectly formed, but which crumbled to dust if touched'.[39]

Another aspect of the Banbury Stone's 'underworld' was described in Dr Derham's *Physico-Theology* of 1712. He wrote:

90 The Banbury Stone, Bredon Hill, Worcestershire (SO 958403). (*Right*) This 10ft high by 21ft long 'mother in labour' is composed of oolitic limestone. (*Left*) The 'birthing gully' through the rock's west end.

> near the [Bredon] precipice facing Pershore, in or near the old fortress, is a cave lined with stalactitical stones... On the top they hung like icicles, great and small, and many lay on the ground ... as an exudation of some petrifying juices out of the rocky earth there.[40]

Whitsuntide games were held at the Banbury Stone.[41] They included wrestling, shin kicking, quarterstaff contests and bare-knuckle boxing, while the Banbury Stone itself was danced around; hence its name may derive from Latin *ambire*, 'to go around'; others connect the boulder's colour with 'amber', a stone once regarded as helpful in childbirth; and 'Banbury' was locally pronounced 'Bambury'.[42]

The stone continued to be viewed seriously in Christian times. On Good Friday many pilgrims climbed the hill to kiss it.[43] By this act, the pagan 'Lady' merged with the Blessed Virgin Mary. Here, as at Silbury, water was an essential element in the Banbury Stone's fecundity. Veneration of a spring 200ft below the stone continued into Christian times. A chapel to St Catherine was built near the outflow.[44]

Roseberry Topping, North Yorkshire

The Danish word *toppen*, 'pointed', explains the second element attached to this 1057ft-high mountain's place name. It rises in isolated splendour on the edge of the Cleveland Hills near Middlesborough. A Nordic connection also underlies the name Roseberry, a corruption of *Othenesberg*, from 'Odin', the chief Norse god.[45] His *Aesir* pantheon was hostile towards the fertility goddess Freyja, yet he was sometimes represented as her husband!

They both had links with the underworld that have seeped into this hill's folklore. For example, when a sick person's shirt was placed in the well at the mountain's foot, 'if yt floated aloft yt anounced recovery to the partie, but ... if yt sanke, there remained no hope of health'.[46]

A local legend tells of a Danish princess who dreamed that her infant son would drown. In order to thwart the presentiment she climbed with him to the summit of Roseberry, high above any dangerous river or lake. However, when she fell asleep on that warm summer's day, he drowned there, in the tiny mountaintop spring.[47]

Perhaps this tale contains a faint memory of harvest sacrifice, acknowledging the two-way traffic between *sid* and surface worlds, which is also apparent in the Roseberry Topping folk custom of 'threading the needle'. As at the Wrekin, so on this mountain there was 'a clefte in the rocke'. Here it was called St Winifryd's Needle, 'whither blynde devotyion led many a syllie soule, not without hazard of a breaknecke tumblinge, while they attempted to put themselves through a needlesse payne, creepyinge through that Needle's eye'. (St Winifred is the English form of Welsh Gwenfrewi, whose decapitated head rolled downhill to create the still-revered well at Holywell, Flintshire. Divine powers from east *and* west converged on Odin's hill.)[48]

Roseberry's many 'sillie soules' had inherited a prehistoric need to identify with the sanctified Mother Earth, for they were the offspring and future replicators of that mountain's fecundity. Accordingly, they undertook to be physically 'born' from the rock. In a similar but reversed vein, a hoard of prehistoric Bronze Age implements, including socketed axes, gouges and hammers, and a bronze sheet with crescent moon-shaped openings, was found hidden beneath a boulder close to the summit. The earth's precious ores were returned with interest.[49]

Cruckbarrow Hill, Whittington

On the western outskirts of Worcester, at junction 7 of the M5 motorway, this 28m-high tump is a major local landmark, which can be seen over a wide area. With a name derived from British *crug*, 'hill', it has been compared to Silbury Hill by J. Allies. He attributed Cruckbarrow's 'extreme regularity of contour to artificial means'.[50] D. Hurst later claimed (wrongly) that 'it is somewhat larger

91 (*Top*) Roseberry Topping, North Yorkshire, 320m, 1057ft high (NZ 579126). This mountain was known as Othenesberg in the twelfth century, after the god Odin. As at the Wrekin, girls ritually squeezed through a rock crevice (here called St Winifred's Needle) on the summit. Nearby, Freebrough Hill (NZ 6812), an isolated Silbury-shaped cone, is probably named after Odin's wife, Frigg. (*Bottom*) Thor's Cave, Staffordshire (SK 098548). The Angles redesignated some prehistoric sacred sites to their own deities.

and higher than the celebrated druidical hill of Silbury'. In fact, the hill is closer to an elongated sow-back shape than Silbury's truncated cone. The Geological Survey classifies Cruckbarrow as 'artificial ground', an assertion that has yet to be tested.

Cruckbarrow was an important gathering spot. F.T. Spackman recalled that until 1914:

> there has always been, once a year, a great concourse of Worcester people on Crookbarrow Hill, with swings, roundabouts and other accessories for merrymaking, to the very great inconvenience of the owners of the estate. This annual exodus of citizens [from Worcester] occurs on Good Friday – perhaps the most sacred of all the fasts observed by the Church. [Yet] so firmly established is the custom, so great are the throngs of people who attend, that … no opposition, as far as I know, has ever been offered to the merrymaking.[51]

This gathering died out in the 1930s.

A Neolithic flint scraper and Roman coins found at the site suggest that in prehistoric times and beyond, Cruckbarrow might have attracted 'harvest hill' rites. As might be expected of a possible First Fruits location, Cruckbarrow, alias 'Cooksey Hill' was involved in the task of converting the white stones that lined the Tything (a Worcester street) back into the men and horses that they had once been. A folk tale asserts that for this transformation to occur a new loaf of bread had to be placed at midnight on each stone, precisely '*when a half moon was rising over Cooksey Hill*'. But the only man brave enough to try was terrified when one stone that he had loaf-crowned changed into a gigantic, rearing horse. The man ran off, failing to complete the task.[52] Does this crumb of folklore fall from a Cruckbarrow 'First Loaf' rite?

92 (*Top*) Whittington Tump (alias Cruckbarrow), Worcestershire (SO 875523) is 28m high. Victorian writers compared this steep-sided 28m-high tump to Silbury. Prehistoric and Roman finds from around this hill's base indicate millennia of human interest in what is probably a largely natural feature. (*Bottom*) The Cruckbarrow Good Friday Fair in 1910. Annual gatherings at Cruckbarrow continued until the 1930s.

Four Stones Hill, Clent

This prominent isolated hill, reaching 304m OD, lies at the north-west end of the Clent hills in Worcestershire. As a natural counterpart to Silbury Hill, it attracted local start of harvest rites. Like Silbury, Clent was named as the centre of a 'hundred' – a group of Anglo-Saxon parishes where law courts were held.[53] (Both Demeter and Ceres were regarded as originators and disseminators of law and order.)

The hamlet at Clent's eastern foot was the scene of a fair, held on three consecutive days in late July and endorsed by royal approval in 1254. Horses, cattle and sheep were traded, as were linen cloth, cheeses and pedlars' wares, with the third day given over to pleasure. Records show that this well-attended market and celebration persisted until at least 1784 'and at nearly every house were sold roast beef and ale … with accommodation for man and horse'.[54]

The fair was linked to a 'Crab Wake', which took place on the first Sunday in August, with the two events spanning the 1 August quarter day. Taken together, they may represent an instance of 'Sillie Season' continuity. (In linguistic terms, 'sillie' derives from Middle English *selli*, 'a wonder, marvellous, supernatural', and from *seli*, 'blessed, prosperous, happy'). The Crab Wake took its name from 'a strange custom of pelting each other with crab apples'. Two barrow loads of these were deposited in the churchyard and flung at the parson and congregation when they emerged from church.[55]

By the mid-nineteenth century the fair had shrunk to 'a few stalls erected by the side of the churchyard, in the narrow road by the brook, at which some trifling articles were sold, the chief commodity being cherries', so Amphlett recalled in 1890. As for the wake, 'being accompanied by great disorder on the hills, it was soon suppressed, and the Fair vanished with it'.[56] The rough behaviour may have derived from the ritual 'faction fights', like those held on the Wrekin, which were also a feature of the otherwise notably peaceful Irish Lughnasa gatherings.

At Clent, history and mythic violence combined with the murder of an Anglian boy-prince, Kenhelm of Mercia. Here, in AD 819, he was supposedly killed and buried by his half sister

93 (*Clockwise from left*) Four Stones Hill, Clent, Worcestershire, 304m (SO 933803); Legends connect Kenhelm, a murdered boy prince of Mercia, with this hill. At its foot a supernatural cow, a church dedicated to him and a holy spring that is revered to this day were merged with an annual 'start of harvest' fair, perhaps Neolithic in origin.

Quendrida and her paramour. 'O Kenhelm, martyr, glory of Mercia, exceedingly sweet is thy memory, for thou surpassest the honeycomb by the delight of thy sweetness,' runs a medieval Latin hymn in his praise.[57] Since Anglian royalty believed themselves descended from their own pagan gods, the boy Kenhelm fell from a divine family tree.

As befits a supernatural harvest child, cut down like John Barleycorn in order to initiate the ripe crop's reaping, Kenhelm's name derives from O.E. *cennan*, 'to beget, to conceive, to bring forth'. He is the symbolic child of O.E. *cenning-tid*, 'the time of bringing forth', subsequently Christianised into Lammas, 'loaf mass'.

After his clandestine burial, 'a white cow … belonging to a certain widow, hastened down from the mountain-top [Clent's summit], to the grave, and there it remained, nor could any force drive it away,' says Richard of Cirencester. In Nordic and Germanic myth the white cow is Audhumla. She emerges from ice at the beginning of time and licks into life the first giant Ymir, progenitor of humankind. Then her udders yield prodigious streams of milk that become the world's rivers.[58]

In Celtic belief, a comparable white cow comes from under the *sidh* as a sacred avatar of the goddess. Pastoralists sang of 'A white cow on the mountain, A fair white cow; She goes east and she goes we, And my senses have gone for love of her. She goes with the Sun, And he forgets to burn, And the moon turns her face with love to her.'[59]

At Clent, when Kenhelm's body was eventually exhumed, a dove flew from the pit, carrying an account of his murder to the Pope in Rome. Then a spring burst forth where the white cow had lain down on his buried body. Directly over the spring a church (rebuilt in the twelfth century) was constructed. As Richard reported 'the stream still flows and has dispensed healing power on many who have tasted it'.[60] In 2002, devoutly hung ribbons still dangled from branches of an ash tree overhanging a subsidiary well 20 yards downstream, the original source having been diverted in the nineteenth century because it made the building damp.

Notable hill, holy spring, sacred cow, sacrificed harvest boy, August quarter day festival and market; here the elements of a Neolithic First Fruits event retained a matrix into which an alternative

Christian theology, other legends, historical particulars and social changes were absorbed. In England nothing is absolutely discarded, yet everything is modified to a degree where the different layers and connections are often hard to decipher. Yet compared to the 200 million-year age of the hill itself, *all* these uses, including a likely Neolithic interest, combine to make a single, recent conglomerate which can be enjoyed in all its confusing variety.

For the thousands of Birmingham and Black Country people, young and old, who climbed Clent Hill on the night of 6 June 1977 to celebrate Queen Elizabeth's jubilee, the communal sense of attachment to a special place for a shared reason was palpable. Around the summit bonfire, a people and their queen were incorporated into a national chain of beacons, blazing from Land's End to John o' Groats, with the neighbouring fires on Malvern and Cannock Chase plainly visible. Thus 'ordinariness' there and then became *extra*ordinary. Hill, fire, monarch and her hilltop throng together generated an unexpected encounter with the sublime.

In that orange glow, among darting silhouettes, something of the spirit of Silbury almost (and briefly) came to life; and it does again (for some readers) in the work of the poet James Thomson (1700–48). He was a frequent visitor to Hagley Park, which laps against the north flank of Clent Hill. There he composed much of his best poem, *The Seasons*.

The Seasons is a reminder that even in an age of reason, such as his (and ours), things can still be seen in the round, despite our concentration on 'linear progress'. Of this poem, Dr Johnson wrote: 'He brings before us the whole magnificence of Nature, whether pleasing or dreadful ... the gaiety of spring, the splendour of summer, the tranquillity of autumn, the horror of winter. Our thoughts expand with his imagery, and kindle with his sentiments.'[61]

Equally radical in their challenge to the monopoly of *linear* time are the architectural follies commissioned by Lord Lyttelton of Hagley Park during the mid-eighteenth century. These include four 'druidical' standing stones, erected on the summit of Clent Hill. On the lower slopes, arcades transported from the ruins of Halesowen Abbey are attached to a mock medieval 'castle'.

Nearby, a Greek Doric temple – the first ever seen in Britain – was built in 1758. Its front was a miniature copy of the fourth century BC Theseion temple in Athens, dedicated to Athena and Hephaestus, the god of divine fire and metalworking.[62] Sited on the fringe of the industrial Black Country, but with a view of rural England, Lyttleton's 'temple' fits, not least because Clent and the neighbouring hamlets were noted for making steel sickles and scythes, the tools of agrarian continuity and peace.

In their beautiful setting, the Hagley follies gathered beneath Clent Hill implicitly speak in favour of an all-time companionship, defying mortality and mediating between differences. If that ambition is folly, then so is Silbury's ability to address the needs of every era, without chronological impediment. Thanks to English Heritage she is still intact, ready to greet us again.

Harvest Hills and Saints

Faced by medieval Christian disapproval and the threat of prohibition, many pagan hilltop ceremonies in England survived by adopting a saintly cover story, such as Saint Catherine's. Her hagiography states that she was a princess of Alexandria, martyred on a wheel, before her body was carried by angels to the top of Mount Sinai and buried there. Her legend was brought to England by returning Crusaders.[63]

From the twelfth century onwards, numerous English hilltop chapels were built in her honour, as at Barmby Moor (Yorkshire), Houghton-on-Hill (Leicestershire), Guilford (Surrey), Chale, (Isle of Wight) and Milton Abbas (Dorset).

At Abbotsbury, Dorset, her chapel tops a hill scored with seven Bronze Age cultivation terraces. Into the south doorpost generations of young women have pressed their elbows and knees, and worn deep hollows there while appealing to the saint on St Catherine's Eve, 24 November, for a husband:

94(a) St Catherine's hilltop chapel, Milton Abbas, Dorset, twelfth century (ST 802024). (b) St Catherine's fourteenth-century hilltop chapel at Abbotsbury, Dorset (SY 573845). The hill is marked by substantial Bronze Age cultivation terraces. (c) St Michael's Mount, Cornwall (Photograph F.E. Gibson). The twelfth-century monastery preserved a pagan 'rough-cut stone seat', later named St Keyne's Chair. Folklore maintains that she decreed its use at weddings to decide whether the bride or groom would be the stronger partner. A similar belief is associated with her mainland holy well. (d) St Michael's thirteenth-century church tower surmounts the prehistoric cultivation terraces of Glastonbury Tor, Somerset; 158m (ST 512385). The tor 'is born' from the surrounding Somerset marshes.

(b)

(d)

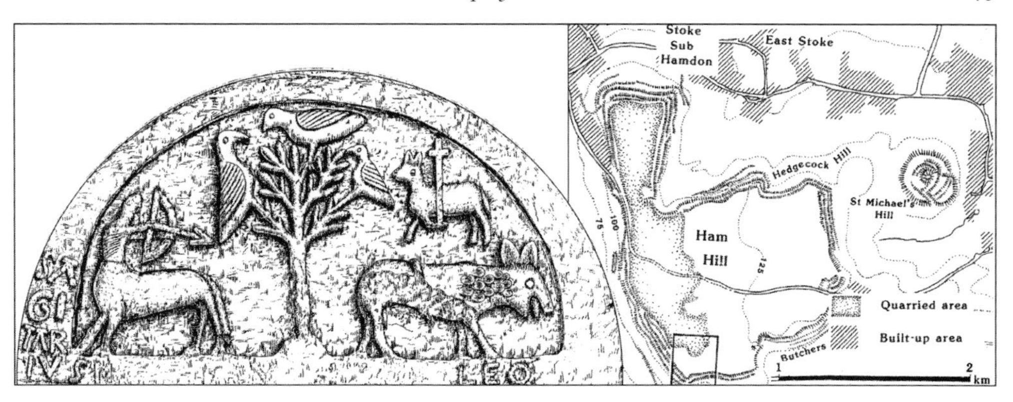

95(a) A twelfth-century tympanum, at Stoke-sub-Hamdon church, Somerset (ST 484173), shows a midwinter Sagittarius firing his arrow at August Leo's rump, with the tree of life rising from a 'harvest hill'. (b) Hamdon Hill, an important Neolithic assembly place (ST 476172), overlooks this church. Some English 'harvest hills' (such as Edge Hill, Warwickshire) now carry churches dedicated to St Peter in Chains (Latin *ad vincula*). St Peter's feast day is 31 July, Lammas Eve, when he was released from a dungeon, just as the first British corn heads were cut and released from their underground roots.

> Sweet St Catherine, send me a husband, a good one, I pray;
> But arn a one better than narn a one,
> O St Catherine, lend me thine aid,
> And grant that I may never die an old maid.[64]

This version is from Cat and Chapel Hill, Piddletrenthide, Dorset. The timing of the chant allowed nine months for the desired mating to turn pregnancy into a Lammas birth. St Catherine provided a hill for all seasons, as her rotating wheel implies.

But Christianity was not always so accommodating. Many former harvest hills were assailed and nullified by the militant archangel, St Michael, Satan's adversary. For example, a late Saxon church and a surviving thirteenth-century tower, both dedicated to him, were built on top of Glastonbury Tor, Somerset. The tor is a steep-side, isolated hill, more than 500ft high, overlooking the marshy Somerset Levels and visible for 20 miles around.

Worked flints from every phase of the Stone Age have been found during excavation of its summit, though this does not necessarily support the view that the dramatic terracing around the tor's flanks are a maze, created in the third millennium BC. St Collen is reputed to have made a cell on the tor in the seventh century and had a vision of Gwynn ap Nudd, King of the Underworld, sitting in his abysmal castle, where a great feast was in progress.[65] (Was it as a concession to the tor's pre-Christian associations that an image of a woman milking a cow was carved in low relief onto the church tower?)

St Michael had much more work to do in Somerset. His churches crown Burrow Mump's conical hillock and St Michael's Hill, Montacute. In Devon, another of his chapels, built by the monks of Tavistock, tops the precipitous Brent Tor. He also claims several Cornish conical hills, including the Isle of St Michael's Mount. Throughout England, the frequency with which St Michael appears on likely 'harvest hills' shows how hard it was to eradicate worship of the prehistoric harvest deity.

Even *within* Christianity, harvest spirits could not be denied. For example, over the north door of Stoke-sub-Hamdon's church (only a mile from Montacute) a twelfth-century tympanum carries the parishioners' corn-growing concerns sky high. It shows Sagittarius firing his midwinter arrow at Leo's August rump, with their names carved on the firmament's edge to make doubly sure he does not miss. Between them, a tree grows from a miniature 'Silbury' creation mound, thereby drawing underworld and celestial vault together. The Neolithic occupants of the Hamdon Hill enclosure, which overlooks the church, would have enjoyed this Norman carving.[66]

Clegyr Boia, Pembrokeshire

One mile west of St David's, Pembrokeshire, a rocky outcrop, approximately 45ft high, rises above fertile fields. Named Clegyr Boia, its 300-yard-long outline, seen from the south-east, makes the classic profile of a reclining lady. On the undulating summit, post-holes of Neolithic houses have been found. Both rectangular and oval, these timber and daub dwellings date from the mid-fourth millennium BC.[67] The inhabitants were believed to have migrated from Lough Gur (Irish *gur*, 'labour pains'), a well-known sacred site in Co. Limerick.[68] At Clegyr Boia, the villagers tilled the surrounding fields, kept cattle, ate, drank, prayed, sang, danced, made love, gave birth, slept and died on their deity's stony breast. They were the human representatives of the Irish *Tuatha de Danann*, 'People of the goddess Anu'.[69]

Occupation of Clegyr Boia continued into the sixth century AD, by which time St David had arrived, intending to set up a monastery nearby. His plan, legend records, annoyed the wife of Clegyr Boia's chief. To drive the saint off, she sacrificed her own daughter, Dunawd. When that had no effect, except to cause a spring named Dunawd to erupt, she encouraged her servant girls to utter obscenities and dance naked in the river Alun before the monks, who were 'disturbed, but did not retreat'.[70] The Alun valley is still known as Merry Vale, and the land around Clegyr Boia continues to be fertile; it grows cabbages. The monks have gone but St David's cathedral flourishes.

96 (a) The Clegyr Boia ridge, Pembrokeshire (SM 737252), has yielded fourth millennium Neolithic evidence of a settlement. (b) Clegyr Boia's 'reclining female' rocky outcrop shape. (c) Carngyfrywy, Pembrokeshire, 364m (SN 147326). This 'reclining mother'-shaped igneous tor is the source of the 'bluestones' that were transported from here and erected at Stonehenge during the period of Silbury's construction.

97 Karn Gluze, Ballowal, Cornwall. This ruined Neolithic double-walled dome is placed near Cape Cornwall (regarded until *c.*1780 as Britain's most westerly point). Here the Earth Mother's womb joined 'land's end' and sun set to her abyss, thereby giving hope beyond death of a voyage to her Scilly or 'Fortunate' Isles.

Carngyfrwy's Bluestones

Twenty-three miles east of Clegyr Boia, on top of the Preseli Mountains, there is a volcanic dolerite outcrop named Carngyfrwy. From the scree around this spectacular natural 'effigy', evocative of the reclining goddess-in-labour, the famous 'bluestones' were collected and somehow transported to Salisbury Plain, where they form a U-shaped setting within the sarsen ring of Neolithic Stonehenge.[71]

The bluestones are Carngyfrwy's natural scree 'offspring'. White egg-shaped spots are a notable feature of this rock. At Stonehenge, 17 miles from Silbury, the bluestones' U-shape makes a well-known symbol for the womb, as seen on Minoan figurines and in much British folklore concerning women's aprons. (In Wales, many a prehistoric cairn is explained and named as a load of boulders dropped from a giantess's apron.)[72]

The Stonehenge bluestones also emphasise the island-wide nature of the 'goddess and her progeny' theme. During the Neolithic, and indeed throughout the succeeding Bronze, Iron and Roman periods, Wiltshire and west Wales apparently spoke the same earth-based visual language. In AD 540 the Welshman Gildas, founder of monasticism here, attacked this long-established earth worshipping tradition, writing:

> I shall not speak of the ancient errors … that bound the whole of humanity before the coming of Christ … I shall not name the mountains and hills and rivers, once so pernicious, [but] now useful to human needs, on which … a blind people heaped divine honours.[73]

His conviction that the new monotheism had brought an end to hill worship was premature. In 1886 Professor Rhys noted that:

> the echoes of a feast or fair on August 1st have not yet died out in Wales. In Cardiganshire till recently the shepherds had a sort of picnic on the hills. A farmer's wife would lend a big kettle for a good broth and everybody present had to put some fuel on the fire.[74]

With those simple gestures, several thousand years' of August hill worship flickered and finally died.

Silbury and the Birth Chairs

Its rites now over, for some observers the Silbury image is hard to recognise, because although the hill and moat together combine to present a clear 'squatting in parturition' pose, most of the figure is laid out on a *horizontal* plane rather than sitting erect. This was necessary because the effigy was largely drawn in water. However, many other Neolithic and later 'squatting goddesses' in Britain *do* employ a vertical format, though on a much smaller scale. A few surviving examples are given here.

A native effigy, carved in sandstone at Roman Caerwent, Gwent, bears (in both senses) a sapling fir tree as a symbol of fertility. She *is* the ground into which the tree is rooted *and* the rocky throne upon which she sits.[75]

In other instances, the chair, stool or throne could, by itself, represent the divine birth event. The 6ft-tall Neolithic menhir at Stackpole Warren, Pembrokeshire, is one of many in Britain with a ledge that suggests an 'abstract' rudimentary image of a seated supernatural figure, and one that invites a human sitter. Similarly, the natural seat within the south portal stone at the Avebury Henge, called the Devil's Chair, was, until the mid-twentieth century, where the May Queen sat on May Day morning.[76] In this way the deity encouraged humanity to join in and engage directly with the world-creating process.

98 Birth chairs. (a) The Hag's Chair, Loughcrew, Co. Meath. The Plough and Pleiades constellation mingle with solar and zigzag water signs on this prehistoric cosmic birthing throne. (b) Cadair Brenhines, or 'Queen's Chair', from Llys y Frenhines, Denbighshire. (c) Seated Attic goddess, *c.*550 BC (Fitzwilliam Museum). (d) Seated goddess, Pazardschik, Bulgaria, fourth millennium BC. (e) The Tressilt Idol, from St Nicholas parish, Pembrokeshire; a seated naked mother and child; soap stone carving, National Museum of Wales (see *AC*, 1900).

The supernatural dimension is also found in the medieval Welsh description of a seated maiden in *The Dream of Macsen Wledig*, when the emperor sees a maiden, whose beauty is brighter than the sun, sitting 'in a chair of red gold'. She is dressed in:

> vests of white silk, with clasps of red gold at the breast; and a surcoat of gold brocaded silk upon her … and a frontlet of red gold on her head, with rubies and gems on the frontlet, and pearls alternately, and imperial stones; and a girdle of red gold around her.[77]

Macsen's intoxication is partly distilled from the Celtic sun goddess tradition.

The deity-*as*-chair was regarded as the source of eloquence. Therefore the 'chair' was awarded to the person who could best access its inspiration; hence the bardic chair, awarded annually to the finest poet at the Welsh national *eisteddfod* (meaning 'sitting together'). Likewise, the Stone of Scone, embedded under the coronation chair at Westminster Abbey, provides the physical link between Britannia, the superhuman rocky island, and her enthroned human representative, the new monarch, who interpreted the divine word into law. All these manifestations may be seen as derivatives of a Neolithic squatting deity prototype, of which Silbury is the grandest surviving example.

The Gop

Surpassed only by Silbury Hill, the Gop is the second largest artificial prehistoric mound in Britain and believed to be Neolithic.[78] This 46ft-high monument, built of rough limestone blocks, is a steep-sided, flat-topped oval in shape. Its long axis measures 223ft, aligned north-west to south-east. Somewhat damaged by stone robbing, Gop stands on a 774ft hilltop in Gwaenysgor parish, Denbighshire, at SJ085724, overlooking the mouth of the Dee estuary.

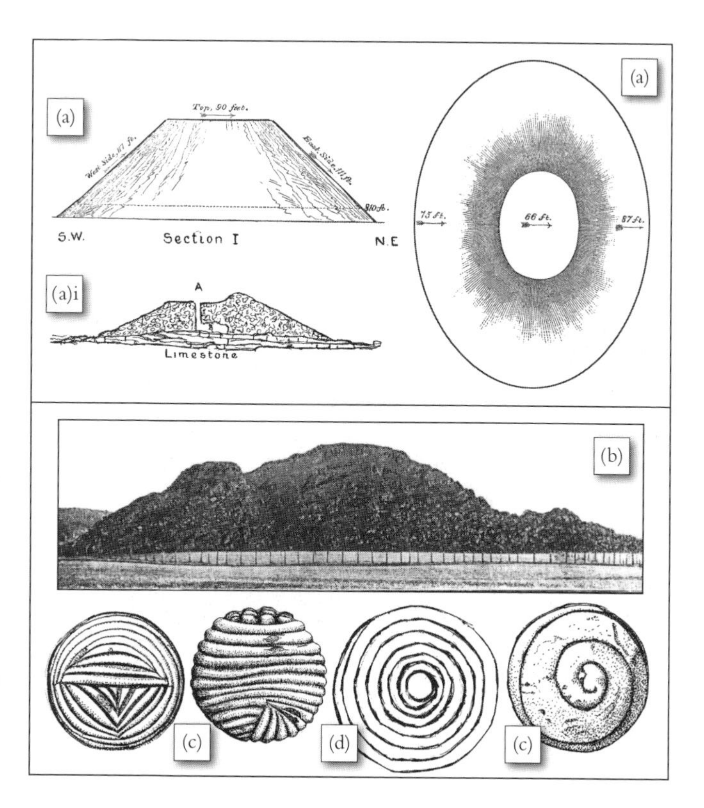

99(a) Gop, Gwaenysgor, Denbighshire (SJ 085724). Excavation has shown that this 46ft-tall Neolithic monument, built of limestone blocks, was not a burial mound and was more likely to have been an August First Fruits ritual site. It was surveyed in 1858 and excavated by Boyd Dawkins in 1902 (a i). (b) Dunadd, Argyllshire, 55m-high seat of the seventh-century Dalriada kings (NR 838936). This 'pregnant female' outcrop rises 160ft above the waterlogged 'Great Moss'. (c) Neolithic carved stone balls from Scotland, *c.*3000–2000 BC. (d) Several of these carved balls show the 'coiled serpent' motif, employed on a monumental scale by the 'spiral ramp' structure of Silbury Hill's chalk walls, as surveyed by D. Field.

The name Dee (Latin *dea*, 'goddess') is a generic form of the river's original Welsh title: *Dyfrdonwy*, 'Waters of the goddess Don'. Don was the mother of an entire Welsh pantheon of deities, listed in the *Mabinogion*, including Lleu and the farmer god Amaethon.[79] Gop may be regarded as their collective birth mound and supernatural home, equivalent to an Irish *side*. *Y Gop* may be a shortened form of *Cop-y-Goleuni*, 'Shining Crown' – a name in use until *c.*1860.[80]

When Boyd Dawkins dug vertically and horizontally into Gop in 1861, he encountered no burials. Like Silbury, it was not a tomb. However, only 40 yards to the south, he discovered, within a limestone cave, a late Neolithic polished axe and skeletal remains of at least 14 people, surrounded by deliberately placed boulders. There were also some woolly rhino, bison and reindeer bones of Palaeolithic age, and some Bronze Age artefacts.[81]

Boyd Dawkins was struck by the close resemblance of the cave's human skeletons to the 'small, dark Welsh who are still to be seen in the fairs and markets of Denbighshire' and concluded that they were descended from the original Neolithic stock that had been settled in the area through more than four millennia.[82]

Willy Howe: A Ruined 'Silbury'?

Willy Howe, at Thwing, is the largest 'barrow' in Yorkshire's East Riding. Its shape, now ruined by treasure hunters, was a flat-topped, grass-covered chalk cone, 25ft tall and 125ft in diameter at the base. Opened by Lord Lonsborough in 1857, 'there was no appearance of a body ever having been interred, yet animal bones found therein proved that any human bones could not have completely decayed away'. Instead, beneath the cone's centre was an oval, or vulva-shaped, shaft, sunk more than 13ft into bedrock and filled with layers of earth and chalk.[83]

The archaeologist W. Greenwell noted that 'on more than one previous occasion … I have found mounds lacking any sign of interment'. He cites one at Folkton, 60ft in diameter, where 'a flat mound of earth was first made, and on this a smaller mound, 42 feet diameter, of chalk and a little soil was placed. This was enclosed by a 1 foot-high wall of chalk slabs, resting on the primary mound.' As at Willy Howe, beneath the entire structure a vulva-shaped pit (in this case 8 x 5ft and 4ft deep) had been sunk, with 'not the slightest indication that a body had ever been buried in it; very difficult to explain'.[84]

Midlothian Harvest Hills

In the villages of eighteenth-century Midlothian, Scotland, 'the celebration of the Lammas Festival was most remarkable,' wrote James Anderson in 1792. Each community built a Lammas tower at some conspicuous place, close to a spring or well. Each tower was built during July and was usually approximately 4ft in diameter at base, 8ft tall, tapering to a point and topped by a 'flag', which was a large table napkin decorated with ribbons. The structure was then closely guarded to ward off attacks from neighbouring villages prior to 1 August. Then, dressed in their best clothes, people marched to the tower, blowing horns and 'making merry', before a meal of bread and cheese was eaten at the tower's foot, and water, fetched from the nearest well, was ceremonially drunk.[85]

Similar, but *prehistoric*, turf stacks, found at West Heath, Sussex, at Six Wells, Llantwit Major, South Wales, and at Crig-a-mennis, Cornwall,[86] indicate that the roots of the Midlothian tradition probably developed with the beginning of Neolithic agriculture in Britain.[87]

As this chapter has attempted to show, Silbury does not stand in isolation. Rather, it belongs among a great company of long-venerated features. They include (i) entirely natural topographical 'pregnant goddess' effigies, regarded as sacred; (ii) hillocks and rock stacks modified by humanity to emphasise their harvest hill character; (iii) entirely artificial structures, created to simulate and wait on the earth deity in labour. All three types served as assembly places, where the Earth

100 (*Top left*) Lough Salt, Co. Donegal, one of 95 Irish hill and lakeside locations where August First Fruits rites are known to have taken place. (*Top right*) Willy Howe, Thwing, East Riding, Yorkshire (TA 063724). With a diameter of 125ft and originally flat-topped, this harvest hill was wrecked by treasure hunters. Local folklore says that fairies could be heard feasting inside the mound. (*Bottom*) A prehistoric non-funerary turf stack at West Heath, Sussex (SU 786226), of a type similar to the eighteenth-century Midlothian Lammas towers.

Mother and the deities of harvest time were honoured, and their stories ritually re-enacted in order to initiate successful reaping and gathering of the ripening crops.

Cesair, Harvest Hill and Lake

MacNeill's account of Lughnasa, the start of harvest festival in Ireland, lists no fewer than 95 hill and mountaintop sites where 1 August celebrations were known in 1942. In addition, near Boyle, Co. Roscommon, there is a 20ft-high flat-topped mound reputed to be the grave of Cesair, Ireland's *magna mater*. According to the medieval *Lebor Gabala*, she was the daughter of Bith (whose name means 'cosmos'). After causing a flood (her breaking waters?), she creates Ireland, its hills and people (Irish *cessair*, 'to carry, to bring forth').[88]

The Irish 1 August rites may be seen as a vestigial repetition of Cesair's primal nativity. As at Silbury, in several locations these celebrations involved both a hill and a lake. For example, on the

101(a) Tan Hill, Wiltshire (ST 086646), 2 miles south of Silbury, was, until 1932, the scene of a two-day fair held annually on 6–7 August, 'the feast and morrow of St Anne'. (b) A carved chalk goddess effigy, 20cm high, from the Iron Age village at All Cannings Cross, immediately below Tan Hill. (c) Dragon's Hill, Uffington, Berkshire (SU 302869), a probable 'harvest hill', set below the Bronze Age Uffington Horse. This gigantic horse was incised into the chalk escarpment as an image of the goddess Epona, alias Welsh Rhiannon. (d) A bronze Romano-British sculpt of Epona in superhuman form, with her colts, platter, grain, and plough (BM).

102(a i–iv) Romano-British bronze sceptre-head from Lowbury Hill, Oxon. (Newbury Museum). This Matres trio may show the young, maternal and aged aspects of the Great Goddess. The sceptre was found close to the former Romano-Celtic temple on Lowbury Hill (scale 1:1, drawn by R. Read). (b) Stylised female images, as a Roman mortarium stamp, found at Lowbury Hill. (c) Bronze head of Diana, the Roman moon and childbirth goddess, found near Lowbury.

shores of Lough Salt, Co. Donegal there was a gathering on the first Sunday before, and the first after, 1 August until *c.*1910, as a man from the district recalled: 'They were very important festivals … eagerly looked forward to'. Young people from four parishes, including fiddlers and melodeon players 'would gather in the evening for dancing, singing, with courting couples very much in evidence and marriages arranged'. Some people came to enquire after lost or stray sheep. Then the steep white quartzite mountain Croc a' Liathain, which overlooks the lough, was climbed. Ripe bilberries growing on the summit were threaded onto long stalks of grass and carried home to give to older relatives.[89]

Lowbury Hill, Oxfordshire (Su 540822)

On the summit of this 185m-high chalk hill that gives magnificent views over fertile down land, a sequence of potsherds has been found running from beakers, *c.*2000 BC, through Bronze Age, Iron Age, Roman and early Saxon vessels. In addition, before AD 100, a Romano-Celtic walled rectangular sacred enclosure, 48 x 60 yards, was constructed on the hilltop. Votive offerings left there include 57 brooches, 22 finger rings, 7 needles, 34 pins, 4 tweezers, 8 bracelets and 1019 Roman coins.[90]

103 Divine hills and implements. (*Top*) Silbury, 2008, with a ripe oats crop. (*Inset*) A reconstructed Neolithic flint sickle (Devizes Museum). (*Bottom*) Two Iron Age rotary corn-grinding querns from Llanidan and Rhyddgaer, Wales. (Welsh *silio*, 'to hull grain, to generate, to spawn'.) Throughout prehistory divine agency was recognised in agricultural tools and processes.

To the archaeologist M.G. Fulford the many sherds of *mortaria* (one stamped with female images) and flat dishes discovered at the site imply the ritual preparation and consumption of food as part of the pattern of worship. Further, the ceremonial 'slots' or deep 'first furrows' that Fulford found within the divine enclosure, and the oval-shaped pits filled with dark loam, may be further signs of earth deity rites there.[91]

That these were orientated towards the Harvest Mother is confirmed by the recent find nearby of a bronze sceptre head, incorporating three images of the Great Goddess, displaying her maiden, mother and old woman forms. These spring from leafy volutes. (Unfortunately, the plump 'mother' has lost her head.) Only 27 miles east of Silbury, this three-in-one cluster of deities 'were deeply involved in the whole of Nature', writes the Roman art expert Martin Henig. He envisages the sceptre being carried in religious processions and relates the object to three similar 'tipstaffs' found within the Lowbury summit enclosure in 1914.[92]

As if to emphasise a Lowbury-Silbury resemblance, a bronze bust of Diana, the Roman goddess associated with the moon, mountains and women-in-childbirth, has been unearthed less than half a mile from Lowbury.

The seventh-century pagan Saxon barrow, constructed a few yards from this Romano-British temple is interpreted by Fulford as a Germanic newcomer's wish to achieve continuity with the spirit and native purpose of the site. This may also explain the burial of a middle-aged Saxon woman in the bank of the temple compound.

Though remote, Lowbury remained an important gathering place, and on 21 June 1887, as *The Times* reported, a traction engine and trailer were used to transport older inhabitants from surrounding villages to join a crowd on the hill, celebrating Queen Victoria's jubilee. Today (late July 2009), as in the Neolithic, fields of wheat and barley continue to wave in the winds that blow around Lowbury's grassy top.

104 The Cramlington Goddess, Northumberland. Designed by the American landscape architect Charles Jencks, this 400-yard-long effigy is to be built in 2010 from the debris thrown up by an adjacent opencast coal mine. It seems ironic that the age-old deity of cyclical renewal is now to be linked to short-sighted fossil fuel extraction and its harmful global impact; but perhaps her message is that life will go on, despite three centuries of industrialised recklessness.

The Cramlington 'Goddess', Northumberland

On 1 July 2009 it was announced that a 400-yard-long 'Goddess of the North', with 100ft-high breasts, would be built from grassed-over debris, thrown up by a proposed opencast coalmine sited 10 miles from Newcastle. It is to be set in a newly created lake and fringed by willow trees. The American landscape artist, Professor Charles Jencks, regards his design as 'a celebration of the earth's natural power'. He added: 'Northumberlandia does not refer to any particular goddess or religion. When finished you will see the most incredible curvaceous woman lying there, with her left leg over her right and her hair spread out.'[93]

Mark Dowdall of the mining group added: 'Visible from the A1, it will be an outstanding artistic achievement, and provide high quality leisure facilities for the local Cramlington community.'[94] Work on the effigy is due to start in 2010.

Unlike Silbury (a land and water deity who was designed to integrate solar rays into her enduring metabolism), the Cramlington goddess presides over fossil fuel extraction, a major cause of global warming. Does Jencks's 'Northumberlandia' symbolise a world going up in flames or faith in its eventual recovery from our carbon burning excesses?

Motherland

Although the genuine harvest hills of Britain and Ireland, whether natural or of human design, have now fallen from use, traces of their previous popularity continues to provide 'Silbury-the-enigma' with a rich and widespread context of meaning, into which that monument readily fits. Far from standing in isolation, Silbury, the Harvest Goddess *par excellence*, is surrounded by a host of evocative knolls and mountain summits that until recently were similarly recognised and worshipped.

Even now, to climb and stand on any one of these up rearing features and to see spread out below a green and gold tapestry of pasture and corn field, is to admire and feel grateful for a 6000-year-old work of farmers' art, made in collaboration with nature and continually renewed. Such a hilltop pilgrimage is an engagement with a numinous present, exemplified by Silbury.

ten

THE VANISHING EFFIGY

Discarding Myth

Silbury is a product of the age of myth, during which it was assumed that all surface 'reality' arose from and depended upon the regularly repeated creations of the gods. When the universe and nature were regarded as the offspring of mythic narrative, human society modelled itself on the supernatural drama believed responsible for these outcomes. By doing so, communities hoped to receive a share of the divine gifts, which included plants and animals, both wild and domesticated.

To aid the transfer, people sought out numinous places where the underlying sacred story was glimpsed, emerging to the surface in a vivid and compelling manner, as at the Swallowhead and Waden springs and the sow-shaped Waden Hill. Because the two springs (regarded as outpourings from a divine underworld) happen to align with the critical sunrise on 1 August, they jointly inspired the construction of Silbury. The monumental image was built to such a height that from its terrace, and just below the sacred corn growing on the flat summit, the *same* sunrise could be observed, riding Waden 'pig's' sacred crest.

From the mythic perspective, an outlook that has provided the basis of almost every human culture, the *super*natural gives birth to, imbues and sustains the entire natural world. This conviction is reflected in the entire group of Avebury monuments.

By contrast, twenty-first-century Britain has adopted a largely secular culture, in which *any* mythic framework, including the Christian, tends to be rejected, marginalised or ignored. In English the very word 'myth' has now been redefined in pejorative terms – both in dictionaries ('untrue, without foundation, a figment') and in general usage.

Given this change, Neolithic Silbury is likely to appear obsolete, or worse, a conveyor of false attitudes. No wonder archaeologists have shied away from any serious attempt to unravel its messages. Though the damaged interior has been successfully plugged with chalk paste, the monument's significance now lies 'out of bounds', sunk in the vanished age of myth from which it rose. Consequently, as a water and earth image of the presiding Neolithic deity, Silbury is invisible to many modern eyes.

The effigy has vanished. Her water body has been more or less ignored, with almost all attention being concentrated on the hill, regarded as a heap of dead matter. Instead of a unified image, antiquaries, archaeologists and the official guardians have effectively dismembered and erased the Silbury goddess. Just as in *Waiting For Godot*, the name Godot was said by the play's author, Samuel Beckett (being true to his times), to have nothing to do with God, so Silbury's presence has likewise been denied in the modern era.

Paradoxically, Silbury's disappearance from expert and public view as an earth and water supernatural image may also be attributed in part to the current glut of television and advertising images that blinds us to the more subtle array of topographic and monumental effigies that earlier generations recognised as multivalent symbols, operating at a *range* of levels. Because they were not saturated by a profusion of electronic imagery and did without a written script and the insulating effect of urbanism, they had far more incentive both to 'read' the land and to produce art and architecture imbued with meanings. What little they added to the natural environment grew out of and remained attached to that source, itself viewed as a manifestation of the supernatural. It is precisely this integration of nature and culture, held within a supernatural frame of reference, which is so superbly demonstrated by Silbury.

As suggested in Chapter 1, the inability of most contemporary archaeologists to see Silbury as an image may stem from a lingering inheritance of Protestant iconoclasm, combined with the potent and continuing influence on academic archaeology of the ancient Greek philosopher Plato. From him the specialism has inherited a distinctly *anti*-mythic epistemology.

Following his teacher Socrates, Plato decisively rejected the myth-centred outlook that had prevailed throughout prehistory. He deposed Greek *muthos*, the revealed divine word of the deities, which was synonymous with their cosmogonic or universe-creating acts. In place of that physical, spiritually and emotionally charged synthesis (expounded at Silbury both in *sil* words and solid matter), he urged the installation of Greek *logos*, the transparent, abstract, supposedly 'objective' word of rational, single issue, linear discussion. A misplaced loyalty to Plato's methodology, which was specifically *designed* to block the way to prehistoric understanding, provides an unpromising starting point from which to launch a search for Silbury's core meaning.

In order to recover Silbury's *pre*-Platonic character, the artificially isolated fields and techniques of study – scientific instrumentalism, comparative religion, folklore, place-name evidence and art history – should again be seen as aspects of the former poetic compound, the basis of prehistoric understanding, which is contained within and radiates from Silbury's apparently simple structure.

This kind of 'knowledge' could more readily re-emerge if those engaged in the academic study of Silbury were willing to see themselves not only as detached observers, but also as members of the one and only human race. Awe in the face of the universe, enjoyment of night and day, full moon and sunrise, a field of golden barley or the birth of a child, are experiences common to all humanity, not least the inhabitants of the Neolithic. Instead, as the Professor of Archaeology at nearby Reading University mournfully admits, in Britain all his colleagues, 'immersed in chronological analysis', suffer from 'an inability to come to terms with experience itself'.[1]

Yet admitting to a sense of the *extra*ordinary and of the *super*natural should not disqualify them from scientific study. Rather, it might help them to appreciate the sanctity of Silbury's moat and Kennet's stream, in which the prehistoric community so gladly waded. With academia thus refreshed, its 'now' and 'then' could reunite around a shared pleasure in creation's gifts, rooted in death's inevitable companionship, which draws all generations, archaeologists included, together.

Meanwhile, 'Silbury-as-enigma' continues to attract both academic analysts and members of the general public. It stands for what we have overlooked or lost, but nevertheless hope to find again.

A Working Model

In fact many of Silbury's previous functions, described in this book, *have* been perpetuated, though often in a different style. For example, if Silbury was a living giantess, intermediate in scale between a woman and a maternal cosmos, a far *greater range* of quantitative scales is explored by modern science, from microbiology to astrophysics; and with a corresponding sense of wonder. On a purely material plane, Silbury's old art of micro-macro interplay has recently been substantially reinforced.

Likewise, the Neolithic 'all-life' family, in which each kind of animal (including us) and every plant participated on equal terms, has been reinstated by Charles Darwin and confirmed by geneticists who also state that our bodies and brains are identical to those of Stone Age people. Similarly, the anxiety, grief and rapture of human life thresholds have not disappeared, nor have the seasons, nor our dependence on grain, flocks and herds, weaving and pots – all products of the Neolithic.

As for religion, in place of pilgrimages to Silbury's moat-body, an August paddle or swim in the sea has been popular in recent centuries, with gleeful shouts, just as loud as those coming from the Ceres's processions at Roman Silbury. Meanwhile, around that great cone, the Marlborough Downs continue to display their compelling beauty, as the unstoppable Kennet slides serenely on. To this day such scenes may underlie the aesthetic vitality currently shown by British artists across many fields.

However obliquely, as a symbol of earth-animal cohesion Silbury still addresses us. Set alongside its great mass, we register as tiny creatures, at one with its soil, rock, grasses, snails and rabbits, blue butterflies, lake and water birds. Through this ingathering, the monument both invites and expresses our thanks for Britain as a whole and for the only known inhabitable planet.

But Silbury, the ever-pregnant pivot of good fortune, also bears the wounds of much rapacious tunnelling, typifying three centuries of industrialisation and fame-seeking vanity. The huge collapse of material that the monument suffered from top to bottom in AD 2000 amounted to a general warning that while the solar, lunar, agrarian and human life cycles have been regularly renewed since 2500 BC, a world cremated or drowned by industrial overheating will not so easily be restored.

Yet as this dire rumour turns into fact, so Silbury's original significance comes more clearly into view. Her grass-cloaked chalk walls again suggest a spiralling umbilical cord, designed to deliver carefully measured nourishment from age to age and to all creation. Silbury is a beneficent prototype, a perfectly balanced, wonder-filled endowment and exemplar, silently addressing our current need for moderation. The monument, skilfully conserved in 2007–08 as a relic from the remote past, is re-emerging as an indispensable working image of a plausible future.

eleven

THE PLOUGH-JAGS AND DURGA

From First Furrow to Harvest Hill

If Silbury was designed to enact one phase of an annually repeated drama, the final chapter of this book attempts to restart the same cycle by digging into mid*winter*'s hard ground, as a necessary prelude to the birth hill's high summer parturition.

That was also the motive underlying the traditional midwinter English Mumming plays, which were performed in villages throughout England, probably from the time of the Anglo-Saxon invasion, *c.*AD 500, down to the twentieth century.

Such rustic shows endured, despite Christian disapproval and 'educated' scorn. So it was that on Christmas day 1852, F.A. Carrington encountered a party of Mummers from Avebury. After performing there, they 'came round the neighbouring villages and, grotesquely dressed, acted their drama from house to house'.[1] Their play dramatised the fight between midwinter's icy darkness and the warm power of returning light, able to bring the start of a new ploughing season. To that extent, the seasonal cycle, as portrayed in Avebury's Neolithic monuments, was given a fresh voice by these English country dwellers.

Harvest Home

Haligmonath, 'holy month', was the pagan Anglo-Saxon term for September, because then the harvest was nearing completion and so 'they sacrificed to their idols'.[2]

A nineteenth century Wiltshire vestige of that long-lost rite (perhaps corresponding to Silbury's maternal fulfilment) was described by Carrington thus:

> At a Harvest home, care is taken that the last load shall be a light one; and when loaded, it is drawn by the best team, with their bells on. A little boy, with a shirt decorated with ribbons over his other clothes, rides the fore horse. [He is the divine harvest child.] On top of the load the rakes etc. are placed. As many as possible of the work people, male and female, ride on the load, with the rest of the party walking on each side. As they go homewards they chant in a monotone:
>
> 'Ploughed well, sown well; Reaped well, mown well; Carried well, housed well; Nur'a load overdrwd.'
>
> On the next evening, the Master regales them all with a hot supper.[3]

Mummers and Goddess

Many Mumming plays from the eastern counties set the 'winter battle' of the Wiltshire performances alongside the need to woo the primordial goddess in her manifestations as maiden, bride, mother and crone, by using costume, music, dance, spoken dialogue and song. As in Avebury, the shows were performed at or close to the winter solstice, when the actors briefly re-entered and reactivated a myth-based, goddess-centred 'other world'. (Writing in the early eighth century, Bede associates Yuletide with pagan Anglian worship of the Mother Goddess at Modraniht, 'Mothers Night' (Old English *modren*, 'maternal').[4]

An East Midlands term for the winter Mumming, which emphasises the farm labourers' role, was Plough-Jag. The performance ritually initiated every new arable round by featuring uncanny animals and supernatural characters, combined with those drawn from ordinary life. In essence, such dramas were probably inherited via an unbroken chain of oral transmission from the prehistoric inhabitants of Europe, as portrayed in the rock engravings at Bagnola, Italy, and Bohuslan, Sweden.[5]

105 West Halton Plough Jags, Lincolnshire, January 1898, outside Normanby Post Office. Back row from left to right: Four Hatmen, Turkish Knight, Ribbon Man. Middle: Soldier, The Lady, Accordionist, Hobbyhorse, Sergeant Drummer, Hobbyhorse, St George, Doctor. Front: Farmer, Lame Jane, Fool, King, Betty Besom? Beelzebub.

106 Burrington Plough Jags, Lincolnshire, pre-1914 (Photo A.H. Singleton, Scunthorpe). Back row from left to right(?): Hobby, The Lady, The Fool, Hatman, Soldier, Sergeant Drummer, Soldier, Hatman, Hobbyhorse. Front: Old Dame Jane, Doctor.

107 Ploughing. (a) Ploughman, ploughboy and ox-team; from Lincolnshire's Luttrell Psalter, *c.*1340. (b) Hu Gadarn, 'the Mighty'. A legend says that he brought the first plough to Wales from India. (c) A Romano-British bronze plough-team, 6cm long, from Piercebridge, Co. Durham (BM), showing bull and cow yoked together to cut the first 'ritual' furrow. (d) Ploughing in prehistoric rock engravings from (i) Seradina, Italy, with a hoer carrying a child; (ii) Bohuslan, Sweden, with phallic ploughman, seed bag and wheatear.

Divine Ploughmen

Sharing the same roots with the ploughboys of the English folk rites, are Demeter's ever-young ploughman, Triptolemus, son of the mortal king of Eleusis,[6] and the former plough god of Ireland, Eochaid Airem (Irish *airem*, 'the ploughman'). From the interior of the *sidh*, or fairy hill underworld, Eochaid obtained the art of making oxen work in the yoke and then became Ireland's original cultivator-in-chief.[7]

Eochaid's double in Wales is Amaethon, the farmer son of the goddess Don.[8] A second legendary Welsh ploughman, Hu Gadarn, was believed to have cut his furrow all the way from India. Of him the fourteenth-century Welsh poet Iolo Goch declared:

Hu Gadarn... The emperor of the land and the seas
And the life of the world was he.
After the Deluge he held the strong-beamed plough, active and excellent;
Thus did our lord of stimulating genius.[9]

Welsh legend asserts that this Hu the Mighty's plough was pulled by large-horned oxen from 'the land of Haf' (Welsh *haf*, 'summer') or from 'the place where Constantinople now is'.[10] This garbled tale probably reflects the original Neolithic spread of agriculture from the Middle East, and folk rites that bear a strong resemblance to the Lincolnshire plays were known during the early twentieth century in northern Greece, Bulgaria and throughout the Balkans.[11] Together (and singly) these rites provide something akin to the missing words and actions that may have animated the winter landscape around Silbury.

Should we be amazed by such a link when the sequence of the seasons, the corresponding agricultural tasks, human life thresholds and humanity's appeal to supernatural forces were repeatedly woven together by rural communities, every year without fail, between 4000 BC and AD 1900?

Plough Monday in Lincolnshire

Well into the twentieth century, the Lincolnshire Plough-Jags performances, albeit crude and by then fast degenerating, remained fundamentally true to the Neolithic spirit.

The words of the play enacted yearly at Bassingham, Lincolnshire, on Plough Monday were written down in 1823 and form the basis of this study.[12]

Plough Monday, the nearest Monday to 6 January (Twelfth Night and old New Year's Day), was the traditional start of the ploughing season throughout England. Like Luna's crescent moon, the plough's sharp blade cutting the sod, was the counterpart to Silbury's full moon birth night. (Monday > O.E. *monan daeg*, 'moon day'.)

But before the first sod was turned it was felt necessary to re-enact the annual cycle of the divine powers, in whose footsteps ploughmen and harvesters would then follow. Therefore at Bassingham, as elsewhere, the rite began with the dragging of an abnormally big, ribbon-decorated plough around the village. It was pulled neither by horses nor oxen, but by the ploughboys themselves, with up to 20 dragging it along; hence the play's 'Plough Jack or Jag' title. In neighbouring parishes the team members could be called Plough Bullocks or Plough Witches. From the outset, therefore, the event retained a prehistoric animal-human ambiguity, together with an evocation of female power, here ascribed to 'witches'.[13]

The close bond between man and beast was also typical of South Wales, where the ploughman's oxen were credited 'with a kind of occult intelligence, like that attributed to bees'. Family events were communicated to the animal and he was sung to continually when working – 'a set measure, with strains gentle and soothing, and a prolonged note or two in each cadence'. The ploughboy chose words that 'pleased the beast's intelligence ... but mixed with some playful nonsense to gratify his [the animal's] sense of humour'.[14]

The Lincolnshire play, performed at various places in and around each parish including outlying farms, involved a range of male characters drawn from the social hierarchy on earth. They try to woo a reluctant 'maiden', also played by a man. After rejecting all these mundane suitors, 'she' is propositioned by the Fool. He fits into no reputable category, yet is infused with a supernatural appeal. With all the coolness of early spring weather, at first she dismisses his advances before eventually agreeing to wed him. After their wedding, a baby is born and the 'mother' eventually reappears, transformed into her 'old crone' or *Modroniht* 'year's end' state, but still clutching their high-summer offspring. The crone is Mother Earth, ready to be ploughed again into her former maidenly self, when the plough will double as the male god seeking sexual congress with the prostrate goddess, Earth.

108 Mummers in Thrace, 1906–10. (*Left*) The 'Old Man', wearing an animal skin mask. (*Top centre*) A 'smith' (*right*), forging a ploughshare with his 'wife' (*left*) flapping her skirt at the bellows. (*Bottom, centre*) 'Flaying the fallen Bull'. (*Right*) 'Bride and Bridegroom'. English Plough Jags and Mummers belong to a Europe-wide tradition.

The Plough-Jag play encapsulates some of the complexity of the Avebury cycle. Both embody cosmogonic myths that annually attempt to rebuild order from a universe fallen into chaos, with the collapse of vegetation and withering of the sun's strength. Thus at Normanby, Lincolnshire, Plough-Jag troupes from several villagers met around a huge Plough Monday bonfire, on which mistletoe was burnt, and through which the ceremonial plough was dragged to simulate the arousal of the sun from winter decline. Then opposing troupes held a tug-of-war across the dying embers.[15]

These acts, combined with the ritualistic miming of the first furrow's incision, were intended to help rouse the underworld powers from hibernation so that the first seeds could be planted in the sacred virgin's ground, there to germinate and sprout.

An Anglo-Saxon 'first furrow' charm speaks with a similar intent. Just as Silbury was aligned precisely east to west, with its north–south axis linking Swallowhead to the middle of the inter-causeway moat, so the Anglian charm begins by urging the supplicant to cut four sods facing the cardinal directions. Milk from every cow in the herd, mixed with parts of every tree and every well-known herb except burdock is then to be poured over the four sods. (As with the birth at Silbury, this act was performed at night.)

The charm adds: 'When you drive forth the plough and cut the first furrow say then: "Hail to thee, earth, mother of men, may you be fruitful under god's protection, filled with the food for the benefit of men".' Invoking both goddess *and* Christian god, the spell is echoed by the coupling of pagan Plough Monday with the Christian Epiphany, celebrated on 6 January.

109 The Scandinavian Goddess. (a) Gold and garnet brooch from Arslev, Denmark; AD 200–400; Stockholm National Museum. (b–c) Bronze Age bronze figurine of a goddess with gilded eyes, offering milk from her right breast and wearing the *crios*, a sacred belt of continuity; from Fardal, Jutland; compared to (d) The Silbury Goddess. (e) The Sacred Marriage between deities, portrayed on a prehistoric plaque from Helgo, Uppland, Sweden.

As in the Stone Age, a good result also depended on sacrifice, so the Saxon recipe continues:

> Then take flour of every kind and have a loaf baked as big as the palm of your hand, and kneed it with milk and with holy water, and lay it under the first furrow ... [saying] Erce, Erce, Erce, mother of earth, may the omnipotent Lord grant you fields growing and thriving, flourishing and bountiful, bright shafts of millet crops, and of broad barley crops, and of white wheat crops, and of all the crops of the earth.[16]

In contrast with these *individually* performed magic acts, the Plough-Jag play was a social event involving the entire community. Yet the intention was similar – namely to encourage divinity to burst through the surface of the mundane. As in antiquity, the Plough-Jag rite employed costumed disguise, dance, song *and* magic word. The leading peasant actors *became* the deities they represented, so infusing sacred vitality into a tired, god-forsaken world.

The Play

In common with most Mumming plays, the Bassingham text has three distinct but inter-related parts: the Combat, the Wooing and the Collection.

The Combat

The combat is between two male protagonists. After an exchange of boasts about their martial prowess, they fight with swords until one combatant falls dead. This fight carries connotations of old age versus youth, winter versus summer and light versus dark; thus the victorious St George is called *Sun* George in one Cornish play.[17] In this text he complains of being locked underground prior to his arrival here after midwinter. His opponent, the Dark Knight, alias the Fool, is killed in the fight. As an uncanny 'nobody', everyone has a small share in him. Yet, like the year, he is immortal and after his death he is always resurrected by a 'Doctor'.

The Wooing

P. Gelling's study of Sweden's Bronze Age rock carvings show combat, wooing and solar adoration juxtaposed. These pictograms portray the fertility goddess Freyja, meaning 'lady', and her husband Freyr.[18]

The 'maiden' of the Lincolnshire plays is also called the Lady. Another resemblance is evident in that Viking Freyja, alias Gefn or Gefion, 'Giver', brought four giant oxen from the underworld. They were her sons. With them she ploughed southern Sweden so deeply that part of it floated off to become Danish Zealand.[19]

Like Gefn and Silbury's sunlit moat, the Bassingham 'Lady' is bedecked with 'gold' jewellery. They bring the underworld, solar power and surface good fortune together, provided they marry. However, the Plough-Jag Lady scornfully rejects prosperous suitors from this world, such as judges, farmers or wealthy old men. Instead she chooses the despised Fool, since only he, as a creature of mixed bits and pieces, hints at *totality* and therefore at the supernatural.

In their censored modern form the birth act is omitted from the scripts, but towards the play's end the Lady reappears in her role of crone or hag (just as Demeter did in *her* wintry guise). She is synonymous with a 'hag' corn dolly, hung in a winter barn. Here called Old Dame Jane or Dirty Bet, she carries the August harvest corn child in her arms, but the Fool denies paternity. Only this old mother appreciates the link between cycles. As the repository of memory, she personifies all crops *and* the sacred, renewable earth. Both she and her corn 'child' are then ploughed into the first furrow to be cut on Plough Monday. Without them, the next year would be barren.

The Collection

When Beelzebub charges in at the end of the play, he raises a club and cooking pan as tools of former combat, doubling as male and female symbols of a divine love match. The pan (a miniature 'Avebury Henge'?) also serves as a collecting box. By dropping in their coins, the onlookers participate in 'seeding' the Lady, and therefore hope to share in her union's prosperous August outcome.

Much of the money gathered was spent on beer for the performers, a drink brewed in Britain since *c*.4000 BC. The remaining coins paid for a candle, lit every night over the ceremonial plough,

110 Harvest images from Britain and Ireland. (a) Medieval harvest jug with dancers (National Museum of Wales). (b) A Sheila-na-gig fertility figure from Clonmel, Ireland. (c) An English 'mother and daughter' corn dolly (Museum of Rural life, Reading). (d) Basalt sickle hone with solar symbol engraved, from Llandudno Junction, Wales.

which was lodged in the parish church until the next Plough Monday. As at Silbury, the moon was believed vital in promoting the successful harvest at which the Plough-Jags aimed. Their solitary candle may have reflected the pagan Anglo-Saxon calendar of 12 lunar months (with a thirteenth added approximately every three years).[20]

Following the Silbury-long barrow-Avebury cycle, the Plough-Jag play integrates seasonal and agrarian concerns with the human life span, in a supernatural drama. The soot-blackened faces of the performers stress their underworld-other-world origin, while the male-female cross-dressing may evoke an original androgynous state, a feature of many myths. Equally typical of genuine myth is the ease with which the play absorbs contemporary characters, such as a Recruiting Sergeant, without losing the thrust of the archaic plot. (Myth is nourished by history.) The urge to 'do the rounds' of the territory and the use of hobbyhorses and musicians are further signs of the play's ancient credentials.

The Bassingham Plough Play (text of 1823)

FOOL Good Evening Ladies and Gentlemen all This merry time … I've made it bold to call I hope you will not take it ill what I am going to say I have some boys and girls drawing on this way I have some little boys stands at the door In ribbons they are neatly dressed For to please you all they do their best Step in Merrymen all.
ALL Good Master and good Mistress as you sit by the fire
Remember us poor Plough lads That runs through muck and mire
The mire it is so deep And we travel far and near
We will thank you for a Christmas box And a mug of your strong beer.
ST GEORGE In come I, St George, the man of courage bold. With my broad axe and sword I won a crown of gold. First in a closet I was put, then into a cave was locked, There did I make my sad and greivus mone. How many men have I slew, And runnd the firche dragon thrue; I fought them all courageously, And still got thire victory, England's wright, England's admorration. Now ear I draw my bloody weepon; Ho is the man that doth before me stand? I will cut him down with my courageous hand.
TURKISH KNIGHT Hear comes I the Turkish Knight, Come from the Turkish land to fight; I will fight St George, that man of courage bold, And if his blood is hot, Soon I will make it could.
… [After an exchange of taunts and boasts they draw weapons and fight. The 'Turk', alias Fool, is stabbed and killed. Then an Old Witch and a Doctor, watched by a King, resurrect the corpse.]
OLD WITCH Five pounds for a Doctor my husband to cure.
DOCTOR I'm the Doctor.
OLD WITCH Pray what can you cure?
DOCTOR I can cure the itch and the veneral and the gout. All akes within and pains without. You may think I'm mistain But I can bring this man to life again…
KING Where do you feel his pulse?
DOCTOR Where it beats the strongest. {sexual by-play}
KING Is that the strongest part of a man?
DOCTOR It's the strongest part about a woman. I've a little bottle in my inside coat trousers waistcoat pocket. He wants a little of my wiff waff just rubbin round 'is tiff taff. This man is not dead. He is only in a trance. Rise up my good man and have a dance.
LADY [enters singing] In comes the Lady, bright and gay Big fortune makes sweet charms With fingers long and rings upon All made of beaten gold, Good Masters and Good Mistresses I would have you behold.
[Her combination of solar and 'landlady' aspects typifies the poetic amalgams found in early Scandinavian myth and art, and the use made of such compound forms throughout prehistory.]
HUSBANDMAN Here comes the farming man Upon my principle for to stand I'm come to woo this fair Lady To gain her love is all my care.

111 (*Right*) Wheat sheaf and marrow placed in the porch of Broad Hinton parish church near Avebury, 4 October 2008, for the Harvest Festival celebration. (*Below*) Man and woman reaping wheat; fifteenth-century misericord from Ripple, Worcestershire.

LADY To gain my love it will not do. You speak too clownish for to woo. Therefore out of my sight be gone. A witty man I'll have or none.
OLD MAN Here comes the poor old ancient man. I'll speak for myself as best I can. My old grey hairs they hang so low I'll do the best for myself the best I know. Methinks me sees that shining star bright On you I've fixed my heart's delight.
LADY Away, away from me begone Do you think I'd marry such a drone?
No, I'll have one of high degree And not such a helpless wretch as thee.
OLD MAN Kick me Lady out of the room I'll be hanged over the kitchen door.

[In his rejection, Baskerville and Chambers see the displacement and slaying of the old year in favour of the new.]
FOOL {to Lady} Come write me down the power above that first created a man to love I have a diamond in my eye Where all my joy and comfort lie I'll give you gold I'll give you pearl If you can fancy me my girl Rich costly robes you shall wear If you can fancy me my dear.
LADY It's not your gold shall me entice Leave off Virtue to follow your advice? I do never intend at all to be at any young man's call.
FOOL Go you away you proud and scornful Dame If you had been true I would have been the same I make no doubt that I can find As handsome a fair one to my mind
LADY O, stay Young Man you seem in haste Or are you afraid your time should waste? Let reson rule your roving mind And perhaps in time She'll prove more kind
FOOL Now all my sorrows is cod and past Joy and comfort I've found at last The girl that used to say me nay She comforts me both night and day
BEELZEBUB In come I, old Beelzebub. On my shoulder I carry a club; In my hand a dripping pan. Don't you think I'm a jolly old man? {All three dance and sing: Tooroориadio Tommy's wed tommorio}
FOOL Stop! Stop! Stop! What's all this dancing and jigging about? 'Ere's a tight boy to dance I can dance on a barley chaff riddle. It will neither bend nor break one strand. I am going to ask all you Stickme jacks to me and Lady's wedding and what you like best you must bring on with you. I know what me and my Lady likes. We're going to have barley chaff dumpling buttered with wool and a gallon of ropey ale to it.
[This bizarre choice reflects the hunger often endured in springtime and early summer, prior to the next harvest. Tantalisingly, in this text there is no August-maternity dialogue covering the climax of the agrarian year. Instead, it cuts to introduce a 'year's end' 'old mother', who is still carrying the 'harvest child'.]
DAME JANE In come poor old Dame Jane Leaping over the meadow. Once I was a blooming girl But now I'm a down old widow {To Fool} Long time have I sought you But now I've found you, Sirrah, come take your Bastard. {She holds him her child}
FOOL {to Lady} Bastard? You Jade, its none of mine Its not a bit like me I am a valiant hero lately come from the sea. You never see me before now did you? I slew ten thousand men with a seed of mustard Ten thousand with an old crushed toad. What do you think of that Jane? If you don't be off I'll see you the same.
BETTY BESOM {enters with broom} [in the Alkborough, Lincolnshire text.] Money I want, and money I crave. If you don't give me money, I'll sweep you into your grave.
ALL [During the collection they sing]
The mire it is so very deep, The water runs so clear
Give what you like to our money box And a mug of your best beer.
Good Master and Mistress You see our Fool is gone
We make it in our business to follow him along. {All exit}

Plough-Jag Postscript

In 1847 the *Stamford Mercury* noted on 8 January that 'the extinction of these heathenish customs from this enlightened and supposedly Christian country has not been achieved altogether', and an 1870 edition of the paper reported that 'the plough boys are still dancing in their uncouth fashion, accompanied by equally rude music'.[21]

What prohibition had failed to eliminate, the following century undermined with increased agricultural mechanisation, urbanisation, secularism and World War I. It was these changes that combined to dismantle the Plough-Jag troupes during the 1930s. Yet in 1932 the equivalent Mummers play, given at Marshfield, Gloucestershire, until 1880 (when a flu epidemic demolished the cast), was revived. In a somewhat corrupt, yet by no means half-hearted manner, it is

112 Burrington Plough Jags, 1934, a tradition in decline. Back row: Hobbyhorse, Soldier-Accordianist Elso Betsy Bug, Tom Fool, Hatman, Hatman, Hatman, Besom Do It, Sergeant Drummer, unknown, Hobby. Middle: The Lady, The Groom, The Collector, Jo Straw. Front: The Doctor, The Collector, The Groom.

performed on Boxing Day morning in the village square.[22] There 'Old Dame Jane' has been converted into 'Saucy Jack'. As the 'bread-winner', he carries several dolls as 'babies' on his back but complains that they have all died from starvation. He tried his best but is no mother.

Plough, Harvest and the Church of England

Decline and demise of the Plough-Jag rites and English Mummers' performances left a gap in religious experience that coincided with the Church of England's belated willingness to conduct 'Plough Blessing' rites inside parish churches on the Sunday following Plough Monday. This persists in several lower Severn Valley villages, including Moreton Valence. There Mr Doug Watts of Moor Farm has adapted a modern plough to replace the horse-drawn implement previously used in the annual ceremony.[23]

In addition, the Church now conducts harvest festival services throughout England and Wales. This was the idea of the vicar of Morwenstow in 1843. He wished to add a sacred dimension to the traditional 'harvest home' suppers given in autumn by farmers for their workers. The Church officially adopted his initiative in 1863. The full moon nearest the autumn equinox (23 September), termed the Harvest Moon, was selected as the time to bring wheat, barley, other vegetables and foodstuffs into the Christian domain. Such produce was afterwards distributed to the 'poor of the parish'. In the Avebury district these festivals are now held in mid-October, when corn sheaves, canned goods and packets of pasta are laid on the chancel steps. As in the Neolithic, is the sacred to be found again within food?

Silbury and Durga

Contrasting with the restrained mood of these church thanksgivings around Silbury, India's October Durga Puja festival is a vibrantly passionate affair. Throughout that country, and especially

113 Mr Doug Watts of Moor Farm, Moreton Valence, Gloucestershire, in 2009, with his specially adapted plough that he takes to the parish church for an annual January blessing by the vicar.

in Bengal, gigantic skilfully painted clay images are made of the ten-armed Durga, the great goddess creator-destroyer. Her cult probably originated in the Neolithic Indus Valley civilisation.[24] Ever since then, her annual task has been to demolish, conceive, recreate and nourish the world, while bringing a harmony of spirit to her devotees through control of destructive forces, represented by a buffalo demon.[25]

Durga's struggle is re-enacted yearly in a carnival, during which (as with the Avebury group of monuments) the goddess is believed to re-live every stage of a woman's life cycle, from infancy to old age and death. 'Durga Ma', as her followers call her, resembles Silbury as cosmic 'Great Mother' and the personification of nature, with its extensions into agricultural and urban life. The nine-day festival ends when Durga's image is thrown into the Ganges or into some other river.

Since 1962 Hindus living in London have celebrated Durga-Puja, but not until 2006 did a team of craftsmen from Calcutta come to London to model a 20ft-high Durga-centred tableau, using Ganges clay and imported cow dung. The festival ended on 2 October when at high tide her icon was ritually lowered into the Thames beneath Putney Bridge. There, water flowing from Swallowhead's Kennet (the Thames's major tributary) helped dissolve her image back into slime. In Sangeeta Datta's words: 'as Ma Durga was immersed mid-stream a huge rainbow arched over the sky. Then Durga floated swiftly downstream, clay to clay, and life was a circle once again.'[25]

The word *durga*, 'inaccessible' or 'difficult to understand', implies that whether richly painted in Bengal or made of Silbury's grass and moonlit water, the Great Goddess ultimately lies beyond the imagination's grasp. (If she did *not* include the unimaginable, she would fail to be comprehensive.) Although Silbury, like Durga, is an embodiment of *shakti*, 'the fountain of power', and incorporates the firmament into her moat-body's reflections, the Wiltshire monument is a noble attempt to envisage the unknowable. For example, the Silbury deity probably never revealed, even to her makers, *why* she gave birth to the universe.

114 Durga in London. (a) The 10ft-high straw and clay image of the Bengali creation goddess, Ma Durga, made in the courtyard of London's British Museum by Calcutta craftsmen, August 2007. At the end of the nine-day Durga Puja she was thrown into the Thames at Putney.

Consequently, when English Heritage saved Silbury from physical collapse by plugging the miners' cavities with solidified chalk paste and rendered the central core permanently inaccessible in order to preserve the hill's external form, they completed a *theologically* appropriate act. Thanks to them, 'Silbury-the-Hidden' is now reunited with 'inaccessible' Durga, her inscrutable partner from the eastern end of the Indo-European alliance.

Yet what *can* reasonably be inferred is that Silbury was designed to represent a divine birth as a positive climax to each cycle of death, chaos, re-seeding, germination and replenishment, on behalf of every kind of life form. For millennia illiterate multitudes could to some degree 'read' and identify with the monument's purpose, through the vicissitudes and pleasures of their own lives and with a sense of connectedness to a universal whole. That was what the monumental figure provided. So, under a summer sun, they were drawn towards Silbury in time for a full moon's *Gwyl Awst*, 'the Vigil of August', and with an urge to participate in the solemn pre-natal ceremony that culminated in the harvest child's delivery and a shout of joy.

That cry has vanished into the past, yet Silbury is no more 'over' than are the Swallowhead spring and River Kennet 'finished'. Just as *their* seasonal dive underground is followed by reappearance, so Silbury, arising from a moonlit moat, epitomises rebirth. The great hill's very shape encourages thoughts of the rotation between death and renewal. Therefore, to revolve (if not resolve) the Silbury enigma amounts to wishing our endangered world many more Happy Returns.

POSTSCRIPT: THE DRAX LETTERS

Unread for centuries, two letters penned by Colonel Drax in November 1776 have recently been found in the British Library, and published in the *Wiltshire Archaeological Magazine*, vol 103, for 2010. Drax, who directed the 1776 vertical dig into Silbury, from summit to base, states that within the organic material at the monument's core he found, instead of the hoped-for hero's burial urn, a polished stone axe 'half a foot long and sharpened at the end', now classifiable as Neolithic.

Then, at 95ft below the summit and penetrating into the bedrock, his four miners encountered 'a perpendicular Cavity that yet appears Bottomless'. It was 6in in diameter. Drax wrote: 'We have followed it already about 20 feet [downwards] and can plumb it about Eleven feet more, but as a great deal of loose chalk as unfortunately fallen in, at that depth is a stoppage'. Yet, he adds, 'at present a Strong wind comes up the Hole, enough almost to blow out a Candle'. Therefore, he believes that this pipe 'must have some communication with a great Cavity somewhere', and notes that 'the country people' believe that an underground tunnel links Silbury to the nearby West Kennet long barrow, where, they claim, there is a similar hole. Thus inherited folk conviction, confirmed by experience of the seasonal and human life cycles, linked Nature and the Supernatural, by means of two abiding architectural goddess images.

The hole beneath Silbury may be explained as a pipe worn by natural chemical erosion of the chalk rock by percolating acidic rain. Silbury may have been deliberately sited over this feature, to facilitate communion with the abysmal powers. Puzzling over how the 'hole' retained its shape, Drax concluded that 'something new perished' must have stood in it. David Dawson, current director of the Wiltshire Museum in Devizes, supports this idea. He envisages 'some kind of totem pole' planted therein. Is so, the vertical axis, uniting sky with underworld, was emphasised from the start of the Hill's construction. Perhaps it was then complemented by the pit, dug into the top of the primary mound that was rediscovered by Cleary in 2007–8; (see page 44 above).

However, no excavator since 1776 has mentioned the underlying pot-hole, described so clearly by Drax. Has consolidated debris hidden it from their view? Concrete infill now precludes further enquiries into this 'hole' issue.

NOTES

Chapter One: Excavators' Tales

1 Dames, M., *The Silbury Treasure*, 1976.
2 Ibid., pp. 56–60.
3 See Dark, K. and P., *The Landscape of Roman Britain*, 1997, pp. 91–2.
4 Dames, M., *The Avebury Cycle*, 1977 and 1996.
5 Field, D., *Silbury Hill, Survey Report*, 2002, p. 65.
6 Dames, M., *The Avebury Cycle*, 1977, pp. 11–2, 16–8.
7 Ibid., pp. 114–6.
8 Douglas, J., *Nenia Britannica*, 1793, p. 161.
9 Merewether, J., *Diary of a Dean*, 1851, pp. 11–6.
10 Ibid., p. 16.
11 Flinders-Petrie, W.M., 'Diggings in Silbury' in *WAM*, No 42, 1922, p. 217.
12 Atkinson R.J.C., *Stonehenge*, 1956, pp. 164–5.
13 Atkinson, R.J.C., *Silbury Hill*, BBC Publications, 1967, p. 2; Atkinson, R.J.C., 'Silbury Hill' in *Ant.*, No 41, 1967, pp. 260–1.
14 Ibid., p. 259.
15 Atkinson, R.J.C., 'Silbury Hill' in *Ant.*, No 43, 1969, p. 216.
16 Op cit., 'Silbury Hill' in *Ant.*, No 41, 1967, p. 261.
17 Ibid., p. 261.
18 *EHSHP*, Update 19, September 2007 and Update 21, October 2007.
19 *EHSHP*, Update 27 and 28, December 2007–January 2008.
20 *EHSHP*, Update 20, September 2007.
21 *EHSHP*, Update 11, July 2007.
22 *EHSHP*, Update 10, July 2007.
23 Bewley, R., English Heritage News Conference, 11 May 2011.
24 Cleary, J., in *CA*, January 2008.
25 Bewley, R., in *Daily Telegraph*, 12 May 2007.
26 Whittle, A., *Sacred Mound, Holy Rings*, 1997, p. 143.
26a Bayliss, A., in *Silbury, The Heart of the hill*, BBC4, 14 June 2009.
27 Bayliss, A., et al in *Ant.*, No 81, 2007, pp. 26–50.
28 Field, D., *Silbury Hill*, 2002, p. 65.
29 Ibid.
30 Atkinson, op. cit., *Stonehenge*, p. 167.
31 Daniel, G., *A Hundred Years' of Archaeology*, 1950, p. 323.
32 Gimbutas, M., *The Goddesses and Gods of Old Europe*, 1982.
33 Gimbutas, M., *The Language of the Goddess*, 1989.
34 Bahn, P., et al, 'Cresswell Crags' in *CA*, No 127, May/June 2005, pp. 217–26.
35 Ucko, P.J., *Anthropomorphic Figurines*, 1968, p. 435.
36 Fleming, A., in *World Archaeology*, Vol. 1, 1969, p. 259.
37 Hutton, R., *The Pagan Religions of the British Isles*; 1992, pp. 20, 38–9.
38 *Folklore*, Vol. 24, 1913, p. 542.

39 Stones of England website, *Silbury and The Devil.*
40 Dames, M., *Merlin and Wales*, 2002, p. 127.

Chapter Two: Earthing the Monument

1 Atkinson, R.J.C., *Silbury Hill*, BBC Publication, 1967, p. 2.
2 Dames, M., *The Silbury Treasure*, 1976, pp. 51–65.
3 Flinders-Petrie, W.M., 'Diggings in Silbury' in *WAM*, No 42, 1922, p. 217.
4 Field, D., *Silbury Hill Survey*, 2002, pp. 60, 63.
5 Dames, M., *Silbury Treasure*, pp. 54, 57, 161.
6 Ibid., p. 53.
7 Pass, A.C., 'Silbury Hill' in *WAM*, No 23, 1887, p. 264.
8 Sherlock, R.L., *London and the Thames Valley*, 1947, p. 22.
9 McAvoy, F., in *EHSHP* Update, 1 July 2007.
10 Evans, J.G., et al in *PPS*, No 59, 1993, pp. 142–3.
11 Malone, C., *Avebury*, 1989, p. 99.
12 Ibid.
13 Dames, M., *Mythic Ireland*, 1992, pp. 169, 179.
14 Personal correspondence, 4 April 2007.
15 Field, D., op. cit., p. 60.
16 Aldhouse-Green, S. and Pettitt, P., 'Paviland Cave' in *Ant.*, No 72, 1998, pp. 756–72.
17 Ibid., pp. 766–7.
18 Williams, J.P., 'Nab Head' in *AC*, 1926, plate 5.
19 Coles, J., 'A Neolithic God-Dolly from Somerset' in *Ant.*, No 42, 1968, p. 254.
20 Wheeler, R.E.M., *Maiden Castle, Dorset*, 1943.
21 Smith, I.F., *Windmill Hill and Avebury*, 1959, figurines c11 and c12.
22 Marshack, A., 'The Female Image' in *PPS*, No 57(1), 1991, pp. 17–31.
23 Cleary, J., Devizes Public Lecture, 9 May 2008.
24 Whittle, A., *Sacred Mound, Holy Rings*, 1997, p. 151.
25 Ibid., p. 30.
26 Ibid., p. 31.
27 Ibid., p. 30.
28 Ibid., p. 151.
29 Quoted on BBC News 24, 11 May 2007.
30 Cleary, J., quoted in *The Guardian*, 25 October 2007.

Chapter Three: Silbury and Swallowhead

1 Evans, J., in *PPS*, No 59, 1993.
2 Dames, M., *Silbury Treasure*, 1976, pp. 98–116.
3 *New Larousse Encyclopedia of Prehistoric and Ancient Art*, 1962, pp. 36, 43.
4 Ibid., p. 48.
5 Ibid., pp. 19–22.
6 Ibid., pp. 34–5.
7 Dyer, J., *Prehistoric England and Wales*, 1982, p. 98.
8 Ibid., p. 335.
9 Sievking, G., 'Kendrick's Cave Horse Skull' in *British Museum Quarterly*, No 35, 1971, pp. 232–40.
10 Dyer, J., op. cit., p. 112.
11 Eliade, M., *Patterns in Comparative Religion*, 1958, p. 243.
12 Stukeley, W., *Abury Described*, 1743, p. 19.
13 Atkinson, R.J.C., in *The Times Literary Supplement*, November 1976.
14 Field, D., *Silbury Hill Survey*, 2002, p. 65.
15 Ibid., p. 63.
16 Chadburn, A., 'A Green Hill Long Ago' in *BA*, January/February 2005, p. 18.
17 Cleary, J., English Heritage News Conference, 25 October 2007.
18 Stukeley, W., op. cit., p. 43.
19 Long, W., in *WAM*, No 4, 1858.
20 Harvey, C., quoted in *Wiltshire Books*, *WAM*, No 42, 1923, pp. 381–2.
21 Thacker, F.S., 'Kennet Country' in *Wiltshire Books*, *WAM*, No 49, 1940, p. 120.
22 Knappert, J., *Indian Mythology*, 1995, pp. 108–9.
23 Eliade, M., *Patterns in Comparative Religion*, (trans.) Sheed, R., 1963, pp. 188–9.
24 Ramat, A.G., (ed.), 'Proto-Indo-Europea' in *The Indo-European Languages*, 1998, p. 34.
25 Smith, I.F., 'Excavation of Bell Barrow, Avebury, G55' in *WAM*, No 60, 1965, pp. 24–46.
25a Ibid., p. 38–40.

26 Cannon, J., *New Myths at Swallowhead*, 2005, pp. 202–6.
27 See Bibliography.
28 Truman, A.E., *Geology and Scenery in England and Wales*, 1938, p. 299.
29 Frymer-Kensky, T., '*Enuma elish*' in *ER*, No 5, 1987, pp. 124–6.
30 Knappert, J., op. cit., pp. 223–4, 227.
31 *New Larousse Encyclopedia of Mythology*, 1968, p. 10.
32 Cleary, J., *Daily Mail* report, Ref. 489618, 6 February 2008.
33 Op. cit., *NLEM*, p. 82.
34 Cleary, J., Devizes Lecture, 9 May 2008.
35 Bahn, P.G., et al, 'Cresswell Crags' in *CA*, June 2005, 98-197, p. 14.
36 Meister, M.W., 'Cave' in *ER*, No 14, p. 370.

Chapter Four: Central Ideas

1 *EHSHP*, Update 23, 26 October 2007.
2 Grigson, G., *An Englishman's Flora*, 1987, pp. 24–6.
3 Meredith, A., *The Fortingall Yew*, 2001.
4 Berresford Ellis, P., *Dictionary of Celtic Mythology*, 2007 and Dames, M., *Mythic Ireland*, 1992, p. 78.
5 Jones, G. and T., *The Mabinogion*, 1993, p. 104.
6 Grigson, op. cit., p. 25.
7 Ellis Davidson, H.R., *Scandinavian Mythology*, 1969, pp. 47–8, 112–3.
8 Frese, P.F. and Grey, S.J.M., 'Trees' in *ER*, No 15, 1987, p. 27.
9 Knappert, J., *Indian Mythology*, 1995, p.258.
10 Frese, op. cit., pp. 30–2.
11 See the sixteenth-century carved ladder on the west front of Bath Abbey.
12 Grigson, op. cit., pp. 250–2.
13 Douglas, J., *Nenia Britannica*, 1793, p. 161.
14 Atkinson, R.J.C., in *Ant.*, No 42, 1968, p. 299.
15 Eliade, M., '*Axis Mundi*' in *ER*, No 1, 1987, pp. 20–1.
16 MacNeill, M., *Festival of Lughnasa*, 1962, p. 223.
17 Ibid., p. 237.
18 Levine, B.A., 'The Biblical Temple' in *ER*, No 2, p. 2.
19 Cleary, J., in *Silbury, The Heart of the hill*, BBC4, 14 June 2009.
20 Heyden, D. and Leon-Portilla, M., in 'Meso-American Religions' in *ER*, No 14, pp. 401, 441.
21 Dames, M., *Mythic Ireland*, p. 232.
22 Eck, D., 'Mount Ida', in *ER*, No 10, pp. 132–3.
23 Baldrian, F., 'Taoism' in *ER*, No 14, pp. 292–3.
24 Walter, M., 'Tibetan Religions' in *ER*, No 14, p. 501.
25 Eck, D.L., 'Mountains' in *ER*, No 10, pp. 130–2.
26 Ramat, A.G., (ed.), *The Indo-European Languages*, 1998.
27 Green, T.M., in *ER*, No 14, p. 583.
28 Padoux, A., 'Kundalini' in *ER* No 8, pp. 402–3.
29 Turner, V., *The Ritual Process: Structure and Anti-Structure*, 1969
30 Chandra, P., *Studies in Indian Temple Architecture*, 1975, p. 40 and Harzer, E., 'Purusa' in *ER* No 12, pp. 106–7.
31 Meister, M.W., in *ER* No 14, p. 373.
32 Michell, G., *The Hindu Temple*, 1987, p. 62. and Eck, D.L., *Darsan (Seeing the Divine Image in India)*, 1985, pp. 59–63.
33 Greenwell, W., in *Archaeologia*, No 52, 1890, Plates 1–2.
34 Hilterbeitel, A., 'Mohenjo Daro' in *ER* No 6, pp. 336–7.
35 Jayakar, P., 'Indian Rural Traditions' in *ER* No 7, pp. 180–1.
36 Trevelyan, M., *Folk-lore and Folk Stories of Wales*, 1909, pp. 197–202.
37 Michell, G., op. cit., pp. 70, 118.

Chapter Five: Silbury's Roman Town

1 Linford, N., in *Wessex Archaeological Report* No 7, 2006, pp. 1–7.
2 Corney, M. in *WAM*, No 90, 1997, pp. 139–50.
3 Bewley, R., reported in *The Guardian*, 10 July 2007.
4 Wilkinson, in *WAM*, No 11, 1869, p. 116.
5 Bewley, R., quoted by Kennedy, M. in *The Guardian*, 10 March 2007.
5a Livy, Book 2, *The Rise of Rome*, (trans.) Luce, T.J., 1998, pp. 102–5.
6 Wacher, J., *The Towns of Roman Britain*, 1990, p. 20.
7 Bewley, R., op. cit., 10 March 2007.
8 Neal, D.S. in *Brit*, No 37, 2007, pp. 72–3.
9 *Larousse Encyclopedia of Mythology*, 1959, pp. 126–7.

10 Robinson, P., 'Religion in Roman Wiltshire' in Ellis, P. (ed.), 1955, pp. 147, 160–2.
11 de la Bedoyere, G., *Roman Towns in Britain*, 1992, p. 103.
12 Field, D., *Silbury Hill Survey*, 2002, p. 70.
13 Barker, C.T., 'Long Mounds of the Avebury Region' in *WAM*, No 79, 1985, pp. 7–38.
14 Piggott, S., *West Kennet Long Barrow Excavation*, 1955–56, 1962, pp. 55–6.
15 Pollard, J., *Avebury*, 2002, p. 178.
16 Corney, M., 'Romano-British Nucleated Settlements' in *WAM*, No 90, 1997, p. 29.
17 Brooke, J.W. and Cunnington, B.H. in *WAM*, No 29, 1897, p. 166–70.
18 *Devizes Museum Catalogue*, Vol. 2, 1934, pp. 68–9.
19 Brooke, J.W. in *WAM*, No 36, 1909–10, pp. 373–5.
20 Green, M.T. in *BAR*, No 24, 1976, p. 52.
21 *Devizes Mus. Cat.*, Vol. 2, p. 68, No 569.
22 Ross, A., *Shafts, Pits and Wells of the Belgic Britons*, 1967, pp. 255–85.
23 Brooke and Cunnington, op. cit, p. 170.
24 Perowne, S., *Roman Mythology*, 1969, pp. 52–3.
25 Ovid, *Metamorphoses* (trans.) Innes, M.M., 1955, p. 136.
26 Ibid., p. 137.
27 Ibid., p. 137–8.
28 Callimachus, *Hymn to Demeter* (trans.) Mair, G.R., 1960.
29 Dames, M., *Silbury Treasure*, 1976, pp. 163–76.
30 Dames, M., *Taliesin's Travels*, 2006, pp. 13, 65, 102, 134.
31 MacNeill, M., *Festival of Lughnasa*, 1962.
32 Wilkinson, J.A. in *WAM*, No 11, 1869, p. 115.
33 Alderman, D. in *Britannia*, No 7, 1976, pp. 366–7.
34 Henig, M. in *Proc. Hampshire Field Club*, No 45, 1989, pp. 83–5.
35 Field, D., op. cit., p. 43.
36 Ibid., p. 53.
37 Ibid., p. 53.
38 Cicero, *The Verrene Orations*, II, v, 72, para. 187.
39 Pliny the Younger, *Letters* of Book 9, (trans.) Radice, B., 1969, pp. 267–9.
40 Dames, M., *Silbury Treasure*, 1976, p. 173.
41 Ovid, op. cit., p. 139.
42 Fowler, W., *Roman Religious Experience*, p. 255.
43 Galinsky, K., *Augustan Culture*, 1995, pp. 94–101.
44 Catullus, T., Book 2, Part 5, (trans.) Postgate, J.P., p. 275.
45 Collingwood, R.G., *Roman Inscriptions of Britain*, 2 vols, 1983.
46 Henig, M. in *Oxford Journal of Archaeology*, Vol. 1, 1982, p. 215.
47 Ovid, op. cit., p. 140.
48 'Claudius' in *Oxford Classical Dictionary*, 3rd edition, 1996, pp. 337–8.
49 Smith, W. (ed.), *Dictionary of Greek and Roman Biography and Mythology*, 3 vols, 1844–49.
50 Toynbee, J.M.C., 'Beasts and Seasons' in *BR*, No 12, 1981, pp. 1–5.
51 Richardson, N.J. (ed.), *The Homeric Hymn to Demeter*, Vol. 2, 1974, pp. 297, 313.
52 Ibid., p. 313.
53 Powell, A.P. in *Wessex Archaeological Report*, Vol. 8, p. 55.
54 Virgil, *The Aeneid* (trans.) Jackson Knight, W.F., 1956, p. 178.
55 Richardson, op. cit., pp. 321–3.
56 Ovid, op. cit., p. 142.

Chapter Six: Cuda, Matres, Sil

1 Dio's *Roman History*, Book 7 (trans.) Cary, E., 1982; and Hind, I.J.F. in *BR*, No 20, 1989, p. 16.
2 Yeates, S.J., *The Tribe of the Witches*, 2008.
3 Toynbee, J.M.C., *Art in Roman Britain*, 1962, pp. 82–4, plate 76.
4 Toynbee, J.M.C., *Romano-British Sculpture in Gloucestershire*, p. 69.
5 Toynbee, J.M.C., op. cit., p. 155.
6 Yeates, op. cit., pp. 1–40.
7 Dames, M., *The Avebury Cycle*, 1977, pp. 185–209.
8 Yeates, S.J. in *BAR*, No 411(1), 2006, p. 89.
9 Moore, T., in *TBGAS*, No 119, 2001, fig. 6, p. 92.
10 Field, D., 'Silbury Hill' in *BA*, No 43, April 1999.
11 Yeates, op. cit., p. 89.
12 Aubrey, J., *Monumenta Britannica*, Vol. 2, 1695.
13 *Chwedl Taliesin* (trans.) Guest, Lady C., 1877, p. 472.

14 Bellows, J. in *TBGAS*, No 5, 1880, pp. 137–41.
15 Cleary, J., Devizes Lecture, 9 May 2008.
16 Toynbee, op.cit., *Romano-British Sculpture*, pp. 64–7.
17 Jones and Jones, G. and T., *The Mabinogion*, pp. 62–3.
18 Toynbee, op. cit., pp. 64–7.
19 Dames, M., *The Avebury Cycle*, 1977, pp. 16–7.
20 Jones and Jones, op. cit., pp. 102–5.
21 Buckman, C.H. and Newmarch, C.H., *Roman Art in Cirencester*, 1850, plates 2–3.
22 Cunliffe, B., *Roman Bath Discovered*, 2000, fig. 24.
23 Henig, M. in *TBGAS*, No 116, 1998, pp. 186–8.
24 Yeates, S.J. in *Glevensis*, Vol. 37, 2004 and Smith, *Place-names of Gloucestershire*, Vol. 4, 1962, p. 50.
25 Morton-Nance, R., *An English-Cornish Dictionary*, 1952, Marazion.
26 Toynbee, J.M.C., op. cit., *Romano-British Sculpture*.
27 Quin, (ed.), *DIL*.
28 Thomas, R.J. (ed.), *Geiriadur Prifysgol Cymru*, Cardiff, 1950–2002.
29 Aubrey, J., *Topographical Collections* (ed.) Jackson, J.E., 1862.
30 Monier Williams, *A Sanskrit-English Dictionary*, Oxford, 1872.
31 Thomas, R.J., op. cit.
32 Quin, E.G., op. cit.
33 Dwelly, E., *The Illustrated Gaelic-English Dictionary*, Glasgow, 1949.

Chapter Seven: Silbury's Roman August

1 *Archaeo News*, 16 September 2006; source *ANSA*, 11 September 2006.
2 Apuleius, *The Golden Ass*, AD second century (trans.) Graves, R., p. 268.
3 Casey, P.J., *Roman Coinage in Britain*, 1980, p. 32 and Levick, B., *Claudius* (Yale), 1990, plate 12.
4 Calpurnius Silicus, *Eclogue*, No 4 (trans.) Duff, J.W. and A.M., 1982, p. 255.
5 Wilkinson, A.C. in *WAM*, No 11, 1869, p. 115.
6 Henig, M. in *Oxford Archaeological Journal*, 1982, p. 215.
7 Callimachus, *Hymn to Demeter* (trans.) Mair, G.R., 1960.
8 Ovid, *Fasti*, Book 1, ii (trans.) Frazer, Sir J.G., 1929, pp. 676–8.
9 Hornblower, S. (ed.), *Oxford Classical Dictionary*, 3rd ed., pp. 15–6.
10 Scullard, H.H., *Festivals and Ceremonies of the Roman Republic*, 1981, 169–70.
11 Dames, M., *Taliesin's Travels*, 2006, pp. 13, 65, 102.
12 Anderson, J., 'Lammas towers in Midlothian' in *PSAS*, Vol. 1, 1792.
13 MacNeill, M., *Festival of Lughnasa*, 1962, p. 10.
14 Levick, B., op. cit., pp. 72–9, 188–90.
15 Warde Fowler, W., *The Roman Festivals*, 1899, p. 195.
16 Tacitus, *Agicola*, (trans.) Hutton, M., 1970, pp. 53–61.
17 Ibid., pp. 63–5.
18 Scullard, op. cit., p. 70.
19 Wheeler, R.E.M., *Lydney Park Excavations*, 1932, pp. 40, 88–9.
20 Scullard, op. cit., p. 170; Warde Fowler, op. cit., p. 190.
21 Dames, M., *Mythic Ireland*, 1992, p. 267.
22 Scullard, op. cit, pp. 171; Warde Fowler, op. cit., pp. 191–3.
23 Dames, M., *The Silbury Treasure*, 1976, pp. 166–73.
24 Scullard, op. cit., pp. 171–3; Warde Fowler, op. cit., pp. 193–5.
25 Scullard, op. cit., p. 175; Warde Fowler, op. cit., pp. 198–200.
26 Scullard, ibid.; Warde Fowler, ibid., p. 199.
27 Warde Fowler, ibid., p. 201.
28 Propertius, *The Elegies*, Book 4, Parts 2–3 (trans.) Butler, H.E., pp. 275–81.
29 Scullard, op. cit., p. 176; Warde Fowler, op. cit., p. 202.
30 Varro, *De Lingua Latina*, (trans.) Kent, R.G., 1967, pp. 189–93 and Warde Fowler, op. cit., pp. 289–96.
31 Williams, D., 'Roman Vineyards in Britain' in *BR*, No 8, pp. 327–34.
32 Scullard, op. cit., 177–8; Warde Fowler, op. cit., pp. 206–9.
33 Hornblower, S. (ed.), op. cit. p. 384; Smith, I., *Dictionary of Greek and Roman Mythology*, Vol. 1, pp. 347–8.
34 Cunliffe, B., *Danebury*, 1986, p. 110.
35 Warde Fowler, op. cit., p. 208.
36 Dames, M., *Mythic Ireland*, 1992, pp. 32, 35, 100.
37 Scullard, op. cit., pp. 178–9; Warde Fowler, op. cit., pp. 209–10.
38 Warde Fowler, op. cit., pp. 211–2; Rykwert, J., *The Idea of a Town*, 1976, p. 97.
39 Rykwert, J., op. cit., p.97
40 *Plutarch's Lives*, Vol. 1, (trans.) Perrin, B., 1914, p. 118.

41 Chadburn, A., 'Inside The Hill' in *BA*, January/February 2005, p. 14.
42 Warde Fowler, op. cit., p. 213.
43 Hornblower, S., op. cit, pp. 1069–70.
44 Warde Fowler, op. cit., p. 213.
45 Ovid, op. cit., Book 6, p. 286; Macrobius, *The Saturnalia*, Book 1, AD 410, p.72.
46 Quintus Ennius, *c.*200 BC (trans.) Warmington, E.H., 1967, p. 413.
47 Pliny the Elder, *Natural History*, Book 18, II (trans.) Rackham, H., 1942, pp. 8–9.
48 Macrobius, op. cit., Book 1, pp. 7–9.
49 Pliny, op. cit., pp. 8–9.
50 Warde Fowler, op. cit., p. 214.
51 Scullard, op. cit., p. 180.
52 Baker, W.J., *Playing With God*, Harvard U.P., 2007.
53 Virgil, *Georgics*, Book 2 (trans.) Fairclough, H.R. and Gould, J., 1999, pp. 169–73.
54 Virgil, op. cit., Book 2, p. 169.
55 Galinsky, K., *Augustan Culture*, 1999, pp. 192–5.
56 Birley, A.R., *Hadrian*, 1997, p. 175.
57 Ibid., pp. 6, 191.
58 Zanker, P., *The Power of Images in the Age of Augustus*, 1990, p. 101.
59 Galinsky, op. cit., pp. 148–9.
60 Cleary, J., *EHSHP*, Update 14, 13–17 August 2008.
61 Cleary, J., Devizes Lecture, 9 May 2008.

Chapter Eight: Transfigurations

1 Merewether, *Diary of a Dean*, 1851, p. 13.
2 Ibid., p. 15.
3 Dames, M., *Mythic Ireland*, 1992, p. 81.
4 Thurnam, J. in *Arch*, No 38, 1860, p. 409.
5 Piggott, S., *Excavation of the West Kennet Long Barrow*, 1955–56, 1962, p. 23.
6 Smith, W., *Greek and Roman Biography and Mythology*, Vol. 1, 1844, p. 960.
7 Ward, J., 'The St Nicholas Chambered Tumulus' in *AC*, 1915, pp. 253–320.
8 Dames, M., *Taliesin's Travels*, 2006, p. 48.
9 Dames, M., *The Avebury Cycle*, 1977, p. 33.
10 Thurnam, J., op. cit., p. 416.
11 Smith, I.F., *'Pre-Bronze Age Barrow, G.55'* in *WAM*, No 60, 1965, pp. 30–3.
12 Aristophanes, *The Frogs*, 405 BC (trans.) Fitts, D., 1958, p. 113.
13 Cleal, R., *Avebury*, 2009, p. 6.
14 Parker Pearson, M. in *Silbury, The Heart of the Hill*, BBC4, 14/06/09.
15 Piggott, S., op. cit., p. 38.
16 Ibid., pp. 37–9.
17 Dames, M., *The Avebury Cycle*, pp 53–9.
18 Evans, T.C. in *Eisteddfod Transactions*, 1885, p. 187.
19 Cunnington, M.E., 'The Sanctuary' in *WAM*, No 45, 1931, pp. 300–19.
20 Dames, op. cit., pp. 74–9.
21 Atkinson, R.J.C. in *Ant.*, No 42, 1968, p. 299.
22 Owen, T.M., 'The Celebration of Candlemas in Wales' in *FL*, No 84, 1973, pp. 238–51.
23 Piggott, S., op. cit. p. 75.
24 Cunnington, M.E., op. cit., p. 313.
25 Mackensie, D.A., *Scottish Folklore and Folk Life*, 1935, p. 188.
26 Field, D., *EHSHP*, 2002, p. 52.
27 Stukeley, W., *Abury Described*, 1743, p. 31.
28 Whittle, A., 'A Later Neolithic Complex at West Kennet' in *Ant.*, No 65, 1991, pp. 150-151
29 Ibid., p. 154.
30 Whittle, A., *Sacred Mound, Holy Rings*, 1997, pp. 151, 160.
31 Whittle, A. in *Ant.*, No 65, 1991, p. 152.
32 Piggott, S., op. cit., p. 53.
33 Smith, I.F., *Windmill Hill and Avebury*, 1959, p. 212.
34 Green, M., *Celtic Goddesses*, 1995, p. 41.
35 Gimbutas, M., *The Language of the Goddess*, 1989, pp. 146–8.
36 Virgil, *The Aeneid*, (trans.) Jackson Knight, W.F., p. 203.
37 Cato, M., *On Agriculture*, cxxxiii.3–cxxxiv.4.
38 Frazer, J., *The Golden Bough*, Part 1, 1925; *The Corn Spirit as Pig*, pp. 298–301.
39 Lucian, the scholiast on; quoted in Farnell, L.R., *The Cults of the Greek States*, Vol. 3, 1907, pp. 86–7, 90.

40 Aristophanes, *The Frogs*, ll. 36–7 (trans.) Henderson, J., 2002.
41 Bromwich, R. (ed.), *Trioedd Ynys Prydein*, 1961, No 26w.
42 Trevelyan, M., *Folklore and Folk Stories of Wales*, 1909.
43 Dames, M., *Mythic Ireland*, 1992, pp. 205–6, 234.
44 See *WAM*, No 20, 1882, p. 346; *WAM*, No 27, 1894, p. 290; *WAM*, No 87, 1994, p. 34; and *WAM*, No 60, 1965, p. 21.
45 Whittle, A. in *Ant.*, No 65, 1991, p. 164. See also Dames, M., *The Silbury Treasure*, 1976, pp. 61–3.
46 Whittle, A., op. cit., p. 151.
47 Cleal, R., *Avebury*, 2009, p. 4.
48 Branston, B., *Gods of the North*, 1980, p. 132.
49 Grinsell, L.V. in *VCH Wilts*, 1957, Vol. 1, Part 1, pp. 31–4.
50 Thomas, N., 'A Neolithic Pit on Waden Hill' in *WAM*, No 56, 1955–56, p. 167–71.
51 Powell, A.B., et al, *Archaeology in the Avebury Area*, in *Wessex Archaeology*, Rep. 8, pp. 13, 30; *Wiltshire Sites and Monuments Record*, History Centre, Chippenham.
52 Bromwich, op. cit., No 26w.
53 Ibid., Nos 26, 26w.
54 Jones, G. and Jones, T., *The Mabinogion*, p. 112.
55 Aldouse-Green, M., *Gwent in History*, Vol. 1, 2004, p. 72.
56 Children, G. and Nash, G., *A Guide to Prehistoric Sites in Monmouthshire*, 1996.
57 MacNeill, M., *Festival of Lughnasa*, 1962, pp. 185–8.
58 Dames, M., *Mythic Ireland*, 1992, pp. 162–3.
59 MacNeill, op. cit., pp. 19, 43–4, 662–3.
60 Devereux, P. in *Ant.*, No 65, 991, pp. 394–5.
61 Baker, W.J., *Playing With God*, Harvard U.P., 2007, p. 13; Whitlock, R., *Folklore of Wiltshire*, London, 1976, p. 52.
62 Dames, M., *The Avebury Cycle*, 1977, pp. 94–5.
63 Conway, D.J., *Mind, Body and Spirit*, 1995.
64 Whittle, A., *Sacred Mound, Holy Rings*, 1997, p. 163.
65 Trevelyan, M., 1909, p. 74.
66 Gimbutas, M., op. cit., pp. 121–2, 127.
67 Cleal, R., op. cit. pp. 14–5.
68 Dames, M., op. cit., pp. 164–5.
69 Merewether, op. cit., p 15.
70 Morris, R., *The Prehistoric rock Art of Argyllshire*, 1997.
71 Lucian, op. cit., pp. 92–3.

Chapter Nine: A Bevy of Silburies

1 See Keiller Museum, Avebury.
2 Aldhouse-Greene, S., op. cit., p. 767.
3 Ibid., p. 766.
4 Rees, Mr, of Tonn in *The Physicians of Myddvai*, 1861, based on oral accounts by Evans, J. and Williams, D.
5 Rhys, J. in *Y Cymmrodor*, Vol. 4, 1881, p. 177.
6 W.J.W. in *AC*, 1858, p. 160.
7 Rhys, J., op. cit., p. 177.
8 Sikes, W., *British Goblins*, 1880.
9 Rhys, J., *Celtic Folklore, Welsh and Manx*, Vol. 1, p. 29.
10 Jones, G. and Jones, T., *The Mabinogion*, pp. 1–20 and 148–9.
11 Bromwich, R., *Trioedd Ynys Prydein*, p. 458.
12 Dames, M., *Mythic Ireland*, pp. 214, 223, 232.
13 Bromwich, R., op. cit., p. 458.
14 Bartrum, C.A., *A Welsh Classical Dictionary*, 1993, p. 90.
15 Ibid., p. 431–2.
16 Bromwich, R., op. cit., pp. 433–5.
17 Ibid., p. 459.
18 Pratt, S., *Gleanings Through Wales* etc., 1795.
19 Rhys, J., 'Welsh Fairy Tales' in *Y Cymmrodor*, No 6, 1883, pp. 168–78.
20 Pennant, T., *Tours in Wales*, 1773, (ed.) Rhys, J., 1883, Vol. 2, pp. 325–6.
21 Baring Gould, S., *Lives of the British Saints*, 1907–13, Vol. 1, p. 164.
22 Conversation with Frank Cowdrey of All Cannings, June, 1973.
23 Coombs, D. in Harding, D.W., *Hillforts*, 1976, p. 147.
24 Camden, W., *Britannia*, 1607.
25 Branson, B., *Gods of the North*, p. 113.
26 Alcock, L. in *PPS*, No 16, 1950, p. 81.
27 Ralph, G.H., 'The Wrekin' in *The Shropshire Magazine*, September 1965, p. 19.

28 Burne, C., *Shropshire Folklore*, 1883, p. 197.
29 Ibid., p. 434.
30 *Bye-Gones*, Vol. 1, 1871, p. 110.
31 *Bye-Gones*, February 1873, p. 141.
32 Rhys, J., 'All Around the Wrekin' in *Y Cymmrodor*, No 21, 1908, pp. 11–60.
33 Ibid., p. 60.
34 Burne, C., op. cit., p. 330.
35 Ibid., pp. 330–2.
36 Ibid., p. 332.
36a Danielou, A., *Hindu Polytheism*, 1964, p. 226.
37 Aldouse-Green, op. cit., pp. 766–7.
38 Partridge, J.B. in *FL*, No 23, 1912, pp. 332–48.
39 Allies, J., *Antiquities and Folklore of Worcestershire*, 1856, pp. 78–81, 363–5.
40 Derham, Dr W., *Physico-Theology*, 1713, p. 70.
41 Palmer, R., *Folklore of Worcestershire*, 2005, p. 296.
42 Partridge, op. cit., p. 342.
43 Palmer, op. cit., p. 6.
44 Fletcher, A.W., *Eckington*, 1933, pp. 130–3.
45 Turton, R.B., 'Roseberry Topping' in *Yorks. Archaeol. Journ.*, No 22, 1913, pp. 40–8.
46 Nichols, J.D., (ed.), *Topographer and Genealogist*, Vol. 2, 1853, pp. 405–30.
47 Gutch, Mrs E., *Folklore of Yorkshire, North Riding*, 1897, p. 31.
48 Anon, *Account of Guisborough*, *c.*1640; BM MS *Cott. Julius*, F.vi, at fol. 431.c.
49 Longworth, I.H., *Regional Archaeology; Yorkshire*, 1985, p. 47.
50 Allies, J., op. cit., pp. 216–20.
51 Spackman, F.T. in *Worcester Naturalist Club*, No 4, 1909–10.
52 Corbett, E.H. in *Transactions Worcestershire Archaeological Society*, 1944, p. 25.
53 Mawer, A. and Stenton, F.M., *Place-names of Worcestershire*, 1927, p. 274.
54 Timmings, W., *The History and Antiquities of St Kenelms*, 1839, pp. 26–7.
55 Ibid., p. 27.
56 Amphlett, J., *A Short History of Clent*, 1890, p. 26.
57 Latin Hymn in Bodleian MS 285, fol. 80–3.
58 Richard of Cirencester (*d.*1402), *Speculum Historiale*, Vol 1, ii, c.67.
59 Wilde, J.F.C., *Ancient Legends of Ireland*, 1888, pp. 102–3.
60 Richard of Cirencester, op. cit., p. 33.
61 Johnson, S., *Lives of the Poets*, 1903 (ed.), Vol. 11, pp. 38–9.
62 Pevsner, N., *Worcestershire*, 1994 (ed.), p. 178.
63 Farmer, D.H., *Oxford Dictionary of Saints*, p. 77.
64 Hole, C., *English Shrines and Sanctuaries*, 1954, p. 160.
65 Watkins, A., 'The Glastonbury Legends' in Carley, J.P. (ed.), *Glastonbury Abbey and the Arthurian tradition*, 2001, pp. 17–8.
66 Dyer, J., *Prehistoric England and Wales*, 1981, pp. 225–6.
67 Williams, A. in *AC*, 1952, pp. 20–47.
68 Dames, M., *Mythic Ireland*, pp. 73–112.
69 Smyth, D., *A Guide to Irish Mythology*, 1998, p. 153.
70 Baring-Gould, S. in *AC*, 1903, pp. 1–4.
71 Dyer, op. cit., p. 282.
72 Dames, M., *Merlin and Wales*, 2002, p. 127.
73 Gildas, *The Ruin of Britain*, Section 2, Para. 4. (trans.) Winterbottom, M., 1978.
74 Rhys, J., Hibbert Lectures, Vol. 2, 1886, p. 421.
75 In Newport Museum, Gwent.
76 Dames, M., *The Avebury Cycle*, pp. 145–6.
77 Jones and Jones, op. cit. pp. 66–7.
78 Burnham, H., *Clwyd and Powys*, 1995, pp. 11–2.
79 Gruffydd, W.J., 'Donwy' in *BBCS*, 7, 1933, pp. 1–4.
80 Jackson, R.H., 'The Gop' in *AC*, 1858, p. 152.
81 Boyd Dawkins, 'The Gop' in *AC*, 1902, pp. 163–71.
82 Boyd Dawkins in *AC*, 1921, p. 413.
83 Greenwell, W., 'Willie Howe' in *Arch*, No 52, 1890, pp. 23–4.
84 Ibid., p. 24; Ibid., p. 9.
85 Anderson, J. in *Proc. Scottish Antiqu. Society*, No 1, 1792, pp. 126–42.
86 Drewett, P., 'Barrows at West Heath' in *Sussex Archaeol. Collections*, No 114, 1976; and Fox, C., *Life and Death in the Bronze Age*, 1914, pp. 150–2; Christie, P.M., 'Crig-a-mennis' in *PPS*, No 26, 1960, pp. 87–9.
87 MacNeill, M., *Festival of Lughnasa*, 1962, p. 357, quoting Cramond, *Extracts from the Synod of Moray*, p. 66.
88 Dames, M., *Mythic Ireland*, pp. 66–9, 146–9.

89 MacNeill, op. cit., pp. 143–4.
90 Davies, J.A., 'Roman Coins from Lowbury Hill' in *Oxonsiensia*, No 50, 1985, p. 8.
91 Fulford, M.G. and Rippon, S.J. in *Archaeological Journal*, No 151, 1994, 158–211.
92 Henig, M. in *Brit.*, No 31, 2000, pp. 358–60.
93 Jencks, C. in *The Telegraph*, 1 July 2009 and *The Times*, 12 September 2009.
94 Downall, M. in *The Times*, 12 September 2009.

Chapter Ten: The Vanishing Effigy

1 Bradley, R., *Altering The Earth*, 1993, p. 65.

Chapter Eleven: The Plough-Jags and Durga

1 Carrington, F.A., 'Ancient Wiltshire Customs' in *WAM*, No 1, 1854, p. 79.
2 Bede, *De Temporum Ratione*, AD 725, (ed.) Jones, C.W., 1943, p. 13.
3 Carrington, op. cit., p. 86.
4 Bede, op. cit. p. 3.
5 Gelling, P. and Ellis Davidson, H.R., *Chariot of the Sun*, 1965.
6 *New Larousse Encyclopedia of Mythology*, 1968, pp. 120, 152.
7 Dames, M., *Mythic Ireland*, 1992, pp. 240–2.
8 Jones G. and Jones, T., *The Mabinogion*, p. 95.
9 Iolo Goch, 1320–98, (trans.) Williams, G., *Welsh Poems, 6th c.–1600*, 1973.
10 *The Cambrian Register*, Vol. 3, 1818.
11 Dawkins, R.M., 'The Modern Carnival in Thrace' in *Journal of Hellenic Studies*, No 36, 1906; Wace, A., 'North Greek Festivals' in *British School of Athens*, No 16, 1909–10.
12 Baskerville, C.R., 'The Bassingham Plough Play' in *Modern Philology*, No 21, 1924, pp. 225–40.
13 Wright, A.R. and Lones, T.E., *British Calendar Customs*, Vol. 2, *Plough Monday*, p. 97.
14 Evans, T.C., 'Folklore of Glamorgan' in *Eisteddfod Transactions*, 1885, pp. 187–8.
15 Wright, A.R. and Lones, T.E., op. cit, p. 97.
16 Gratton, G.C.H. and Singer, C., *Magic and Medicine in Anglo-Saxon England*, 1952, p. 173–7.
17 Chambers, E.K., *The English Folk Play*, 1933, pp. 23–4.
18 Gelling, P. and Ellis Davidson, H.R., op. cit., fig. 30.
19 Ellis Davidson, H.R., *Gods and Myths of Northern Europe*, 1964, p. 113.
20 Harrison, K., 'The Primitive Anglo-Saxon Calendar' in *Ant.*, 1973, pp. 284–5.
21 *The Stamford Mercury*, 8 January 1847; in Lincolnshire Local History Library.
22 Palmer, R., *Folklore of Gloucestershire*, 2001, pp. 266–7.
23 E.V. in *Notes and Queries*, 3rd series, 3, 1863, p. 428; Chambers, op. cit., p. 91.
24 Larousse, op. cit., p. 325.
25 Knappert, J., *Indian Mythology*, 1995, p. 97.
26 Sangeeta Datta in Wikipedia, *Durga Puja*, London, 2007, pp. 1–12; Low, V. in *The Evening Standard*, 3 October 2006.

BIBLIOGRAPHY

Abbreviations:

Antiquity, Ant.; *Archaeological Journal, AJ*; *Archaeologia, Arch*; *Archaeologia Cambrensis, AC*; *Britannia, BR*; *British Archaeological Reports, BAR*; *British Archaeology, BA*; *Bulletin of the Board of Celtic Studies, BBCS*: *Current Archaeology, CA*; *Dictionary of the Irish Language DIL, Encyclopedia of Religion, 1987, ER*; *Folklore, FL*; *Journal of Roman Studies, JRS*; *London and Middx. Arch Soc., LAMAS*; *Modern Philology, MP*; *Proceedings of the Prehistoric Society, PPS*; *Proc. Scottish Archaeological Society, PSAS*; *Revue Celtique, RC*; *Transactions of Bristol and Gloucester Archaeological Society, TBGAS*; *Wiltshire Archaeological Magazine, WAM*; *Victoria County History, Wiltshire, VCHW.*

Adkins, L. and Adkins, R., *Dictionary of Roman Religion*, London, 1996.

Aldhouse-Green, S. and Pettitt, P., 'Paviland Cave' in *Ant.*, 1998, pp. 756–72.

Anati, E., *Camonica Valley* (trans.) Asher, L., New York, 1961.

Ashby, T., 'Statue of Ceres, Ostia' in *JRS*, Vol. 2, 1912, pp. 153–94.

Apuleius, L., *The Golden Ass* (trans.) Graves, R., London, 1950.

Aristophanes, *The Frogs* (trans.) Fitts, D., London, 1958.

Atkinson, R.J.C., *Silbury Hill*, BBC pamphlet, 1968.

— 'Silbury Hill' in *Ant.*, 41, 1967, pp. 259–62.

— 'Silbury Hill' in *Ant.*, 42, 1968, p. 299.

— 'Silbury Hill' in *Ant.*, 43, 1969, p. 216 and in *Ant.*, 44, 1970, pp. 313–4.

Alcock, J.P., 'Celtic Water Cults in Roman Britain' in *AJ*, 1955.

Aubrey, J., *Monumenta Britannica*, parts 1 and 2; MSS Bodleian, *c.*1665–90 and Devizes Museum Library, *Aubrey MS*, p. 74.

Aver Falk, N.E., 'Feminine Sacrality' in *ER*, Vol. 5, 1987, pp. 302–5.

Bachofen, J.J., *Myth, Religion, and Mother Right*, London and Princeton, N.J., 1967.

Bahn, P.G. et al, 'Cresswell Crags Cave Art' in *CA*, June 2005, pp. 98–197.

Banks, M.M., *British Calendar Customs*, Scotland, 3 vols, London, 1937–41.

Baring, A. and Cashford, J., *The Myth of the Goddess*, London and New York, 1991.

Baring-Gould, S., *The Lives of the Saints*, Edinburgh, 1914.

Baring-Gould, S. and Fisher, J., *Lives of the British Saints*, 4 vols., London, 1907–13.

Bartrum, C.A., *A Welsh Classical Dictionary*, Aberystwyth, 1993.

— 'Fairy Mothers' in *BBCS*, 19, 1961, pp. 6–8.

Barker, C.T., 'The Long Mounds of the Avebury Region' in *WAM*, Vol. 79, 1984.

Baskerville, C.R., 'The Bassingham Plough Play' in *MP*, Vol. 21, 1924, pp. 241–6.

— 'Mummers Wooing Plays in England' in *MP*, 21, 1924, pp. 225–40.

Bateman, T., *Ten Year's Digging in Celtic and Saxon Grave Hills*, London, 1861.

Bayliss, A., McAvoy, F. and Whittle, A., 'The World Recreated: redating Silbury Hill in its monumental landscape' in *Ant.*, 81, 2007.

Billington, S. and Green, M., *The Concept of the Goddess*, London, 1996.

Blagg, T.F.C., 'The London Arch' in *BAR*, 329, 2002, pp. 168–70.

Bolle, K.W., 'Myth: An Overview' in *ER*, Vol. 10, 1987.
Boyd Dawkins, W., 'Robin Hood's Cave, Creswell' in *Quart. J. Geol. Soc.*, 1877.
— 'On the Cairn and Sepulchral cave at Gop, near Prestatyn' in *AC*, 1902, pp 152–81.
Bram, J.R., 'The Sun in Religion' in *ER*, 14, 1987, pp. 132–43.
Bromwich, R. (ed. and trans.), *Trioedd Ynys Prydein*, Cardiff, 1961.
— *Culhwch ac Olwen*, Cardiff, 1988.
Brooke, J.W., 'The Excavation of a Roman Well near Silbury Hill in October 1908' in *WAM*, 36, 1910, pp. 373–5.
— and Cunnington, B.H., 'Excavation of a Roman Well near Silbury Hill' in *WAM*, 29, 1897.
Brown, P.W.F., 'The Luxuriant Pig' in *FL*, Vol. 76, 1965, pp. 288–300.
Brouwer, H.H.J., *Bona Dea*, Brill, 1997.
Buck, C.D., *A Dictionary of Selected Synonyms in the principle Indo-European Languages*, Chicago, 1949.
Burkert, W., *Greek religion* (trans.) Raffan, J., Harvard U.P., 1995.
Burnham, B. and Wacher, J., *The Small Towns of Roman Britain*, London, 1990.
Burnham, H., *Clwyd and Powys*, London, 1995.
Callimachus, *Hymn to Demeter* (trans.) Mair, G.R., London, 1960.
Campbell, J., *Creative Mythology*, London, 1968.
— *Primitive Mythology*, London, 1960.
Cannon, J., 'New Myths at Swallowhead' in *The Avebury Landscape* (ed.) Brown, G., Oxford, 2005.
Cato, M., *On Agriculture* (trans.) Hooper, W.D., Harvard U.P. and London.
Catullus, Tibullus, *Poems* (trans.) Warre Cornish, F., London and New York, 1928.
Chadburn, A., McAvoy, F. and Campbell, G., 'A Green Hill Long Ago' in *BA*, 80, Jan./Feb., 2005.
Chadwick, A. and Wickstead, H., 'Gray Hill' in *Archaeology in Wales*, Vol. 42, 2002, pp. 101–3.
Chandra, P. (ed.), *Studies in Indian Temple Architecture*, New Delhi, 1975.
Chemery, P.C., 'Cosmic Trees, in Vegetation' *ER*, 15, Chicago, 1987.
Coles, J., 'A Neolithic God-dolly from Somerset' in *Ant.*, 42, 1968.
Collins, A., *The Rotherwas Serpent Ribbon and Mound*, Hereford, 2007.
Connah, G., 'Knap Hill' in *WAM*, 60, 1965, p. 21.
Cool, H.E.M., 'The Significance of Snake Jewellery Hoards' in *BR*, 31, 2000, pp. 33–9.
Coombs, D.J. and Thompson, F.H., 'Mam Tor' in *Derbyshire Archaeological Journal*, 99, 1979, pp. 44–5.
Corney, M., 'New Evidence for the Romano-British Settlements by Silbury Hill' in *WAM*, 90, 1997, pp. 139–50.
Crawford, O.G.S., *The Eye Goddess*, London, 1957.
Cunliffe, B., *The Temple of Sulis Minerva at Bath*, 2 vols., Oxford, 1988.
— *Danebury*, Vol. 6, Oxford, 1995.
Cunnington, M.E. '"The Sanctuary" on Overton Hill' in *WAM*, 45, 1931.
— *All Cannings Cross Iron Age Village*, Devizes, 1923.
— 'Romano-British Wiltshire' in *WAM*, Vol. 45, 1930.
Cunnington, W., 'Overton Hill Barrow' in *WAM*, 20, 1882, p. 346.
Dames, M., *The Silbury Treasure*, London, 1976.
— *The Avebury Cycle*, 1977 and 1996.
— *Roman Silbury and the Harvest Goddess*, London, 2007.
— *Mythic Ireland*, London, 1992.
— *Merlin and Wales*, London, 2002.
— *Taliesin's Travels*, London, 2006.
— *The Silbury Treasure*, London, 1976.
Dark, K. and P., *The Landscape of Roman Britain*, Stroud, 1997.
Davies, J.A., 'Roman Coins from Lowbury Hill' in *Oxoniensia*, 50, 1985, p. 1–13.
Davies, J.G., '[Sacred] Architecture' in *ER*, Vol. 1, 1987, pp. 383–91.
'Deiniol', 'Llyn Caws' in *AC*, 1873, p. 208.
De la Bedoyere, G., *The Golden Age of Roman Britain*, Stroud, 1999.
— *Roman Towns in Britain*, Stroud, 1992.
Devereux, P., '3-D aspects of the Avebury complex' in *Ant.*, Vol. 65, 1991, pp. 894–8.
Devizes Museum Catalogue, Vol. 2, 1911, pp. 68–9. *Finds from Silbury's Roman Wells.*

Collections, Vol. 114, 1976, pp. 127–42.
Eck, D.L., '[Sacred] Mountains' in *ER*, 10, 1987, pp. 130–4.
— *Darshan; Seeing the Divine Image in India*, 3rd ed., New York, 1988.
Eliade, M., *Images and Symbols*, London, 1961, New York, 1969.
— *Myths, Dreams and Mysteries*, London, 1960, New York, 1969.
— *Patterns In Comparative Religion*, London and New York, 1958.
— *The Forge and the Crucible*, London and New York, 1962.
— *Birth and Rebirth* (trans.) Trask, W.R., New York, 1958.
— *Myth and Reality* (trans.) Trask, W.R., New York, 1963.
— *Symbolism, the Sacred, and the Arts*, New York, 1986.
— (ed.), *Encyclopaedia of Religion*, 16 vols, Chicago, 1987.
Ellis, C.J. et al, 'An Early Mesolithic Hunting Site in the Kennet Valley' in *PPS*, 69, 2003, pp. 107–35.
Ellis, F., 'Bronze Figurine from Aust Cliff, Gloucestershire' in *TBGAS*, Vol. 23, 1900.
Ellis, P. (ed.), *Papers for K. Annable*, Bournemouth U.P., 1955.
Ellis Davidson, H.R., *Scandinavian Mythology*, London, 1969.
— 'The Sword at the Wedding' in *FL*, 71, 1960, pp. 12–28.
English Heritage, 'Silbury Hill Conservation Project' Website, March 2007–April 2008.
Evans, J.J. et al, 'An Environmental History of the Upper Kennet' in *PPS*, 59, 1993.
— 'A Romano-British interment on the bank of the Winterbourne near Avebury' in *WAM*, 61, 1966, pp. 97–8.
Farnell, L.R., *Cults of the Greek States*, London and New York, 1907.
Ferguson, J., *The Religions of the Roman Empire*, Cornell, 1970.
Field, D., *The Investigation and Analytical Survey of Silbury Hill*, English Heritage, 2002.
— 'Silbury Hill' in *BA*, 70, May 2003.
— 'Surface Story' in *BA*, Jan./Feb. 2005.
Fawcett, I., *The Symbolic Language of Religion*, London, 1970.
Ford, P.K., 'A Highly Important Pig' in Matonis, A.T.E. and Melia, D.F., *Celtic Language and Culture*, pp. 293–303, New York, 1990.
Frese, P.F. and Grey, S.J.M., 'Trees' in *ER*, 15, Chicago, 1987.
Fulford, M., *A Guide to Silchester*, 2002, Stroud.
Fulford, M.G. and Rippon, S.J., 'Lowbury Hill, Oxon.' in *Archaeol. Journal*, 1994, pp. 151, 158–211.
Galinski, K., *Augustan Culture*, Princeton U.P., 1996.
Gelling, P. and Ellis Davidson, H.R., *Chariot of the Sun*, London, 1969.
Gildas, *The Ruin of Britain* (trans.) Winterbottom, M., Chichester, 1978.
Gillings, M. and Pollard, J., *Avebury*, London, 2004.
— *Landscape of the Megaliths*, Oxford, 2008.
Gimbutas, M., *The Goddesses and Gods of Old Europe*, London and New York, 1982.
— *The Language of the Goddess*, London and New York, 1989.
Gratan, J.H.C. and Singer, C., *Anglo-Saxon Magic and Medicine*, London, 1952.
Graves, R., *New Larousse Encyclopedia of Mythology*, London and New York, 1968.
Green, M.J., *Animals in Celtic Art*, London, 1992.
— *Dictionary of Celtic Myth and Legend*, London, 1992.
— *Symbol and Image in Celtic Religious Art*, London, 1989.
— 'Ritual Wells' in *BAR*, 24, 1976, pp. 51–2.
— *The Gods of the Celts*, London, 1986.
Grinsell, L.V., 'Wiltshire Gazetteer of Monuments, and Archaeological Gazetteer' in *VCHW*, Vol. 1, Part 1, London, 1957.
Gruffydd, W.I., 'Mabon mab Modron' in *RC*, Vol. 33, 1910–11, pp. 452–61.
— 'Donwy' in *BBCS*, 7, 1933, pp. 1–4.
Gutch, M. and Peacock, M., *The Folklore of Lincolnshire*, London, 1908.
Hanfmann, G.M.A., *Roman Art*, London, 1964.
Haverfield, F., 'The Mother Goddesses' in *Archaeologia Aelina*, Vol. 15.
Hawkins, E., '… Ornaments [from Backworth, Co. Durham] connected with the worship of the Deae Matres' in *AJ*, 8, 1851.
Hemp, E.P., 'Bryn Celli Ddu' in *Arch*, 80, 1930, pp. 179–214.

— 'Culhwch, the Swine' in *ZCP*, 41, 1986, pp. 257–8.
— 'The Pig in Ancient Northern Europe' in Skomal and Polome, 1987, pp. 185–90.
Henig, M., *The Art of Roman Britain*, London, 1995.
— 'Seasonal Feasts in Roman Britain' in *Oxford J. of Archaeol.*, Vol. 1, No 2, 1982.
— 'The Crookhorn Stand' in *Proc. Hampshire Field Club*, Vol. 45, 1989, p. 83–4.
— 'Water Cults' in *AJ*, Vol. 122.
— 'A Sceptre-head for the Matres cult from West Berkshire' in *Brit*, 31, 2000, pp. 358–60.
Hesiod, *Theogony* (ed. and trans.) West, M.L., Oxford, 1966.
— *Works and Days*, (ed. and trans.) West, M.L., Oxford, 1978.
Hind, I.J.F., 'The Invasion of Britain in AD 43' in *BR*, 20, 1989, pp. 1–21.
Hole, C., *English Shrines and Sanctuaries*, London, 1950.
Horace, *Odes* (trans.) Bennet, C.E., London and Harvard, 1927.
— *Satires* (trans.) Rushton Fairclough, H., London and Harvard, 1978.
Hornblower, S., *Oxford Classical Dictionary*, 3rd edition, Oxford, 1996.
Howey, M. O., *The Cult of the Dog*, London, 1972.
Hymes, D. (ed.), *Language in Culture and Society*, New York, 1964.
Jackson, G.F., *Shropshire Folklore* (ed.) Burne, C., London, 1883.
Jones, G. and T. (trans.), *The Mabinogion*, London, 1974.
Keiller, A., 'Avebury' in *Ant.*, Vol. 13, 1939.
Keiller and Piggott, S., 'The Recent Excavations at Avebury' in *Ant.*, Vol. 10, 1936.
Kinsley, D., 'The Hindu Goddess' in *ER*, 6, 1987, pp. 52–3.
Knappert, J., *Indian Mythology*, London, 1991.
Leach, E. R., 'Primitive Time Reckoning' in Singer, C., *A History of Technology*, Vol. 1, London, 1954.
Leary, J., 'Silbury Hill, A Last Look Inside' in *CA*, Jan. 2008.
Linford, N., 'Silbury Hill Environs, Geophysical Survey' in Wessex Archaeology Report, 2006.
Livy, T.L., *History of Rome*, Book 3 (trans.) Foster, B.O., London, 1900.
Lorenzen, D.N., 'Durga Hinduism' in *ER*, 4, 1987, pp. 516–7.
Lynch, F., *Prehistoric Wales*, Stroud, 2000.
— 'Silbury Hill and the New Age Angle' in *BA*, 36, July, 1998.
Macalister, R.A.S., *Ireland in Pre-Celtic Times*, Dublin, 1921.
— 'Centre of The World' in *ER*, 3, Chicago, 1987, pp. 166–71.
Mack, R.P., *The Coinage of Ancient Britain*, London, 1953 and 1964.
Mackenzie, D.A., *Scottish Folklore and Folklife*, London and Glasgow, 1935.
— 'A Highland Goddess' in *The Celtic Review*, Vol. 7, 1911–12, p. 339.
McKim, F.W., 'Resistivity Survey of Silbury Hill' in *WAM*, 1959.
MacNeill, M., *The Festival of Lughnasa*, Oxford U.P., 1962.
Makepeace, G.A., 'Gray Hill' in *BAR*, 427, 2006, pp. 66–72.
Malone, C., *Avebury*, English Heritage, 1989.
Manningworth, W.H., 'The Piercebridge Plough Group' in *British Museum Quarterly*, 35, 1971, pp. 125–7.
Marlborough College Natural History Society Report, vols 37-41, *Roman Coins found at and around Silbury.*
Marshack, A., 'The Female Image: A Time-Factored Symbol' in *PPS*, 57, 1991.
Marshall, D.N., 'Scottish Carved Stone Balls' in *PSAS*, 108, 1976, pp. 60–4.
Merewether, J., 'Examination of Barrows and Earthworks near Silbury' in *Proc. Archaeological Institute*, 1849.
— *Diary of a Dean*, London, 1851.
Merrifield, R., *The Archaeology of Ritual and Magic*, London, 1987.
Michell, G., *The Hindu Temple*, University of Chicago, 1988.
Milne, G., 'The Thames in London in mid 1st century AD' in *LAMAS*, 34, 1983, p. 27.
Morris, R.W.B., 'Prehistoric Rock Art' in *PPS*, 55, 1989.
— 'The Petroglyphs at Achnabreck, Argyll' in *PSAS*, 103, 1970–71.
Morton Nance, R., *An English-Cornish Dictionary*, Marazion, 1952.
Neal, D.S. and Cosh, S.R., *Roman Mosaics in Britain*, 2 vols, London, 2002–05.
— *Art and the Creative Unconscious* (trans.) Mannheim, R., Princeton, 1971.
Nilsson, M.P., *The Religion of Eleusis*, New York, 1947.
Nuttgens, P., *The Landscape of Ideas*, London, 1972.

Osborne White, H.J., *Geology of the country around Marlborough*, London, 1925.
Ovid, *The Metamorphoses* (trans.) Innes, M.M., London, 1955.
— *Fasti* (trans.) Frazer, Sir J.G., London, 1967.
— *The Amores and Heroides* (trans.) Showerman, G., Harvard and London, 1971.
Owen, T.M., *Welsh Folk Customs*, Cardiff, 1959.
Pass, A.C., 'Recent Explorations in Silbury Hill' in *WAM*, Vol. 23, 1887.
Passmore, A.D., 'The Avebury Ditch' in *AJ*, Vol. 2, 1922.
Pearson, J. (ed.), *Paganism in the Modern World*, Edinburgh, 1998.
Pennant, T., *Tour in Wales*, 1773, 3 vols (ed.) Rhys, J., London, 1883.
Petrie, Sir Flinders, W.M., 'Diggings in Silbury' in *WAM*, Vol. 42, 1923.
Piggott, S., *Excavation of the West Kennet Long Barrow, 1955–56*, London, 1962.
— 'The First Agricultural Communities' in *VCHW*, Vol. 1, Part 1, London, 1973.
— *The West Kennet Long Barrow*, HMSO, London, 1963.
Pitts, M., 'Excavating The Sanctuary' in *WAM*, 94, 2001, pp. 1–15.
Pliny the Younger, *The Letters of*, (trans.) Radice, B., Harvard, 1969.
Pollard, J., 'The Sanctuary, Overton Hill' in *PPS*, 58, 1992, pp. 220–5.
Pollard, J. and Reynolds, A., *Avebury, The Biography of a Landscape*, Stroud, 2002.
Powell, A.B., Allen M.J. and Barnes I, 'Archaeology in the Avebury Area' in Wessex Archaeology Report, No 8, Salisbury, 1993.
Quintus Ennius, *The Annals* (trans.) Skutsch, O., Oxford, 1985.
Rawson, P., *Primitive Erotic Art*, London, 1973.
Rea, Carleton, 'Crookbarrow' in *Trans. Worcester Field Club*, Vol. 4, 1909–10.
Rees, A. and B., *Celtic Heritage*, London, 1973.
Rhys, Sir J., 'The Lady of Llyn y Fan Fach' in *Y Cymmrodor*, 4, 1881, pp. 164–70.
— 'Welsh Fairy Tales' in *Y Cymmrodor*, 6, 1883, pp. 168–78.
— 'All Around The Wrekin' in Y Cymmrodor, 21, 1908, pp. 11–60.
— *Celtic Folklore, Welsh and Manx*, 2 vols.
Rhys, S.D., 'Welsh Giants' in *Y Cymmrordor*, 27 (trans.) Owen, H., 1917, pp. 124–52.
Richardson, N.J., *Homeric Hymns to Demeter*, Oxford, 1974.
Robinson, P., 'Religion in Roman Wiltshire' in *Papers for K. Annabale*, (ed.) Ellis, P., Bournemouth U.P.
Rogers, R., 'Female Representation in Roman Art' in Scott, S. and Webster, J., *Roman Imperialism and Provincial Art.*, London, 2003.
Rivet, A.L.F. and Smith, C., *The Place-names of Roman Britain*, London, 1979.
Ross, A., *Pagan Celtic Britain*, London and New York, 1967.
— 'Shafts, Pits and Wells … of the Belgic Britons' in Cles, J.M. and Simpson, D.D., *Studies in Ancient Europe*, 1968, pp. 255–85.
Scott, S., *Art and Society in 4th Century Britain*, Oxford, 2000.
Scullard, H.H., *Festivals and Ceremonies of the Roman Republic*, London, 1981.
Skomall, S.N. and Polome, E.C., *Proto-Indo-European*, Washington, 1987.
Smith, A.C., 'Excavations at Avebury' in *WAM*, Vol. 10, 1865.
— *Guide to the British and Roman Antiquities of the North Wiltshire Downs*, London, 1885.
— 'Silbury' in *WAM*, 7, 1861, pp. 185–91.
— 'Wiltshire Superstitions' in *WAM*, Vol. 14, 1874.
Smith, I.F., *Windmill Hill and Avebury*, London, 1959.
— 'Excavation of a Bell Barrow, Avebury, G.55' in *WAM*, 60, 1965, pp. 24–45.
Smith, W. (ed.), *Dictionary of Greek and Roman Biography and Mythology*, 3 vols., London, 1844–49.
— (ed.), *Dictionary of Greek and Roman Geography*, 2 vols., London, 1887.
Spence, I, *Myth and Ritual in Dance, Game and Rhyme*, London, 1947.
St George Gray, H., 'The Avebury Excavations' in *Arch*, 84, 1934, p. 158.
Stukeley, W., *Abury Described*, London, 1743.
— *Gough Maps*, p. 231, MS Bodleian, Oxford.
— *Itinerarium Curiosum*, Vol. 1, London, 1724.
— 'Letters and Diaries' in Surtees Society, Vols 1 and 3, London, 1885.
Stutley, M. and J., *A Dictionary of Hinduism*, London, 1977.

Tacitus, *Agricola* (trans.) Hutton, M. and Ogilvie, R. M., London and Harvard U.P., 1911.
— *Annales, Book 2* (trans.) Moore, C.H., London and Harvard U.P.
— *Germania* (trans.) Hutton, M., revised Winterbottom, M., London, 1970.
The Gloucester Journal, 9 Nov. 1736, *Report on Silbury Hill Games.*
Thomas, N., 'A Neolithic Pit on Waden Hill, Avebury' in *WAM*, 56, 1955–56, pp. 167–71.
Thomas, R.J. and Bevan, G.A. et al (eds), *Geiriadur Prifysgol Cymru*, Cardiff, 1950–2002.
Thurnam, J., 'Examination of a chambered long barrow at West Kennet, Wilts.' in *Arch*, Vol. 42, 1869.
Timmins, W., *The History and Antiquities of St Kenelms*, 1839, Stourbridge.
Toynbee, J.M.C., *Art In Roman Britain*, London, 1962.
— *Art In Britain Under The Romans*, Oxford, 1964.
— 'Romano-British Sculpture in Gloucestershire' in McGrath, P. and Canon, J., *Essays in Bristol and Gloucester History*, Bristol, 1976.
Trevelyan, M., *Folklore and Folk Stories of Wales*, London, 1909.
Varro, M.T., *De Lingua Latina* (trans.) Kent, R.G., London and Harvard U.P., 1967.
— *De Re Rustica*, (trans.) Hooper, W.D., London, 1934.
Virgil, *The Aeneid* (trans.) Jackson Knight, W.F., London, 1956.
— *Georgics* (trans.) Rushton Fairclough, H., revised Gould, J., London, 1999.
Wace, A.J.B., 'North Greek Festivals' in *British School of Athens*, Vol. 16, 1909–10.
Wacher, J., *The Towns of Roman Britain*, Oxford, 1974.
Wainwright, G. J. and Longworth, I. H., *Durrington Walls Excavations, 1966–8*, London, 1971.
Warde-Fowler, W., *The Roman Festivals of the period of the Republic*, London and New York, 1899.
— *Roman Religious Experience*, London and New York, 1911.
Wheeler, Sir M., *Report on the excavations of the Prehistoric, Roman, and post-Roman site in Lydney Park, Gloc.*, Oxford, 1932.
— *Maiden Castle, Dorset*, Oxford, 1943.
White R., *Britannia Prima*, Stroud, 2007.
Wilkinson, Rev. J. A., 'A Report of diggings made in Silbury Hill' in *WAM*, Vol. 11, 1869, pp. 113–8.
Wiltshire Gazette, August, 1824–1914, Tan Hill Fair Reports.
Whitley Stokes, 'The Rennes Dindsenchas' in *RC*, Nos 15, 16, 37, 50, 160, 1894–95.
Whittle, A., 'A Late Neolithic Complex at West Kennet, Wilts.' in *Ant.*, Vol. 65, 1991.
— 'Millbarrow, West Monkton' in *WAM*, 87, 1994, p. 34.
— 'The Neolithic of the Avebury Area' in *Oxford Journal of Archaeology*, Vol. 12, 1993.
— 'West Kennet' in *WAM*, Vol. 82, 1988.
— *Sacred Mound, Holy Rings*, Oxford, 1997.
Whittle, A. and Smith, R., 'West Kennet' in *CA*, Vol. 118, 1990, pp. 363–4.
Whittle A., Pollard, J. and Grigson, C., *The Harmony of Symbols: Windmill Hill*, Oxford, 1999.
Woodroff, J., *Shakti and Shakta*, Madras, 1914–16.
Wright, A.R. and Lones, T.E., *British Calendar Customs*, (England) 3 vols, 1936–40.
Yeates, S.J., *The Tribe of Witches, The Religion of Dobunni and Hwicce*, Oxford, 2003.
— 'Evidence for a Cotswold Cult of Cuda' in *Glevensis*, 37, 2004.
Zevi, B., 'Architecture' in *Encyclopedia of World Art*, Vol. 1, New York, 1968.
Zuntz, G., *Persephone*, Oxford, 1971.

SOURCES OF ILLUSTRATIONS

(All photos, maps and drawings are by the author, unless otherwise stated. Abbreviations follow those used in the Bibliography)

Front Cover: Katie Beard. **Back**:'Storm over Silbury', painting by David Inshaw.
1a *Abury Described*. 2b G.C. Ashmead. 3 Wiltshire Newspapers. 6b Cahors Museum. 8 *Current Archaeology* 10a *BBC Publications* 10ci-cii M. Gimbutas. 11a Swansea Museum. 12a I.F. Smith. 12b Sir Mortimer Wheeler. 12ci-cii *The Times*. 12d *AC*. 13a P.V. Glob. 13c C.F. Evans. 13d S. Piggott. 21a J.G. Evans. 21b P.J. Fowler. 24a-b J.Rykwert 24e I.F. Smith. 24f *Journal of the Royal Irish Academy*. 24g P. Mookerjee. 25a,c. P.Chandra. 27(above) BM. 28 Taunton Castle Museum. 29 *English Heritage*. 30a J.M.C. Toynbee. 31a J.W. Brooke. 32a-f *WAM*. 33a Hatfield House. 34a Nasonii tomb, Rome. 34b *VCH Hants*. 34c *New Larousse Encyclopedia of Mythology*. 35a,c. *Hampshire Field Club*. 35b *VCH Somerset*. 35c *VCH Hants*. 36b *WAM*. 36c Vatican Museum. 37a Corinth Museum. 37b Corney, M., in *WAM*. 38 Powysland Museum. 39a-b, Corinium Museum. 41(right) Corinium Museum. 43a Corinium Museum. 44 (top inset) *Archaeo News*. 44 (bottom inset) S. Piggott. 45a *Numismatic* Journal. 45b R. Ling. 45c Reading Museum. 45d Terme Museum, Rome. 46a *TBGAS*. 46b Sir Mortimer Wheeler. 47b *AJ*. 47c Koln Museum . 48c *VCH Hants*. 48d Ostia Museum. 49 (top right and left) Corinium Museum. (bottom left Skokloster Slott, Stockholm. 50a Nasonii tomb. 50b Palatine Museum. 50c *VCH Somerset*. 51a Ashmolean. 51b Louvre. 51c English Heritage. 51d Devizes Museum. 51e *VCH Wilts*. 51f J. Hawkes. 52c University Museum, Cambridge. 52 e Gloucester Museum. 53a K.M. Barron. 53b *VCH Wilts*. 54a S. Perowne. 55 (bottom) *BR*. 57a , bi, cii. *The Avebury Cycle*. 57d *Arch*. 57e *Ant*. 57f BR. 58 (top right) Bignor Roman Villa. 59 (top left) *The Avebury Cycle*. 60a S. Piggott. 60b J. Aubrey. 61a *Maiden Castle Report*. 61b *Book of Days*. 61d S. Piggott.62d *Abury Described*. 62e-f *WAM*. 62g G. Wainwright. 63 (left) *Cumberland Archaeological Society*. 65a English Heritage. 65b Aegyptische Museum Berlin. 65c Ashmolean. 67ai-aii S Aldhouse –Green. 67aiii Newport Library. 67c St Fagans Folk Museum. 70a *Abury Described*. 70b Neumann *The Great Mother*. 74(top) National Museum, Scotland. 74(bottom inset) *AC*. 75 *Current Archaeology*. 76 Salisbury Museum. 77b *TBGAS*. 77c BM. 77d Devizes Museum. 78a *Abury Described*. 78ci-cii I.F.Smith. 78d *AJ*. 79b Pompeii.79c *Archaeologia Aeliana*. 79d F. Lynch. 79e *PSAS*. 79f P.Gelling. 81b *Henley Wood Excavation Report*. 81c London Museum. 83 (inset) W.W. Sikes. 84 (top right) *AC*. 84 (bottom right) J. Moore. 85 (inseto St fagans Folk Museum. 86b–c *Derbyshire Archaeological Journal*. 92 (bottom) Worcestershire Record Office. 93 (right) *Gentlemens' Magazine* 94c F.E. Gibson. 95a–b *Somerset Archaeological Society*. 96a–b *AC*. 97 F.E. Gibson. 98a *Proc. Royal Irish Academy*. 98d Univ. Museum Cambridge. 98e Fitzwilliam. 99a–ai *AC*. 99b–d *PSAS*. 100c *Sussex Collections*. 101b M.E. Cunnington. 101d BM. 102 ai–aiv R. Read. 102 b–c Reading Museum. 103 (inset) Devizes Museum. 103(bottom) *AC*. 104 C. Jencks. 105 –6 Scunthorpe Library. 107c *British Museum Quarterly*. 107di G.Anati. 107dii P.Gelling. 108 Journa of Hellenic Studies. 109 National Museum Stockholm. 108b–c Copenhagen Archaeological Museum. 110a National Museum of Wales. 110b National Museum of Ireland 110c Museum of Rural Life, Reading. 110d *AC*. 112 Scunthorpe Library.
Colour Photos 4 (right) St Fagans Folk Museum. 10(top right) Sally Matthews. 10(bottom left) *TBAGAS*. 11 (top) *The Gloucester Citizen*. 13 (bottom right) Newport Museum.

INDEX

INDEX OF ILLUSTRATIONS

(Colour plates are referenced in **bold**)